KITCHEN LIFE

ALSO BY ART SMITH

Back to the Table

ART SMITH

KITCHEN

LIFE

Real Food for Real Families—Even Yours!

HYPERION

NEW YORK

Photographer: Lori Allen Soderholm
Food Stylist: Josephine Orba
Assistant Food Stylist: Judy Lockhart
Stylist: Tom Hamilton
Project Manager: Constance Pikulas
Shoot Assistant: Charles Falarara

Special thanks to Mick De Giulio, de Giulio kitchen design, inc.
and to Crate and Barrel.

Library of Congress Cataloging-in-Publication Data

Smith, Art
    Kitchen life : real food for real families, even yours! / Art
Smith—1st ed.
        p. cm.
    ISBN: 1-4013-0773-6
    1. Cookery. I. Title.

TX714.S58845   2004
641.5—dc22
                                                        2004047589

Hyperion books are available for special promotions and
premiums. For details contact Michael Rentas, Manager,
Inventory and Premium Sales, Hyperion, 77 West 66th Street,
11th floor, New York, New York 10023, or call 212-456-0133.

Book design by Richard Oriolo

FIRST EDITION

10   9   8   7   6   5   4   3   2   1

Thanks to all the families who, through the years, have allowed me into their kitchens and opened a window to their personal lives. All of us seek to be family and very often find ourselves looking to the kitchen as the heart of the home.

I hope that *Kitchen Life* will help you with that age-old question "What's for dinner?" and allow you and those you love to spend more—and more meaningful—time together.

I get letters from people from around the world, and the common thread through all is that no matter where we live, we share the same concerns and love for our families. What is most important is that love be our intention.

I owe a special thank you to all the visitors to Oprah.com who shared their kitchen questions and lives with me. This book is for you.

So America, celebrate your family! Make time to cook a meal for your loved ones, and I promise, you will see a difference in your lives.

CONTENTS

PART THREE

ABOUT THIS BOOK

Imagine coming home after a busy day at work. You've picked up the kids at soccer practice and dance class, helped them lug backpacks and equipment from the car to the kitchen, and now everyone is hungry for supper.

Open the refrigerator and take out the container of homemade marinara sauce defrosting on the shelf. Remove a package of chicken breasts, lightly season them with salt and pepper, slice up some mushrooms, and open a box of frozen artichoke hearts. Put a pot of rice on the stove, and while the chicken and vegetables are simmering, pull some fresh, crisp lettuce, cucumbers, and carrots from the vegetable bin. Thirty minutes later, toss the greens with your legendary "house" balsamic dressing and put the rest of the food on platters. The kids have finished setting the table, and everyone happily sits down to a lovely meal.

If this does *not* sound like your life, welcome to the club!

The scene I describe here is not impossible to achieve. I will help you get there. If you have the right ingredients in your pantry and the right equipment in your cabinets, and have mastered just a few basic cooking techniques, mealtimes will cease to be a chore and become a pleasant family event. I promise!

This is why I wrote *Kitchen Life*.

WHAT IS KITCHEN LIFE?

Kitchen life is the joy we find in the heart of the household where we nurture our families. And it's soulful, too. It's the feeling of well-being we get when we give our time and our love to those we care about most. But it's also down-to-earth, nuts-and-bolts stuff, from stocking our shelves and refrigerator to planning meals and snacks that keep our kids happy and healthy.

I want to hand you the keys to the cooking kingdom so that preparing a meal is never overwhelming or a chore but is instead a pleasure—or at least a good experience. I don't want to scold or dictate; I want to arm you, the home cook with too little time and too little energy, with the tools and confidence needed to get the job done.

Organization is the key. Bite the bullet and decide to get organized. When you have a good shopping list, a sensibly stocked pantry, and an arsenal of cooking tips, you will find that cooking is not a task to dread. If you already like to cook, I will help you become even better at it.

These days everyone has to work hard to maintain a family life. Preparing and eating food is critical to this dynamic, but too many people are conflicted. Here are just a few examples.

- Jennifer from North Dakota pleads: "My kitchen needs to be organized, and I need to learn not to fear the kitchen. I want to feel comfortable making a wide range and variety of foods."

- Diana from Illinois told me what bothers her the most is that "every time I cook a new recipe, I have to go out and buy the ingredients. I don't really know how to keep my kitchen cupboards stocked with the things I really need."

Help may be at hand, Jennifer and Diana. Read Chapter 2, Getting Organized, to learn what to have in the kitchen in terms of foodstuffs and equipment.

- Kim in Texas confesses that "shopping can be such a chore. I just want to get in and get out as fast as I can."

In Chapter 3, Shopping Styles and Secrets, I explain my own hard-won strategies for getting in and out of the market rapidly and for keeping my kitchen "cooking ready."

- Debra, a young mother and college student from Florida, says she cooks "on the fly mostly because once we get home, I am tired and have to study for my courses."

- Susan from Tennessee admits that "dinner gives me the most stress. I usually get home at around 6 P.M., and by then I'm starving!"

- Wendi from Indiana chases three little girls around all day and says, "When four or five o'clock rolls around, I am too exhausted to even think about what to make."

These women share time challenges that can be relieved somewhat by using the ideas in Chapter 4, Maximizing Time. No truer words were ever said than that there never seems to be enough time. But with some forethought and commitment to a system, time can be mastered. I have discovered that while planning is perhaps a bore, it actually saves time. And that's a beautiful thing.

- Martha from New Jersey says her family "seems to eat chicken, chicken, and more chicken."

- Denika from California worries because her "cooking has gotten so bland I don't even enjoy cooking much anymore."

Turn to Chapter 5, Eating Right, for ways to broaden your culinary choices while keeping them healthy and kid-friendly.

- Nicole from Alabama writes: "I'm not Wonder Woman and would love some great tips on quick-fix items and how to plan a menu, shop for that menu, and know what foods complement each other."

- Alayne from Idaho says she has "forgotten how to cook. I used to fix things, and my kids hated everything I fixed. I never use an onion or green pepper in their food."

- Heather from Texas, a busy young mother, says she "would love some ideas for quick meals that I could prepare in stages throughout the day (I usually have to work in ten-minute increments!) and have ready for my hardworking husband when he arrives home."

I urge all three women to read Chapter 6, Different Ways of Cooking, for solid advice. I offer some ideas on how to coordinate the cooking process so that it becomes easy and fail-safe.

- Jennifer from Louisiana has trouble pleasing her young son. "His favorite dish is tacos, but we can't eat tacos every day."

- Linda from Kentucky is wary of cookbooks. "I don't know how to cook some of the food in the books and I haven't even heard of a lot of the ingredients listed. I need something different to eat than what I've been eating ever since I was a kid."

- Kelley from New York complains that it is "hard to plan just one meal for all five of us. Usually I end up making three separate meals, which means I sometimes make eight meals a day."

If these readers check out Chapter 7, Satisfying Your Family's Taste, they will get some ideas about how to choose the right foods for their families.

HOW THIS BOOK WORKS

Take the quiz on the following pages. It's fun and quick and will give you some insight into how you like to cook for your family. The idea is to help you tailor how you cook to how you live, not the other way around.

If you get a kick out of advice columns such as Dear Abby and Hints from Heloise, turn to Chapter 1, Real People, Real Solutions, and read some of the letters I've received from home cooks around the country and Canada. These letters should resonate with many of you; my solutions will help you, too.

Read Chapters 2 through 7 to learn from my experience in the kitchen. I address everything from how to save time to how to organize your kitchen cabinets.

When you see a recipe called a *Kitchen Workhorse*, know that it is one that will save you time and work in the long run. The initial cooking may take some effort, but these dishes are meant to be used in any number of spin-off recipes that will save time as the week goes on. For anyone tempted by the large cuts of meat sold in food clubs and discount warehouse stores, the *Kitchen Workhorse* recipes for meat are perfect!

Throughout the book are questions and answers titled "Ask Art." I have put them near recipes where they are most useful, but as you flip through the pages and read them, you will discover some of my most effective tricks and tips.

The last chapter of the book, Real People, Real Meals, will help you select recipes that meet your needs in terms of time, cooking style, and dietary preferences. I have identified seventeen categories of recipes that, for instance, have very few ingredients, are great for freezing, or are ideal for vegetarians and fish lovers.

ABOUT ME

I grew up in rural Florida where family meals were a cherished, familiar tradition. Not only did we sit down every night for supper, but on weekends cousins, aunts, uncles, and stray friends found their way to my grandmother's house for a big, riotous meal. This happened every Sunday after church, and I think it was these large family gatherings that led me to a career of cooking for families.

I have cooked for small and large families in times of great joy, happy conviviality, and terrible sadness. The food I cooked was often the glue that kept people together and provided the centerpiece for whatever activity was being marked, from a simple supper to a grand wedding celebration.

Observing how universally reviving and comforting good home-cooked meals are helped me decide to be a home cook rather than a restaurant chef. I couldn't be happier with my choice. I love seeing families congregate and eat together, whether it's to share Hot Italian Beef Open-faced Sandwiches (page 97) for Saturday lunch, a big bowl of Capellini with Summer Tomato-Basil Sauce (page 216) on a weeknight, or Butterflied Roast Chicken with Herbs and Garlic Oil (page 173) for a more formal occasion.

In my first book, *Back to the Table*, I outlined my philosophy and beliefs about the importance of cooking for our families. In *Kitchen Life* I get down to the nitty-gritty of making it happen.

IT'S ALWAYS ABOUT THE FOOD

Without recipes you can really use, this book wouldn't be much help. Not everything will fit into your cooking style or meet your family's needs, of course, but I have worked hard to come up with recipes that appeal to the way we cook today.

I've tried to pay attention to freshness, health concerns, ethnic flavors, and simple methods. Every recipe is not for everyone, which explains why some are easier than others, some will appeal more to meat eaters than vegetarians, and some will happily satisfy sweet tooths. Because I believe home cooking is a treasure, I hope that as you become more adept, you will try slightly more difficult or unusual recipes.

Take it from me: Nothing in this book is beyond you! I am confident you will find at least one or two items in every chapter that you'll proudly put on the table. Even picky kids will like my Macaroni and Cheese Soup (page 109), Make-Ahead Salsa (page 92), and Chicken Drumsticks with Lemon-Pepper Marinade (page 191). And I guarantee everyone will happily gobble up my unabashedly old-fashioned desserts, from Gingersnaps (page 294) to Carrot Cupcakes with Cream Cheese Frosting (page 280).

This may be a cookbook, but I hope you find it to be much more: a real guide in the kitchen. We all deserve it!

ART'S
KITCHEN LIFE
QUIZ

Take the following quiz and discover what kind of cook you are. Then look at the lists of recipes I have selected just for you. It's fun to see what other cooks like to make, too, and of course there are no right or wrong answers. My advice? Have fun, try new things, and enjoy your kitchen life.

What kind of shopper are you?

a. I religiously keep a running shopping list.

b. I check my supplies before I leave for the store and write a list of what I am missing.

c. I write down what I need only if it's something unusual.

d. I don't use a shopping list.

---

a. I know what I will cook in the next few days and have all the ingredients on hand.

b. I read recipes and jot down ideas.

c. I buy food with an idea for a meal in mind.

d. I wait until I get to the store for inspiration and shop accordingly.

---

a. I buy only what is on my list.

b. I am always on the lookout for interesting ingredients and build a meal around them.

c. I buy in bulk whenever I see a good deal.

d. I buy food that catches my eye and figure it out when I get home. I buy a lot of prepared food.

---

a. I always check prices and remember them at the register. It saves time in the long run.

b. I don't pay much attention to prices. I figure it all evens out in the end.

c. I make sure to use my shoppers' card and/or coupons. Every penny counts.

d. I catch up on reading in the checkout line. I look forward to these few minutes.

What are your time challenges?

a. I have time to prep food in the morning.

b. I have time to prep food in the evening.

c. I find time to prep when needed.

d. I never have enough time.

---

a. I don't mind prepping food but like quick-cooking recipes.

b. I don't like a lot of prep but don't mind if the dish has a long cooking time.

c. I have time for prepping and cooking.

d. I have no time for prepping or cooking

---

a. I know which appliances I use most often and keep them handy.

b. I periodically clean out my equipment and utensil drawers.

c. I can always find what I need even if my drawers are a jumble.

d. I don't mind clutter in the kitchen.

---

a. I always clean up as I work in the kitchen. It gives me a sense of accomplishment.

b. I pile all dishes and utensils in the sink before I leave the kitchen.

c. The kitchen looks like a tornado hit it after I cook.

d. I do the cooking; someone else cleans up.

What kind of cook are you?

a. I never think about using the oven unless I am baking.

b. I like to put a casserole or roast in the oven and be done with it.

c. I use the microwave for most cooking.

d. I use countertop grills, slow cookers, and rice cookers.

---

a. I like to organize all ingredients and utensils before I begin to cook.

b. I prepare my ingredients and measure everything before I cook.

c. I don't pay much attention to measuring. I "guesstimate" and taste as I go.

d. I jump into cooking and find things as I need them.

---

a. I always read recipes through at least once. I like to know what's coming next.

b. I trust the times given in recipes but appreciate the visual and textural tests for doneness.

c. I pay special attention to heat intensity.

d. I prefer dishes that don't require much tending. If they cook a little longer than required, it's no big deal.

---

a. I have a wide variety of pots and pans for different purposes.

b. I have a small selection of pots and pans but have a good sense of how to use them.

c. I like the way my cookware looks and hang it proudly on a pot rack.

d. My key consideration is how easy the pot is to clean.

Are you eating right?

a. I prepare one meal for the entire family, and we eat it together.

b. Each person tends to fix his or her own meals, and they often overlap.

c. I prepare different foods for everyone, but we try to eat at the same time.

d. We rarely eat together. Our schedules are so crazy, it just doesn't work for our family.

---

a. I believe breakfast is the most important meal of the day.

b. I try to have healthful snacks in the house.

c. I am never sure if everyone in the family had a good lunch.

d. We love takeout.

---

a. I always read food labels.

b. We all try to eat healthfully.

c. Someone is always on some kind of special diet.

d. I try to make sure we eat healthfully, but I know we often don't.

---

a. We get our protein from chicken, meat, fish, and legumes.

b. We get most of our protein from meat.

c. We all like to get our protein in different ways.

d. We eat what we like.

What are your taste preferences?

a. My favorite snack foods are salty, such as potato chips.

b. My favorite snack foods are creamy, such as ice cream.

c. My favorite snack foods are vinegary, such as pickles.

d. Fruit is my favorite snack food.

---

a. I like crunchy things.

b. I like smooth things.

c. I like puffy things.

d. I like chewy things.

---

a. I like foods that are piping hot.

b. I like foods that are frosty cold.

c. I like everything at room temperature.

d. I like different things at different times.

---

a. I like spicy food.

b. I like bland food.

c. I like sweet food.

d. I like different things at different times.

ANSWERS

*If most of your answers are **a**,* you are a seasoned and careful cook who cares as much about the process as about the final outcome. You are organized and precise. You read recipes often and like to try new things. You never shy away from a challenge in the kitchen. Your kitchen is extremely well stocked. You like to use your equipment, and you appreciate having the right tool for the job. You love getting the newest and sleekest kitchen gadget or appliance. You might want to try the following recipes:

snacks and beverages

Habanero and Garlic Popcorn, page 89

Tropical Fruit Cooler with Ginger Syrup, page 100

soup and salad

Smoked Turkey and White Bean Soup, page 106

Chopped Grilled Vegetable Salad, page 120

main courses

Steak Hoisin with Stir-fried Broccoli Slaw, page 142

Lamb Chops with Asparagus, Tomatoes, and Feta, page 168

Bacon-Wrapped Chicken Breasts with Gorgonzola and Walnut Stuffing, page 175

Chicken and Peas Risotto, page 184

Cod with Cashews Baked in Foil Envelopes, page 202

Striped Bass with Clam Sauce, page 210

Potato Gnocchi with Pesto, page 224

Soba Noodles in Miso Broth with Roast Pork and Vegetables, page 228

side dishes

Portobello Caps with White Bean–Pesto Puree, page 266

Corn and Rice Pilaf, page 268

Baked "Risotto" Pudding, page 277

sweets

Chocolate Custards, page 279

Coconut Caramel Sauce, page 307

*If most of your answers are **b**,* you are a confident cook who likes the process but cares most about the final result. "As long as it tastes good," you might say. You read recipes carefully and are not afraid to improvise. You are organized but not frantic. You measure and prep correctly, but if your 1-inch dice are 1½ inches, you don't really mind. Your kitchen is well stocked, but your equipment may not be up-to-date. You might want to try the following recipes:

snacks

Spiced Honey-Glazed Nuts, page 88

Smoked Salmon and Scallion Spread, page 91

soups and salad

Cabbage and Bacon Soup, page 108

Cream of Tomato Soup with Shrimp, page 116

Salmon Steaks with Citrus Couscous Salad, page 128

main courses

Kitchen Workhorse Italian Pot Roast, page 144

Roast Leg of Lamb with Pesto, page 167

Butterflied Roast Chicken with Herbs and Garlic Oil, page 173

Grilled Jerk Chicken Thighs with Pineapple-Cilantro Salad, page 188

Spicy Catfish on Succotash, page 200

Turkey and Black Bean Pie with Polenta Crust, page 240

side dishes

Roasted Beets with Walnuts, page 251

Mashed Cauliflower and Parsnips, page 259

Creamy Parmesan Spinach, page 271

sweets

Coconut Cupcakes with Fluffy White Frosting, page 284

Banana–Peanut Butter Cupcakes with Peanut Butter Frosting, page 302

If most of your answers are **c**, you are a pretty good cook but don't consider yourself a star in the kitchen. You like easy and quick meals, and you are not afraid of a little prep or a little tending once the food is in the pot or pan. You take shortcuts when you can. You buy pre-cut veggies and fruit, bags of lettuce greens, frozen fruit, and marinated chicken breasts from the meat counter if they look good. Your kitchen is stocked with serviceable cookware, and you never ask for pots and pans for your birthday. You might want to try the following recipes:

snacks and beverages

Fruit-and-Nut Bagel Spread, page 90

Make-Ahead Salsa, page 92

Barbecued Ribs and Slaw Sandwiches, page 96

Three-Citrus Iced Green Tea, page 99

soup and salad

Roasted Chicken Soup, page 114

Romaine Hearts with "Caesar" Dressing, page 122

main courses

Peppered Roast Eye of Round with Pesto Vegetables, page 146

Java Beef Stew, page 148

Barbecued Orange-Maple Country Ribs, page 162

Honey-Mustard Chicken Breasts, page 177

Cajun Chicken Wings, page 190

Roasted Shrimp with Lemon-Lime Dipping Sauce, page 212

Capellini with Summer Tomato-Basil Sauce, page 216

Quick Vegetable Chili Tostadas, page 244

side dishes

Baby Carrots with Orange Glaze, page 253

Corn Pudding, page 254

If most of your answers are **d**, you are a cook in a hurry. Home-cooked meals are great, but not every night! You love fast and easy, and the easier the better. You don't like fussy prep work, and you don't pay a lot of attention to culinary details; for instance, you are apt to use a dry measuring cup for liquid measurements or vice versa and you chop vegetables a little haphazardly, but it seems to work out. You have the same pots and pans you had when you moved into your first house, and you don't really care about adding new ones. You have the basic kitchen appliances and really love your microwave and Crock-Pot. You might want to try the following recipes:

PART
ONE

REAL PEOPLE,
REAL SOLUTIONS

Nearly every day I receive letters and emails from home cooks around North America, and, frankly, it's because of them I wrote this book. Again and again I hear that no one has enough time, but we all want to feed our families right and enjoy our time in the kitchen. This is good news! And these are very achievable goals.

While I have addressed home cooks' needs elsewhere in the book, here is a handful of representative letters I have gotten in the past year from people needing help. Many of these came to the Oprah.com website after I posted a message asking people to tell me about the challenges they face in their kitchen lives. These same problems are shared by many of my readers. I hope my answers help them and you.

NOT ENOUGH TIME

Dear Art,
I have four children between the ages of three and ten, and I am always making something special for someone to fit in with his or her activities (hockey, figure skating, gymnastics, piano and guitar lessons, art classes, and horseback riding). I have an awesome gourmet kitchen but barely have time to cook. I would love some time-saving tips so that I can enjoy my wonderful kitchen.
Anne
Age 39
Indiana

Dear Anne,
It's fun to cook in a great kitchen, so I suggest that when you find time, take full advantage of it. Make sauces and soups; both can be doubled to stretch your efforts, and both can be reheated. Take a tip from my mother, who always bought vegetables when they were at their best. She then blanched them lightly and froze them. A vacuum-sealing device such as the FoodSaver® packaging system makes this more efficient than ever. When you want them, they are ready to go!

Dear Art,
My husband works from ten until six, and I am a stay-at-home mom with two small children. I don't have enough hands or time to fix the recipes in cookbooks, and I rarely find good old-fashioned meals in them. Everything is so fancy and intricate. Please help!
Liza
Age 34
Nevada

Dear Liza,

Isn't it crazy how fussy some books have gotten? Some of the older cookbooks have recipes for good old-fashioned meals, and I have incorporated many of these same ideas in *Kitchen Life*, modernized slightly for today's tastes. I also find really good recipes in newspapers and current magazines; these publications know what their readers want. As you build a file of recipes, you will become more and more comfortable cooking them.

Dear Art,

I am the mother of two children, aged two and a half and eight months. I commute to the city and have trouble trying to prepare ahead because I have no time! I would love to learn some techniques and menus that will help me cook for my family.

Marianna

Age 35

New Jersey

Dear Marianna,

If I had two kids and had to rush to work, I would focus on soups and stews that can be cooked ahead of time and put in the freezer. When your schedule is hectic, try easy things that you can make on a weekend and eat during the week.

Dear Art,

How can I feed a family of four in forty-five minutes? Both my husband and I work, and both of our older children are very involved in sports. Games and practices take up four evenings a week, and we end up buying and eating too much microwavable junk food such as mini pizzas, chicken fingers, and fries.

Gayle

Age 38

Manitoba, Canada

Dear Gayle,

Since your family is so into sports, they obviously need lots of good protein. Stick with boned chicken breasts, pork tenderloin, and even a good steak now and then. Toss the steak on the grill, add a salad and a green vegetable, and you're off. Carbohydrates are important for active families, but stick with the better carbs such as beans and brown rice.

BORED WITH THE SAME OLD STUFF

Dear Art,

I enjoy cooking, and my husband and teenage son enjoy eating—but I am running out of ideas for new meals. Every day I hear the same thing: "What are we going to eat?" I've cooked chicken every way I can think of and would appreciate any suggestions or ideas you have for anything that is good and healthful.

Deborah
Age 47
Georgia

Dear Deborah,

I would ask your husband and son what they like. How about a chalkboard in the kitchen where they can jot down their cravings? You'll soon have a list of good ideas! Make the plunge and try fish now and then. It's easy to cook, and your son is old enough to give it a try.

Dear Art,

I desperately need help! I don't know what to buy in the grocery store and need some new recipes. I make the same thing over and over again, and it seems nearly every meal includes chicken in some form. My fiancé and I panfry everything, and when we have a side dish, it's usually macaroni and cheese, green beans, or whole kernel corn.

Angela
Age 32
Oklahoma

Dear Angela,

Why don't you and your fiancé make a list of the foods you really like and not just those you cook now because they are easy. For instance, if you like burgers, try turkey burgers or meat loaf for a change of pace and as a way to get away from too many fried foods. Don't forget about a nice salad. I have a terrific recipe for a balsamic dressing that you can use over and over with greens, tomatoes, and other raw veggies.

Dear Art,

I am an "almost empty nester," but my busy household means we play a guessing game at mealtimes. I never know who will be there and how many. My husband and I have a college student and a high school sophomore at home, as well as my mother and my daughter's fiancé living with us. I am embarrassed to admit how many times I throw up my hands and order pizza!
Patricia
Age 50
Wisconsin

Dear Patricia,

Why don't you make a few quarts of my Marinara Sauce (page 234) and freeze it in small containers? In the time it takes to order pizza and wait for delivery, you could defrost it for pasta or for your own homemade pizza (buy the dough in the supermarket). That's the beauty of this sauce—it stretches for a crowd. Or make a big casserole, chili, or stew and freeze it. Eat these for one or two meals, depending on how many folks turn up.

Dear Art,

My daughter is in college and my son is fifteen, and I confess my life seems easy compared to how it was when the kids were younger. But I am a full-time public defender and still don't have time to fix the meals I would like. I like to cook and would love to entertain, but I'm out of practice. Please help!
Peggy
Age 50
Florida

Dear Peggy,

When you decide to entertain, plan the party. Organization is key. Check the calendar, set a date, and then get busy. Focus on a recipe you know how to cook and then build your menu around it. Just as you keep files for your life as a public defender, you should keep files for your life as a host—sort of a battle plan. Spontaneous entertaining is fun, but I find it a lot more exhausting than a well-planned party, not to mention a lot more expensive.

PICKY EATERS

Dear Art,

I am happily married and expecting my fifth child. My oldest child is nine, so my time is scarce. It is a major blow when nobody wants to eat what I have taken the time to prepare. Each child is picky in his or her own way, and it is an ongoing challenge to find "please-all" meals. Can you help?
Genae
Age 32
Utah

Dear Genae,

When I cook for families, I like to give the kids a choice and then make what they ask for. But I keep the choices to two or three things I know are healthful and easy. This way you will discover some dishes your kids will eat, they will feel empowered, and everyone should be happy!

Dear Art,

I have a five-year-old, a three-year-old, and a two-year-old, so life is very busy. The kids are picky eaters and usually refuse to eat what I make for dinner for my husband and me, which means I make a couple of dinners. It's difficult to shop with the kids, so I end up buying more than I need but I keep trying to find meals that will appeal to all of us.
Lauren
Age 28
California

Dear Lauren,

I love kids' honesty. Unlike a lot of adults, they are never shy about telling me their likes and dislikes. Believe me, trying to prepare more than one dish in an evening will blow your mind, so don't even try. I like to get the kids excited about the food. I make turkey meatballs or a pasta dish. I have also found that kids often prefer raw vegetables, such as carrots and cucumbers, and if I serve them with a little cheese or tomato sauce for dipping, they are happy.

Dear Art,

I am a stay-at-home mom with three children under age seven. I often feel like a short-order cook because everyone eats something different at mealtimes. I never seem to have the right items in the house. My son lives on peanut butter and jelly sandwiches and "pink yogurt." I would like the family to sit together and enjoy a meal, but the only one we seem to agree on is pizza, which we have at least twice a week.
Lisa
Age 37
New Jersey

Dear Lisa,

I completely agree with you that sitting down to a meal is more important than almost anything else you can do as a family, but it's nice if the kids like what you make, too! My mom used to add vegetables to our pizzas to make them more healthful, which is a good idea. As I have suggested to other moms, ask your kids what they like, keep a list, and then make a plan for the week to come.

Dear Art,

I am a recent college graduate on a tight budget. Like many of my friends, I was never taught to cook by my mother and grew up on frozen, packaged, and takeout foods. I want to break the cycle. How do you learn to cook if your mother doesn't teach you?

Laura

Age 23

Massachusetts

Dear Laura,

My advice is to set very easy goals and stick to them. First, make a decision to limit takeout to three or four days a week, tops, and then decide on something you want to make. I suggest you start with soup. Not only is it easy to make, but it's filling, lasts a day or two, and is inexpensive. When you try a casserole, don't worry if it makes more than you need for a meal. This is a good thing! You can eat it over a few days. Try my easy Marinara Sauce (page 234) and spoon it over pasta. Soon you will have a group of great-tasting recipes that you know you can make, and you will have enough confidence to cook for yourself.

Dear Art,

Take-out food is an issue in our family. Both my husband and I work full-time and rarely have time to cook for our two young children. Too often we pull up to the drive-through window. Not only is this expensive, but it's not nutritious. And this is not a habit I want to instill in my children.

Lea

Age 27

Illinois

Dear Lea,

Cooking at home takes a little planning but doesn't have to take much effort. Make a one-dish meal, such as a stew or casserole, and make sure you have enough for two meals. Add a green salad, which is very easy to assemble. You may have to set aside time to cook one day, but you will save time the next day when all you need to do is reheat.

HELP WITH LEFTOVERS

Dear Art,

Please help a mom who likes to cook but doesn't have time to spend one or two hours a day. I am looking for nutritious meals that can be frozen, easily reheated, and served as leftovers. I have found that recipes which actually taste good the next day are laden with "white food" (such as flour, rice, and pasta) or lots of cheese.

Renee
Age 28
California

Dear Renee,

Think about roasted meats and chicken, pot roast, a wonderful casserole, or a soup. None of these takes a lot of time, and all taste good the next day. You can also take a store-bought rotisserie chicken and dress it up with a coating of marinara sauce or simply serve it with a few good side dishes. As you may know, I hate the word "leftover" because it conjures up something that is second-rate, but any food you prepare yourself, even if you freeze the extras for later, is a gift to your family (and to yourself).

Dear Art,

I wish we could prepare a meal once that could be eaten several ways during the week. I like the idea of fixing meals on Sunday that freeze well, but I am also looking for ways to cook a specific meat or other protein that can be served for several different meals. I also find that when I want to try a recipe, I don't have

the soy sauce, ginger, or fresh herbs, for instance, that I need.
Grisel
Age 35
New York

Dear Grisel,

How about a roast chicken, turkey breast, or pork loin? Any of these can be turned into a casserole, a savory salad, or even a soup. When you have time, read through several recipes and make a list of the ingredients you want to have on hand, such as soy sauce, hoisin sauce, fresh ginger, shallots, and garlic.

SHOPPING LISTS AND SHOPPING PROBLEMS

Dear Art,
I am a stay-at-home mom who can't understand why I am having trouble
deciding what to prepare for my young family. I need a plan, both at the grocery
store and in my kitchen cabinets at home. I love to cook but have a mental block
when it comes to deciding what to buy and cook.
Becky
Age 29
Pennsylvania

Dear Becky,

You're right about needing a plan. Nothing ends up saving time more than good organization. Decide on a few easy recipes with just a few ingredients, develop a shopping list from the recipes, and then stick to the list when you shop. You will find it easy to prepare these meals quickly once the shopping is done.

Dear Art,
Our family lives in the middle of nowhere, and I'd love some suggestions for
simple ways to prepare foods because many ingredients in the recipes I read are
too obscure for our region. We can't even get fresh fish. We are limited by distance

and monotony when it comes to the restaurants around here and so have developed a real love for cooking.

Susi
Age 36
Texas

Dear Susi,

You're already halfway there since you have developed a love for cooking. The good news is that supermarkets, even in rural areas, get better all the time. If yours doesn't have fresh fish, it might have an interesting variety of vegetables or fresh herbs. There are lots of ways to prepare chicken and pork, for example; to be good, meals do not have to be complicated. The best thing is to feel comfortable with the food you prepare and not worry if it seems too simple.

Dear Art,

During the week our days begin at 5:30, and none of us gets home until 6:30 or 7:00. On Saturday morning I go to the grocery store without a list or any idea of what to cook for the week because I haven't had time to cook the food I purchased the week before. My pantry and refrigerator are nightmares of unused food! I think my biggest problem is making out the shopping list and planning dinners to make everyone happy.

Dorinda
Age 37
Georgia

Dear Dorinda,

You need a plan of attack. Start by getting rid of the food your family is not eating. Donate it to a soup kitchen or food bank if possible. Now you can begin with a clean slate. Decide on a few recipes and then make your list. Never go to the store without the list and try not to overshop. Stick to the list. It may take some time to get used to this, but in the end it will save you a lot of headaches and money.

Dear Art,

Grocery shopping is extremely difficult. I can spend what seems like hours at the meat counter trying to decide what to buy and how to cook it. My children and husband are getting tired of eating meat loaf, pizza, and spaghetti.

Jackie

Age 34

Michigan

Dear Jackie,

I, too, have stared at the array of meats in the meat department of the supermarket, but I put those days behind me when I decided never to shop without a list. Don't waste time in the store. Instead, decide on a few recipes, write a detailed list, and then head for the market. Once you get in the habit, you will feel odd turning up at the store without a list.

Dear Art,

I would love to figure out how to keep my pantry and refrigerator stocked so that I am not always trying to decide what to have for dinner. I remember when I loved to cook, and I really want to get back into the swing of things so that my husband can come home to a home-cooked meal.

Jo

Age 38

California

Dear Jo,

I applaud your desire to "get back into the swing" of cooking. You will be so happy once you do. Read Chapter 2, Getting Organized, to see my Top Five lists of foods to have in the pantry, refrigerator, freezer, vegetable bin, and so forth. Your lists may vary from mine, but you'll get the idea. Shop for several days at a time, don't overdo it, and determine to stick with this organization.

NUTRITIOUS MEALS AND SNACKS

Dear Art,

I really could use help with how to make sure my three kids eat healthful, nutritious meals. At the end of the day I try to figure out what to have for supper. My eight-year-old son never likes what I make, and so the war begins. We eat out two or three times a week for convenience and because I am too tired and too hungry. I need help!

Nicole

Age 40

Ontario, Canada

Dear Nicole,

During years of cooking for families, I have learned that kids know only what tastes good to them, and it's our job to sort out what is actually good for them. Talk to your kids and ask them to help you figure out several dishes they like and that you know are good for them. Tell them you are making one of these dishes on a certain night. They'll look forward to it.

Dear Art,

I would like my kitchen to be well organized and a fun place to be because my family does not eat right, and that's not right! We are always buying lots of groceries, probably overspending, and still coming up with boring and unattractive meals. This has to stop.

Veronica

Age 45

Alberta, Canada

Dear Veronica,

Grocery shopping is not easy, and I suggest you try to shop by yourself so that you can focus on what you need and what is most healthful for your family. Read Chapter 2, Getting Organized, make a good list, and stick to it. Resist the temptation to buy more than you need.

Dear Art,

Can you help me with my crazy balancing act? I need quick, healthy meal ideas that can be adjusted to suit the needs of a few (during the week) and the whole crew (on weekends when my husband's three kids come to us). There has to be a happy medium somewhere between grilled salmon and chicken (my choice) and frozen lasagna (the kids' choice).

Carrie

Age 28

Michigan

Dear Carrie,

Everyone likes roast chicken or pasta dishes. Make my easy Marinara Sauce (page 234) and use it to dress up grilled chicken or to make lasagna. The kids might like a big pot of soup on a cold weekend, or a main-course salad in the warmer months. Whatever you cook at home, whether it's easy or challenging, nourishes your family any day of the week.

Dear Art,

My kids are older now, and I have started to cook "nice dinners" on the weekends. My husband and children are good sports and usually try everything I cook, but they still prefer fattening comfort foods. They won't eat any fish, are not big on salads, and demand huge portions.

Nancy

Age 48

California

Dear Nancy,

It sounds as if your family likes filling foods, so why not try my Chunky Beef Chili (page 150) or one of its spin-off recipes? They also might go for my Roasted Chicken Soup (page 114) or Spicy Black Bean Soup (page 113). Top these with bean sprouts, grated cheese, or dollops of plain yogurt to work some extra nutrients into the meal.

Dear Art,

My husband is in the army, and my kids are two and a half and one year old, so spare time is a novel idea. I have tons of cookbooks and love to cook. My downfall is finding quick and delicious side dishes. If I were to write a cookbook, I would write one on side dishes only. Right now I am in a rut and need help to spice up old dishes.

Melissa

Age 28

South Carolina

Dear Melissa,

I am so glad you asked this question. I love side dishes, and once I figured out that they did not have to be boring, I went to town. Look at Chapter 15, On the Side, for some great ideas. You might even want to make an entire meal of side dishes (I sometimes do). When you're in the mood for a side dish you know is not too good for you—macaroni and cheese comes to mind— eat just a little. If you decide you like rice and veggies, change the ratio so that there are more vegetables than rice. Try my Baby Carrots with Orange Glaze (page 253) or Roasted Beets with Walnuts (page 251), or perhaps the Creamy Parmesan Spinach (page 271). Wow!

Dear Art,

Although I work from home, and my desk is literally about eight feet from the stove, I still can't get supper on the table until eight or nine o'clock! I hardly ever get around to dessert, and my five-year-old feels deprived.

Brenda

Age 37

Arkansas

Dear Brenda,

One of the easiest and healthiest desserts is fresh fruit, so if you have it on hand, your child won't ever feel deprived. Cut it up and serve it plain or spooned over fruit sorbet or ice cream. I also suggest keeping a few dessert sauces in the fridge, such as my easy Homemade Fruit Sauce (page 306) or Chocolate Sauce (page 308). These turn an ordinary bowl of fruit or ice cream into a special treat. I also think easy-to-bake cupcakes (pages 280, 284, 286, and 302) are terrific desserts. They are small, portable, and a festive ending to any meal. Read the label on those cans of whipped cream sold in every market. They are low in carbs and can dress up cakes and fruit like nobody's business!

KITCHEN ORGANIZATION

Dear Art,

My kitchen is totally disorganized, and while I have tried organizing it, somewhere along the line bowls end up in two different places, the silverware drawer is a mess, and my canned foods are used for building blocks. What can I do?

Darcy
Age 30
Nebraska

Dear Darcy,

To have an organized kitchen you need a plan. While you may never feel that you have enough storage space, if you map out how your kitchen would work best for you, you will be ahead of the game. I would get a labeler from a stationery or office-supply store and then label your shelves and cabinets. Walk your family through the kitchen and impress on those old enough to understand that they should put things in the right place. You might find that the kids like the idea of matching the equipment with its label.

Dear Art,

I have a horrid kitchen. It's small and old, with very little counter space and no dishwasher. If dinner is not cooked efficiently, it can get real ugly! My cabinets are full to bursting, and I would like to learn how to store utensils and supplies.

Aimee

Age 32

Michigan

Dear Aimee,

Your kitchen sounds a lot like kitchens I have had over the years. Frankly, I love small kitchens because I find them easy to keep clean, but they can also feel cramped. It's time to be ruthless! Discard all but your most essential equipment and ingredients. When you restock supplies, make sure you store them in the same place all the time. If you lack drawers, put those tools you use most often in canisters or crocks.

Dear Art,

I love to cook and prepare nutritious meals for my three kids and husband, but there are not enough hours in the day. I would love to get my pantry organized and figure out how to prepare things ahead of time. I would like to freeze foods that my fifteen-year-old can pop in the oven for me.

Ellie

Age 42

Florida

Dear Ellie,

You are an ideal candidate for a vacuum-sealing tool such as the FoodSaver device. You can store food packed in one of these plastic pouches in the refrigerator, freezer, or pantry (depending on what it is), and your teen will quickly figure out how to reheat the food.

KID-FRIENDLY RECIPES

Dear Art,

My four-year-old son loves to help me in the kitchen. Other than making the salad, are there recipes that would allow him to have a more hands-on role when I make dinner?

Mary Jo

Age 37

New Jersey

Dear Mary Jo,

It's a great idea to encourage your son to help in the kitchen. I hope he keeps it up. When I run children's cooking classes, I instruct them not to touch anything sharp or hot. This still leaves them with a lot to do. Teach your son to wash vegetables, to stir batters and other mixtures, and to measure.

Dear Art,

I have noticed that my children will eat things if they have something to do with making it. Do you have ideas for recipes that are not too involved or complicated but still taste fabulous and that my kids can help make?

Laurie

Age 41

Texas

Dear Laurie,

Many of the recipes in *Kitchen Life* are easy enough for kids. I don't think they need special cookbooks or "dumbed down" recipes. I have found that they like to read recipes and then round up the ingredients. Even if the dish is a little complicated, the kids are still helping.

Dear Art,

To get dinner on the table by six o'clock, I have to start preparing it by three or four. I constantly have to stop to break up fights or meet the demands of one of my older children. I hate to resort to take-out food and would like to limit it to once a week. Do you have kid-friendly recipe ideas that are quick and easy?
Shannon
Age 33
New Hampshire

Dear Shannon,

Kids like to make pasta dishes and salads. They love raw vegetables. They also like shakes and soups. They like to mix the batters for cupcakes and then to frost the cooled cakes. They like to stir and operate the blender and mixer. The important thing is to get them involved.

GETTING ORGANIZED

My job takes me to the supermarket nearly every day, and I can tell from a quick look at people's carts what kind of shopper they are. Do they plan every meal for a week? Do they buy basics and then "wing it" when they get home? Or are they spontaneous shoppers who buy what looks good or what is on sale or what strikes their fancy at that moment?

It sounds tedious, but if you plan even a few days' meals, your kitchen life will be far happier. And if you keep your kitchen stocked with the foods you like and that make cooking easier, you will be relaxed about cooking. This is why I have created Top Five lists that enumerate the equipment and foods I think everyone should have in the kitchen. Your lists may vary from mine, but I hope mine help you get going.

KEEP A JOURNAL

You may keep a journal for many reasons (to catalog your baby's progress, perhaps, or to reflect on your personal growth), but have you ever considered keeping a kitchen journal? I strongly recommend this.

The journal can be a loose-leaf notebook with pockets for stray recipes, a spiral notebook, or an online file. What's important is that you jot down what your family likes, doesn't like, tries, rejects, and embraces. Keep track of storage problems and cooking triumphs and disasters. Write a wish list for future improvements to the kitchen.

Once you start keeping this journal, you will be amazed at how much fuller and more energized your kitchen life will be. Trust me!

SIMPLIFY

We hear this all the time: simplify your life, trim the fat, get back to basics. Nowhere is this more important than in the kitchen. Here more than elsewhere in the house it's about priorities.

Stocking your kitchen with equipment is easy. Nothing makes cooking more pleasurable than having the right tool for the job; conversely, nothing is more frustrating than working with dull knives or the wrong pans. Start slowly and add equipment only as you need it.

TOP FIVE PIECES OF EQUIPMENT

1 saucepan with lid (2 to 2½ quarts)
1 nonstick skillet (10 inches)
1 sauté pan (8 or 10 inches)

1 roasting pan

2 oven- and flameproof casseroles (1½ and 2½ quarts)

TOP FIVE ITEMS FOR BAKING

2 heavy baking sheets (avoid flimsy, inexpensive ones)

One 12-cup muffin pan

2 mixing bowls

2 to 3 rubber spatulas

Measuring spoons and measuring cups (liquid and dry measure)

TOP FIVE TIME-SAVING APPLIANCES

Blender

Food processor

Handheld mixer

Electric citrus juicer (not a juice extractor)

Vacuum-sealing kit (such as the FoodSaver device)

Beyond these essentials, identify what your family likes and then stock your kitchen with the necessary equipment. Do you like soups? Invest in a good soup pot. Do you like stir-fries? Buy a wok. Does everyone like quick grilled foods? Consider a countertop grill. Do you like to make omelets? You'll need an omelet pan.

This is what I mean about prioritizing. The same principles hold true for utensils. You don't need many for most cooking applications, but those you have should be well made and pleasing to work with.

TOP FIVE UTENSILS

2 or 3 high-quality knives (see About Knives, below)

2 or 3 long-handled wooden spoons

1 pair of tongs

1 pancake turner

2 wire whisks

About Knives

Most of us use two or three knives. Make sure you have a good paring knife, an eight- or ten-inch chef's knife, and a serrated bread knife. If you use a cleaver or a boning knife, augment your collection with these and others as you go along. Buy the best you can afford and take care of your knives. Having three truly fine blades is a lot more sensible than buying an expensive set of knives you'll never use or struggling with inexpensive ones that don't hold an edge.

When you buy a knife, hold it in your hand and select the one that feels best. It should feel balanced and comfortable. Don't worry about brand loyalty; buy individual knives that you like. You'll use them almost every day!

I recommend high-carbon stainless-steel blades, which hold their edge for a relatively long time, won't rust or stain, and can be sharpened easily. Make sure the blade extends all the way through the handle and is secured with three rivets.

Always wash your knives by hand, dry them right away, and store them in a knife block or on a rack. Don't put them in the dishwasher or let them rattle around in a drawer. Not only will the blades nick and dull if you do, but it's dangerous to have loose knives in a drawer with other utensils.

TIME, NOT MONEY

I constantly hear from visitors to Oprah.com and receive hundreds of letters from *Oprah* viewers about the challenges they face in the kitchen. Over the years the most common plea is that there isn't enough time to cook a family meal. It's not the money but the time.

Our lives are busy and complicated, and time is a precious commodity (I address the subject in Chapter 4). We rush from work to home, and it's often easier to stop at a take-out restaurant or call for pizza from a cell phone than to cook a meal. But if you're organized, if you're just a little bit focused, you can do it.

And here's a nice side benefit: You'll save money in the process. It's a lot less costly to cook a meal than to buy it already prepared.

HOME-COOKED MEALS

Moms and dads from coast to coast tell me they want to feed their families nutritiously. They also value the time they spend around the supper table with their kids. The best way to get the most from that time and to ensure that your children are eating healthfully is to cook meals yourself.

First, decide on a few meals for the week. The recipes on these pages should help. All are easy; most are easy *and* quick and, for the most part, don't have a lot of ingredients. Others are easy to assemble and require slow roasting in the oven. If you know what you are going to cook, you can put a good meal on the table in about thirty minutes. Enlist the kids to wash lettuce, set the table, or, if they are old enough, chop vegetables. If you're organized, everyone will find this relaxing and pleasant, a good time to catch up on the day and decompress. Believe me, it's better than television!

"LEFTOVER" IS NOT A DIRTY WORD

I am waging a campaign to remove the stigma from the word "leftover." I love to have extra food when I take the time to cook. It's wonderful and certainly better than anything you can buy. Use leftover vegetables in stir-fries or soups; put leftover meat in casseroles. Wrap extra food in plastic and a freezer bag or use a FoodSaver device and freeze it for later use.

Start to think of leftovers as gifts. You have shopped for and prepared this food with love; don't diminish its value. Properly stored, leftovers can become an unexpected meal for you and your family to enjoy.

STOCK UP!

If you keep your cupboard shelves, refrigerator, freezer, vegetable bins, and fruit bowls stocked with the foods on these lists, you will be able to make most of the recipes in this book. Honestly, I think this, along with keeping a food journal, is the secret to a happy kitchen life.

TOP FIVE PANTRY ITEMS

Olive oil

Vinegar (cider, wine, balsamic, rice)

White and brown rice (not instant)

Pasta (strand and chunky)

Peanut butter

TOP FIVE CANNED GOODS

Canned beans (white, red, black)

Canned tomatoes (diced and whole plum)

Canned chicken broth

Evaporated and condensed milk

Canned tuna

TOP FIVE BAKING ITEMS

Flour (unbleached all-purpose)

Sugar (white granulated, light brown, and dark brown)

Pure vanilla extract

Semisweet chocolate chips

Leaveners (baking soda and baking powder)

TOP FIVE ITEMS FOR THE REFRIGERATOR SHELVES

Large eggs

1% and 2% milk

Unsalted butter

Cheese (soft, such as cream cheese and ricotta; medium, such as cheddar; and hard, such as good-quality Parmesan)

Cured meat (bacon, prosciutto, ham)

TOP FIVE ITEMS FOR THE REFRIGERATOR DRAWERS

Lettuce (red and green leaf, romaine, iceberg)

Bell peppers (green, red, orange)

Celery

Carrots

Fresh herbs (parsley, thyme, rosemary, tarragon)

TOP FIVE ITEMS FOR THE FREEZER

Frozen vegetables (peas, broccoli, corn)

Frozen fruit and berries (peaches, raspberries, strawberries)

Frozen shrimp (I recommend IQF, which means "individually quality frozen.")

Frozen chicken

High-quality ice cream

TOP FIVE ITEMS FOR THE VEGETABLE BIN

Onions

Garlic

Potatoes (all-purpose, baking)

Sweet potatoes

Tomatoes (in season)

TOP FIVE ITEMS FOR THE FRUIT BOWL

Seasonal fruits (whatever is best and freshest)

Bananas

Citrus (lemons, limes, and oranges)

Berries (strawberries, blueberries, raspberries)

Apples

TOP FIVE SEASONINGS

Sea salt and peppercorns

Dried herbs (bay leaves, oregano, thyme, tarragon)

Dried spices (cumin, cayenne, cinnamon, allspice, cloves)

Chili powder (the best you can find)

Hot pepper sauce

TOP FIVE VERSATILE SPECIALTY ASIAN INGREDIENTS

Sesame oil

Chili sauce with garlic

Hoisin sauce

Miso

Soba noodles

THREE

SHOPPING STYLES AND SECRETS

I try to get in and out of the market in the least amount of time possible. I don't think anyone loves shopping in a supermarket, but it's a fact of life and this type of super-sized store is convenient. Having everything under one roof is efficient, but it's also distracting.

As discussed in Chapter 2, some folks plan, some shop for foods they like and then wing it once they get home, and some shop spontaneously. Shopper number one, the planner, is the most effective. He knows what he will cook that week, knows what basic ingredients are running low at home, and keeps close track of cost. Shopper number two may feel confident in the kitchen. She buys food she likes to cook but may walk out of the store without some crucial ingredients. Shopper number three is hopeless. Buying what strikes your fancy is fun, and buying what is on sale may seem wise, but without the kernel of an idea of what you will cook or what is waiting for you at home in the pantry, refrigerator, and freezer is a good way to spin your wheels. And believe me, this disrupts your kitchen life!

My goal is to turn you all into shopper number one! I like to have a good time as much as the next person, but I have never found the supermarket a place to party. Once you make the decision to plan your shopping trips, I have lots of ideas for streamlining the process. To do so, you need to:

- have a good shopping list;

- know the layout of the store;

- know the recipes you want to cook.

I ALWAYS HAVE A SHOPPING LIST

Whenever you set out to shop, you are on a mission, and if you don't have a shopping list clutched in your hand every time, watch out! When a customer enters the store, the supermarket's mission is to convince him to buy more than necessary, while your mission is to buy only what you need and only what will make your kitchen life better. These missions are pretty much opposed, and with luck you will be the winner.

This is where the list earns its keep. Stick to it. Don't be tempted by fancy displays and impulse purchases. (There's also a lot of truth to the old saying about not shopping when you're hungry.)

If you know your pantry, refrigerator, and freezer, you can very easily make a list. A quick glance will tell you when you are running low on olive oil, frozen vegetables, eggs, or butter. Keep a running list in your food journal, on a kitchen blackboard, or on the computer. Avoid scraps of paper with scribbled notes; they are too easy to lose. And unless your brain works a whole lot better than mine does, don't rely on memory!

Before you set off for the market, decide on several recipes you want to prepare in the coming week. Jot down the ingredients and the amounts. If the recipe calls for a large measure of, say, flour, check the flour canister to make sure you have enough. If the recipe calls for a spice you rarely use, check to see if it's in the spice drawer and make sure it's not more than about six months old. Just taking a moment to double-check details saves a lot of frustration later on.

I LIKE TO KNOW THE STORE

Most of us know our supermarkets pretty well, which is a big help when we shop. We're thrown off if the market manager reorganizes the shelves even a little. Wasn't the milk at the end of aisle 3? What's it doing at the end of aisle 4? Bring on the supermarket police! But we adjust.

You may have a favorite route up and down the aisles, but take time to re-assess that route. If you start in dairy, for instance, perhaps you should rethink this. Perhaps you should begin in produce or canned goods and save the items that need refrigeration or freezing for last.

When I find myself in a new or unfamiliar market, I walk it before I start shopping. This way I get a sense of where the perishables are, where the frozen foods are, and which aisles I can avoid if, for example, I am not looking for soft drinks or cold cereal.

I prefer to shop late in the evening or early in the day. If at all possible, I avoid the homeward rush at the end of the day. Know when you do best in the market and when the store is apt to be the least crowded, and then plan your time accordingly.

BOUTIQUE SHOPPING IS FUN

I love to shop in specialty stores and gourmet shops. The extra attention may well be worth the extra cost for the food, particularly if you are looking for an unfamiliar or exotic ingredient or if you are planning a party. This is one place where a little impulse buying is in order. If you are thinking of one or two cheeses for a cheese board, go ahead and buy a third if it looks tempting. Buy a loaf of freshly baked bread if it will complement your meal. Indulge your inner food lover!

These small markets cater to discriminating shoppers, and if they are properly run, the employees are well trained. Ask questions and take advantage of their expertise.

It's a lot of fun to shop at green markets and farmers' markets, too. In the summertime especially, these places burst with color, and I'm tempted to buy far more than I usually need. A good shopping list and a recipe plan make a difference, and while a little impulse buying is acceptable—great-looking peaches or plump, glistening raspberries, for instance—be realistic.

All of these, including supermarkets, are great places to shop depending on your taste, time, and budget.

MY BEST SUPERMARKET TIPS

I shop daily; it's my job. I have logged years of time in supermarkets and have some tips to make it a better experience.

Get to know the employees. Being naturally gregarious, I find it completely natural to strike up acquaintances with supermarket workers. Markets with full-time employees tend to be better run than those with part-time help, but in either case, if you know a few folks in the market and take time to say hello when you shop, you will be rewarded. These people are knowledgeable and ready to help—particularly if you go out of your way to be friendly. I've given the produce manager home-baked cookies. Now, that makes an impression!

Be aware of expiration dates. You should never buy perishable food with an overdue expiration date, and knowing that your market rarely, if ever, has out-of-date items on display tells you that you're shopping in a well-managed market. Conversely, if the milk or orange juice is frequently on sale beyond its expiration date, you can be pretty sure that management is careless. Look for another market.

Buy fruits and vegetables in season. The strawberries you buy in June will be far less expensive and probably taste better than those you buy in January. For one thing, they aren't shipped from South America and so are likely to be fresher. The same goes for most seasonal ingredients, such as sweet corn, squash, peaches, and tangerines.

Buy non-grocery items separately. I suggest you buy cleaning supplies once a month or less often if you have room to store them. Buy them when you don't need to concentrate on food shopping. Some other products, such as shampoo and toothpaste, may be less expensive at a large pharmacy. Check prices.

Make sure all items are priced. If you check everything for a price tag or bar code (those white boxes with the black lines), you'll avoid those endless price checks at the cash register.

Know how produce is priced. Fruits and vegetables don't carry price tags, so make mental notes when you buy them. Watch for these prices at the checkout; mistakes are often made when foods priced by weight are rung up.

Choose a checkout line wisely. The shortest line is not always the best. Look for a fast checker and a line with a bagger.

Arrange food into categories in the cart and again at the checkout. As I put them in the cart, I organize my groceries—all the protein together, all the frozen foods together, all dairy together, and all the fruits and veggies together. I drive checkout people insane by arranging my purchases again on the belt before they are rung up. This way they are bagged together and it makes my life easier when I get home. I can put the perishables away immediately and tend to the rest of the groceries at my leisure if it suits me.

Use a store shopping card and coupons. Most supermarket chains provide shopping cards for regular customers, which save you money. Coupons are another good way to save money.

Be vigilant at the checkout. Watch the computer screen when your food is rung up. Check your receipt before you leave the store. Mistakes happen, and you might save money if you pay close attention.

Save receipts. In a perfect world (one I don't always live in), we would all staple receipts in our food journals and keep track of what everything costs. Even if you aren't this organized, keep receipts in an envelope and go through them once a month or so. Jot down in your journal what you spend. Over the months you will get a good sense of what you spend and figure out ways to spend less. Saving money without scrimping is always good for a happy kitchen life.

SIMPLY DELICIOUS
Prep in the morning; cook in the evening.

Chinese Curried Noodles with Chicken and Vegetables *(page 222)*
Cod with Cashews Baked in Foil Envelopes *(page 202)*

FOR PICKY EATERS
Family tested to please even the least adventurous palates.

Mini Meat Loaves with Really Good Gravy *(page 152)*
Two-Potato Mash *(page 263)*

DOUBLE-DUTY VEGETARIAN (opposite)
You don't have to be a vegetarian to love this meal.

Cauliflower and Penne Gratin *(page 218)*
Roasted Asparagus with Lemon Zest and Black Pepper *(page 250)*
Roasted Beets with Walnuts *(page 251)*

UNDER 15 MINUTES

When time is the only ingredient you don't have.

FEWER THAN 7 INGREDIENTS
No shopping list required.

Bacon, Spinach, and Cheddar Frittata *(page 164)*

KITCHEN WORKHORSE
From one dish, many.

Chunky Beef Chili *(page 150)*
Soft Beef Tacos *(page 98)*

PANTRY MEAL
Making the most of what you've got.

BAKE SALE

Watch these disappear.

Chocolate and White Chocolate Chunk Brownies *(page 283)*

FOUR

MAXIMIZING TIME

No one has enough time these days, it seems, and yet the same twenty-four hours are still in the day, the same seven days still in the week. What's going on? I believe a lot of our lost time is due to poor organization. As a home chef for more than twenty years, I have learned the hard way about organization. It's part of my job and, to be honest, is not something I was born knowing how to do. Every day I just try to do my best. I am as human as anyone and have had my share of organizational nightmares, but each time I fall down on the job, I focus on what I have done right and learn how to turn it into something great.

I live by my calendar. With a glance I can see which weeks are busy and which, blessedly, are more relaxed. This allows me to gear up mentally for the day, the week, and the month, and it also forces me to decide what I am going to cook and eat on any given day. If you take a close look at my calendar, you will see notations about meals and foods eaten as well as lists of appointments.

GIVE YOURSELF A BREAK

Don't think of getting organized as drudgery. Think of it as giving yourself the gift of freedom. With a clearly delineated schedule you have peace of mind. If you plan three or four meals in a week, you can spend time thinking about other things.

I frequently see people gazing at the food on supermarket shelves with a dazed expression. I just know they are trying to figure out what to make for supper. What a waste of time!

Instead, take a few minutes at the beginning of the week—Sunday evening might work for you—and decide on several meals you will prepare for the family. Read through my tips on how to extend a particular recipe, especially if it's labeled as a "workhorse," and consider making more than one meal from the same ingredients.

List what you are going to cook on your calendar or in your kitchen journal, check the ingredients you have on hand, and make a shopping list for any you are missing. Now turn off the kitchen light and join your family. You have just carved out some leisure time. Enjoy it.

I LOVE MY JOURNAL

As discussed in Chapter 3, Shopping Styles and Secrets, keeping a kitchen journal is a great idea. Write down everything that has to do with your kitchen life, and you will have a lot more luck keeping track of what your kids like and don't like, what meals you've served on holidays and for parties, what food costs, and what your hopes and aspirations are for the kitchen itself in terms of renovations and upgrading appliances.

Your journal may be very different from mine, and as you get in the habit of keeping it, you will decide what works best for you and your family. I suggest a binder or clipboard so that you can add paper as you go along. I also like a binder with pockets for coupons, clipped recipes, and grocery receipts. Some folks prefer a spiral notebook, an online journal, or a small box to hold notes, recipes, and receipts. Teach the kids to use the journal. This will make it a family affair that contains far more input and useful information.

Whatever your choice, I urge you to keep the journal for the kitchen only. It is not the place for notes about family vacations, soccer schedules, or landscape renovations.

As important as it is to keep the journal, it's equally important to review it now and then. Study what you have jotted down, make notations, and discard anything you no longer need.

SAVE TIME BY ORGANIZING

Those who spend their days in an office know how important it is to keep the workplace orderly. No business runs efficiently if files and other work-related documents are organized higgledy-piggledy. Why should your kitchen life be any different?

After you read Chapter 3, you will know that I like to organize my groceries in the shopping cart and in the grocery bags (some might say I am a little obsessive). I am extremely cautious about storing food at the right temperature; I make sure to put all my perishables away the moment I get home from the supermarket. In this way chilled or frozen food does not sit on the counter for any length of time and lose its freshness.

It's not crazy to label shelves. I punch out adhesive labels with a labeler and put them on the shelves so that I know where oil and vinegar are stored and where the canned soups and broths go. Even if you can visualize where everything is kept, it's reassuring to see it on a nice, neat label.

I also like to keep my herbs and spices alphabetized. This makes them easy to find and check; since they are so expensive, it's a good habit to get into. Store herbs and spices in a dark cupboard or drawer, and date them or keep track of them in your journal. Both sunlight and long storage zap their potency, so you should replace them every six or seven months at the least.

Before you cook, read the recipe several times. You have heard this before, and like so much common wisdom, it is rooted in good sense. I suggest you read recipes at least a day before making them. Then you can shop for what you need without rushing. Make sure you have the right-sized pans and paper goods, too (does a recipe call for aluminum foil or waxed paper?).

Restaurant cooks never start cooking until their mise-en-place is in order. This means their ingredients and equipment are prepped and lined up. Home cooks can do the same. If I am making more than one dish, I put the ingredients next to the pan and utensils, organizing several little workstations around the kitchen. You may not have room for this, but if you do, it saves time.

For all meals, I decide what can be done ahead of time. For instance, I make the dessert ahead of time, wash and dry the salad greens, and prepare the marinades.

Finally, I highly recommend that you clean up and put things away as you go. Cooking teacher and cookbook author Marion Cunningham taught me to keep a tub of soapy water in the sink for small dishes, utensils, and measuring cups. What a good lesson! Cleanup is much easier if you do. I put the flour and sugar sacks away after I have measured them. Ditto for herb and spice jars. I make sure to put everything back exactly where it belongs.

Get rid of clutter in your drawers and storage areas. You don't need clusters of spatulas and stirring spoons. Two or three good knives will serve you very well. If you don't use a standing mixer very often, store it away from the work area. Don't keep foods in the pantry, refrigerator, or freezer that you don't eat. Food is sacred and I hate waste, but saving every little bit is nuts! When it comes to your kitchen, less is more once you have decided how you cook and what tools work best for you.

This may be foreign at first, but you will come to embrace this tidy, practical approach to cooking. With a logical strategy the act of getting a meal on the table becomes not only easier but pleasurable, and you will enjoy your kitchen life—and have time to spare.

FIVE

EATING RIGHT

I try to eat right, but it is a daily struggle. Whether you work in the food business, as I do, or just like to eat, eating healthfully is not always easy and not always an option. Nevertheless, I honestly believe it's one of the most thoughtful things you can do for your loved ones. The more I learn about how my diet affects my overall well-being, the harder I try to feed my body in sensible ways. In the process I have come up with some ideas that might help you.

When it comes to food, we all have choices. Making the right ones is not as difficult as you might think. Sure, we have to give up cheeseburgers, French fries, and chocolate shakes for the most part, but these are not forbidden foods. Instead, they become occasional foods.

Families have it tough when it comes to controlling what the kids eat. Even when they are very young, children have strong ideas about what they like and don't like, and that doesn't change much as they grow up. Some families cope by preparing multiple meals every day to satisfy everyone's likes and prejudices. Others let the older children fend for themselves, which might mean a lot of microwave meals and delivered pizza. Some families insist that everyone eat what Mom or Dad cooks, regardless of personal prejudices.

What is the best way to make sure we all eat right?

EAT TOGETHER

Meals are important and shouldn't be grabbed on the fly. Try to establish regular mealtimes so that everyone knows what to expect and when. It's never wise to eat erratically.

Plan to eat as a family as often as you can. Even if you don't subscribe to a strict rule of "Clean your plate" or "Eat what I cook, period," it's important for family life to gather the kids around the table for a meal. Turn off the television and let the machine answer the telephone. Cooking a nourishing family meal is wonderful for your kitchen life, too.

Keep the lines of communication open. Ask the kids what they want for dinner. Encourage everyone to share ideas and get excited about planning meals. Make a point to note in your kitchen journal what meals please a family member, and then make it again later on. What a thoughtful way to show your love.

Start early by making sure that everyone gets up in time for breakfast and eats a wholesome one. A bowl of hot cereal or cornflakes and fruit carries you to lunch without hunger pangs. Stay away from sugary cereals. If your family likes eggs, they are fine a few times a week.

For lunch, eat soup and a salad or a moderate-sized sandwich made on whole wheat bread. Encourage your kids to avoid super-sized servings at delis and other popular lunch places. Send a bagged lunch to school with healthy food that your kids like. It may not always get eaten, but much of the time it will!

Eat dinner about four hours before bedtime and avoid snacking afterward. The food we eat just before bed metabolizes more slowly than other food. I have lots of good ideas for lunch and dinner recipes on these pages. Some folks like sticking with the tried and true during the week and experimenting with new recipes on the weekend. This might work well for you. The key is to cook at home, and the trick is to keep portions realistic.

IT'S ALL ABOUT PORTIONS

If you learn only one thing from this book, I hope it's how to read a food label. These are chock-full of useful information, but they can be misleading. Begin by reading what the manufacturer has deemed as the number of portions. Remember that the calories, fat, sodium, and other nutritional values are based on a single portion of that food. If the can or package contains 2.5 servings . . . well, do the math.

When you cook for your family, keep portions reasonable. Many of my recipes are geared for six to eight servings, which means you may have more than you need depending on the size of your family. Instead of eating large amounts, store the uneaten food for another meal. Read my tips for freezing and defrosting food for storage on page 74.

I also like the concept of the bowl or plate. Eat only what fits in a bowl or on a plate. No more. This way you are never tempted to overeat—unless you have extremely large plates!

When you eat in restaurants, ask for a half portion or steel yourself to eat only some of what is on the plate. Take the rest home. If you are splurging on dessert, consider sharing it.

Kids love fast-food restaurants, and occasional visits can work into family life. Turn meals at these places into sometime treats and don't encourage anyone to order more than he or she can eat. It's also a good idea to discuss the negative health aspects of fast food—without hammering away at them. It doesn't take much for fast food to turn into much-desired forbidden fruit.

WE NEED SNACKS

Everyone gets hungry between meals. This may not happen every day, and there will be some days when you are running around so much that you don't have time for a snack. On the other hand, it's often when you are on the go that you grab exactly the wrong snack, such as a candy bar, a bag of corn chips, or a sugary soda.

I keep jars of nuts and dried fruit in the house and snack on them instead of crackers or cookies. A handful is all I need to fend off the kind of hunger that might encourage more fat-laden snacking. Unsalted and unbuttered popcorn is a tasty snack. (I've even been known to sneak a small bag into the movie theater.)

The best snacks are the easiest, such as an apple or low-fat yogurt. If you are home, cut up chunks of a good firm cheese, such as cheddar or Monterey Jack, and keep them in a plastic bag in the refrigerator. The same goes for slices of turkey or cold chicken. These foods, which are powerful sources of protein, stave off hunger and are more healthful than chips or chocolate.

Drink water. I am sure you are weary of hearing about the benefits of water, but they're true! Water really helps control your intake of food, and it's always good for you. Feeling sleepy? Headachy? Hungry? Your body might need hydrating.

WHAT'S HEALTHY?

The food that is best for you and your family is the food you prepare yourself. This way you know how much fat, sugar, and salt is in each dish. You know how fresh and nutritious the meal you put on the table is, and this knowledge makes you feel great.

Commonsense guidelines allow us to recognize what is healthful and what is not. Everyone knows that our families can't live on deep-fried foods and baked goods, yet we all know how easy it is to fill up on fried chicken, potato chips, and brownies.

Feed your family good protein such as chicken, turkey, pork, fish, dried beans, and lentils. Eat red meat only once a week or so. Eat lots of vegetables, whole fruits, and low-fat dairy products, and, for the most part, stay away from processed foods.

Minimally processed foods such as frozen vegetables and fruit (without syrup), canned plum or chopped tomatoes, water-packed tuna, and canned broths are great time savers and make cooking easier and more enjoyable. It's the ready to eat foods you should avoid, such as snack cakes and frozen meals that you pop in the microwave.

Pasta, rice, potatoes, and bread are out of favor right now because they fall into the dreaded category of "bad carbohydrates." Serving these foods several times a week and in sensible portions is more than okay. They satisfy our appetites and enhance other foods. I would rather eat a small baked potato or serving of brown rice than a carton of French fries any day!

Fats are confusing. Olive oil is a monounsaturated fat and is considered the best choice for oils. Polyunsaturated oils such as canola, corn, and safflower oils are nearly as good for you, so you never need to worry about using these in cooking. Minimize fats from animals, such as butter, and very fatty meats, such as bacon.

Margarine is tricky. If you want to use it, choose one that lists unsaturated liquid vegetable oil as the first ingredient on the food label. Avoid those that list hydrogenated or partially hydrogenated oil as an ingredient. Buy soft or liquid margarine rather than sticks; soft margarines tend to contain more unsaturated fats.

SOME OF MY FAVORITES

If you think of your body as sacred, you will want to feed it right. I have discovered some healthful foods that I really enjoy eating.

I eat whole fruits in their natural state. Eat a whole orange instead of drinking a glass of orange juice. The same for pears, peaches, apples, and pineapple. Fruit is high in sugar, which is why we love it so.

Berries are great, and if you can't get them fresh, look for frozen ones that are not packed in juice or syrup. Freezing technology is advanced, and sometimes the best of the crop is frozen. Take advantage of this.

Tomato juice is also great, although you will have to watch the sodium counts. Vegetable juices you make with a juice extractor are lovely. I like carrot-apple juice, among others, but you have to remember that carrots are sweeter than other vegetables.

I eat a lot of chicken breasts, pork tenderloin, and white-meat turkey. I love fish such as halibut, sole, cod, salmon, and tuna. I also like shrimp, although if you watch your cholesterol levels, you shouldn't eat it more than once or twice a month.

When I crave ice cream, I indulge in a small helping of really good, high-quality ice cream; nothing beats it. I have also found some excellent frozen yogurts. I eat graham crackers instead of cookies when I need something sweet and crunchy.

Establishing healthful eating patterns is a long-term challenge, and the best time to start is today. If you are already eating right, keep it up and look through my recipes for good ideas as well as ideas for meals when you throw caution to the wind! Enjoy what you cook and eat with your family. It's vital to your kitchen life.

SIX

DIFFERENT WAYS OF COOKING

W hen I ask people what they like to cook, invariably they reply, "Anything that's quick and easy." I don't blame them; quick and easy are good things, and there are many ways to achieve both. Understanding how you really like to cook makes your kitchen life more rewarding.

Food cooked in the microwave can be quick and easy, for sure, but so can food cooked in the oven or on the stovetop. Examine what you like to eat and then define how you like to cook. Knowing your favorite techniques will help you choose recipes as much as identifying preferred foods.

Do you like to put something in the oven and forget about it for an hour or two? Do you prefer sautéing or stir-frying? Is your idea of cooking heating a frozen meal in the microwave?

Most home cooks avail themselves of all these cooking methods, but with careful scrutiny you can identify what makes you most comfortable. Now you know your preferred style.

What does this tell you? If you like oven roasting or baking, you are someone who is able to plan ahead in order to leave ample time for the hour or two that an oven-cooked meal requires. You like easy, one-pot meals that require little cleanup. You may also be a good candidate for a slow cooker.

On the other hand, if you are comfortable grabbing a sauté pan or skillet and searing chicken breasts or sautéing fish fillets while a pot of rice simmers on the back burner, you are the kind of cook who feels capable of juggling several tasks at once.

If you are nervous about doing much more than heating food in the microwave, you probably feel that you have a lot to learn. I am here to help!

Microwaves are great for some cooking tasks. For instance, I blanch vegetables for stews, salads, and other dishes by sprinkling them with water and microwaving. Blanching, which can also be done in boiling water on top of the stove, does not cook the veggies but softens them a little and heightens their color. It rarely takes more than a minute. The hot food is then immediately shocked in ice water to halt the cooking. Blanching is also an important step if you plan to freeze fresh vegetables for later use.

I also like the microwave for melting chocolate and softening butter for baking. It is kitchen technology that has a place in everyone's kitchen life.

Other cooking implements that I find useful are countertop grills (such as the George Foreman Grill), electric steamers, which are terrific for vegetables, and rice cookers. Look around. See what appliances fit into your kitchen life and buy only those you think you will use with some regularity.

MY COOKING STYLE

My life as a chef is predicated largely on the fact that I have a reliable repertoire of recipes. I cook them over and over—with variations so that not everyone catches on to my tricks! Look at the workhorse recipes in this book. Once you make a pork pot roast, for example, it's easy to use the same cut of pork to make pork marsala or a toasted Cuban sandwich.

I learned a lot about preparing ingredients and timing meals by observing how line cooks in restaurants work. These guys have it figured out. They have the ingredients prepped (chopped, minced, sliced, and so forth) and the amounts portioned out. When it's time to cook, they are ready. No false starts, no searching for anything.

Home cooks may not have the luxury of studying really good restaurant cooks, but they can follow many of the same principles. For instance, if I am cooking a dish that requires chopped or minced vegetables, I do this ahead of time, put the ingredients in small bowls, and refrigerate them until I need them. I measure the ingredients that don't need refrigeration, such as flour and oil, and leave these on the counter. (If your pantry is well organized, it's not hard to do this.) Before I cook, I put everything for that recipe on the counter, lined up in some order. Only then do I actually cook.

If you don't already do this, try it. You will be amazed by how easy cooking becomes. By doing it this way, you pay attention to heat intensity, timing, stirring, seasoning, and tasting, all so important to culinary success. Think about it. If you are chopping the garlic while the onion is already cooking, you will very likely burn the onion. This leads to frustration, which leads rather quickly to the conviction that cooking is hard or no fun.

If we lived in a perfect world, everyone would read recipes through well ahead of time and make sure every ingredient was on hand. If you are like me, your world is far from perfect. Perfection aside, it is important to read recipes before you begin to cook. This way, beyond checking if you have the ingredients, you can decide if you have the time, the skill, and the right equipment for the job.

If you can follow the instructions on the back of a box, you can follow a recipe. A good recipe will tell you the kind of pan to use, whether you need to whisk or stir the food gently, and how much time the food needs to cook. It will also give you visual hints to determine when it is done.

Knowing how long to cook something is one of the hardest things for a home cook to master. Remember that the times given in recipes are estimates and that you need to use tests for doneness, too. This might mean an amount of browning, such as for a cake or a crispy-topped casserole; a certain internal temperature, especially for meat and poultry; or a degree of thickness, as for a sauce or gravy.

Experiment a little and take the time to understand how heat works. Not everything cooks better on high heat, although you may believe this will speed things up. Some foods need gentle cooking; others absolutely need quick searing or browning.

Stovetop burners cook differently. Not only do some stoves put out more heat (BTUs), but my idea of "medium-high heat" might be different from yours. A heavy-bottomed pan will cook food more slowly than a thin aluminum pan.

Ovens vary, too. This is mainly because many home ovens are not accurate. Just because you turn the dial to 350°F doesn't mean the oven's chamber heats to that temperature. It's a very, very good idea to calibrate your oven. To do this, buy an oven thermometer; these are inexpensive and sold at supermarkets, hardware stores, and kitchenware shops. If the temperature on the oven thermometer does not match the temperature on the dial after twenty minutes, your oven is off. It's easy to compensate by adjusting the dial 25 or 50 degrees one way or the other, depending on your findings, and checking the thermometer again. It's an even better idea to ask the electrician or gas company to adjust the oven for you.

UNEXPECTED MEALS

Leftovers are discussed in Chapter 2. Anything you have cooked with your own two hands is not a leftover. It's food you have lovingly prepared and deserves to be eaten and enjoyed. This extra food should not be given second-class status but should be treasured.

If you have a FoodSaver machine, which vacuum-packs the food so that it keeps at its peak for weeks in the refrigerator and for months in the freezer, use it. When you are ready to cook the food saved in the plastic pouch, just drop it in boiling water and presto! It tastes as delicious as the day it was prepared.

You can also pack cooled food in airtight containers and zippered plastic bags for storage. If you refrigerate the food, use it in a day or two. If you freeze it, use it within months. See About Freezing and Defrosting below. In your journal, keep track of what you have stored and make a point to eat it. Your food bills will diminish and you will enjoy your own cooking twice as often!

GET EQUIPPED

I have known people who buy a set of nice cookware and then don't use it. Are they afraid to mess it up? Use your pots and pans, see what they can do, and decide on those you like best.

I caution anyone against buying a "set" of cookware. Buy good-quality pots and pans, ones that will last a lifetime, but collect them as you need them. You will develop favorites, and just as you cook the same recipes over and over, you will use the same pans over and over; you will also buy the sizes that best fit your family's needs.

About Freezing and Defrosting

Freezing is an efficient way to preserve food, and most foods freeze well. These include vegetables, fruit, meat, fish, bread, and many cooked dishes such as casseroles, soups, and stews. Butter is a good candidate for the freezer. I store my butter there to have it on hand for baking. Foods that do not freeze well include cooked potatoes, rice (unless it's in a casserole), creamy preparations such as sauces and custards, greens and cucumbers, and cheese.

Use a freezer thermometer to determine how cold the freezer is. Keep it at 0°F. A well-packed freezer stays colder than a half-empty one.

Make sure the food is cool before transferring it to a freezer bag, heavy-duty plastic wrap, or plastic container, or use a FoodSaver machine. It's more efficient to freeze food in small amounts, so divide the soup or stew into portions. Remove as much excess air as you can from the wrapping or bag (this is where the FoodSaver device is tops!), because too much air surrounding the food results in freezer burn (dried out, white, or dark surfaces).

Date all food you freeze and plan to eat it within three months. Meat, with its relatively high fat content, cannot be kept frozen as long as vegetables and fruit. Plan to eat meat and poultry within two months of freezing at the most. Keep track of what is in the freezer in your journal. Plus, don't refreeze defrosted meat. The texture and flavor will be compromised.

Defrost food in the refrigerator. This is particularly important for meat and poultry, which should never be left on the countertop. With practice you can learn how to defrost vegetables and fruit in the microwave, but take care they just thaw and don't start to cook.

You don't have to be a physicist to understand the materials used for cookware, but a little comprehension helps.

- Aluminum heats quickly and evenly but is not the best choice for long, slow cooking. It's great to boil water for pasta or blanching. It also reacts with acidic ingredients, such as tomatoes and vinegar, imparting a metallic taste.

- Anodized aluminum and aluminized steel are alloys that often have a stainless-steel core and are used to make a host of quality pots and pans. You won't go wrong with these.

- Cast iron is an old-fashioned material that nonetheless can't be beat for retaining consistent heat, even at very high temperatures.

- Glass holds heat well but does not conduct quite as efficiently as metal. Tempered glass works on both stovetops and in ovens.

- Nonstick cookware is very effective these days. I like to use good, heavy, nonstick skillets and other pans, although I don't recommend them for browning meat.

When you are buying pots and pans, hold them while you are in the store and decide if you like the way the handle feels. Imagine hefting a large pot full of liquid. Make sure at least some of your pans have tight-fitting lids. My only real warning is to stay away from bargain-basement brands. They will warp and dent and eventually make you unhappy.

Identifying how you cook and which style makes you happiest will enhance your kitchen life. Whether you prepare the dishes described in this book—and I hope you do!—or stick with your own tried-and-true repertoire, enjoy the process. It's worth it.

SEVEN

SATISFYING YOUR FAMILY'S TASTE

If you analyze taste preferences, we respond to four basic sensations: sweet, sour, salty, and bitter. Some of us like salty foods while others go for sweets. I pretty much like everything, although if I had to choose, I would eat more salty foods than others (but sure would miss my sweets!). When it comes to textures, I like crispy more than soft, but if I had to eat only crispy, crunchy foods for the rest of my life, I would crave creamy rice pudding!

I suspect most people are like me. We have preferences but in general like an array of tastes and textures. Knowing what you like will help you order your kitchen life. Just as it's useful to identify your style of cooking—which is discussed in Chapter 6, Different Ways of Cooking—knowing your preferences in tastes and textures makes it easier to select recipes from these pages and other sources. If you like spicy, salty, crunchy foods, try the Asian Snack Mix on page 87 or Flounder Fillets with Cornmeal-Mustard Crust on page 205. If you like your crunch a little sweet, try Chocolate and Pine Nut Biscotti on page 298.

You get the idea.

TASTE MEMORIES

We hear a lot about taste memories these days. These are the flavors in certain foods that, with one bite, transport us back to our grandmother's kitchen, the corner candy store, or the school cafeteria. By the second bite we generally find ourselves very much in the present, and the flavors may or may not lose their allure.

When I was a kid, my mother "fixed" frozen pizza for me on Sunday night. This meant she took a store-bought pie and added her own touches, such as extra cheese, really good pepperoni, or sliced mushrooms and peppers. I still associate pizza with casual Sunday evening meals. She also spread egg salad on whole wheat toast as breakfast for me, and to this day I think of egg salad as breakfast food.

Think about your own taste memories. Chances are they shape how you eat today, but do you really like them? If not, file them along with other childhood memories. On the other hand, most of us revel in the flavors of our childhood and truly enjoy eating food that reminds us of simpler, happier times. This explains the interest in so-called comfort foods, such as mashed potatoes, pot roast, and chunky chocolate brownies (all of which are included in this book with my own twists and turns).

But we shouldn't stop there when identifying the foods we like best. Examine how you eat day in and day out and note which foods you and your family continually return to. Try this experiment: Without paying special attention, just jot down the meals you prepare over the course of the next several weeks.

Go back over your notes (use your kitchen journal), and I think you will find a pattern or several patterns. This information is valuable. Use it when you plan new menus or decide to try something new.

WHEN YOU WANT TO CHANGE

If you are concerned that you and your family should eat more healthfully, consider taste preferences before making any major changes. When you know your family's eating patterns, dietary changes are easier, too.

When we make adjustments, most of us change our diets for the better. That's the good news. We are more aware than ever about the food we eat, but, still, obesity is on the rise in this country. That's the bad news. Concentrate on the good news, and your family's health and your kitchen life will be enhanced.

Don't ditch all the "bad" foods you truly like. Eating better does not mean life without French fries or chocolate pudding. Just eat them less frequently. Treat the foods you really like but know are not good for you as special occasion foods. I have battled my weight my entire life and have come up with strategies that work for me. For instance, I try to be "good" all week and then allow myself to indulge on weekends. You may come up with a similar plan.

Health and diet experts may be rolling their eyes about now. Eating healthfully does not mean depriving yourself of good-tasting food, they say. Broiled fish and chicken, sautéed vegetables, and steamed rice are delicious. I agree, and I never feel deprived when I cook them. But let's get real. I love a bag of potato chips or a bowl of ice cream now and then. And why not?

FEAR OF FOOD

We're bombarded with information about what we should and shouldn't eat. By now most of us know that we should cut back on fats, carbohydrates, and sugars (which are carbohydrates). We should eat lots of vegetables and some fruit. We should drink water and avoid soda and too much alcohol.

But if you think about it too much, you will lose the enjoyment of cooking, eating, and appreciating good food. I want everyone who reads this book to have a joyful and rewarding kitchen life, and the best way I know to accomplish this is to embrace food and cooking—and to get rid of our fears.

We fear fat. We are terrified of eating too many carbohydrates. We run from chocolate. We gasp at the idea of heavy cream. What's going on? I am not addressing allergies, which afflict many people and which must be taken seriously. I am talking about plain, unadulterated fear of food.

Get over it, people! A little fat tastes good, as does a slice of freshly baked bread or a baked potato. I think eating healthfully is crucial for a happy kitchen life, but this is not and never will be a diet book. All food has a place in my heart and in my kitchen.

My recipes are full of flavor and are planned to meet the way American families cook and eat. For instance, I have not deep-sixed all pasta dishes. (I love pasta and it's a great way to stretch a family meal.) I have plenty of recipes for red meat but temper them with just as many for chicken and fish. And when you get to the dessert chapter, you'll have to control yourselves. Because my intention is to share easy, straightforward recipes with you, none of the desserts (or any other recipe in the book) is difficult to make, but all are indulgent and sinfully delicious.

BEYOND THE KITCHEN

Just as you will be happier and more connected as a family once your kitchen life reaches its full potential, there's life beyond the kitchen. I am talking about eating out.

I love to go to restaurants, from the most elegant to the funkiest dive. My number one criterion is that the food be worth my time and money. This explains why I stay away from chain restaurants for the most part, and instead frequent local ones and, in particular, ethnic places. This way I support my neighborhood businesses and broaden my taste preferences at the same time.

I have learned a lot about what I like to eat by eating at Chinese, Thai,

Vietnamese, Korean, Mexican, Ukrainian, Greek, and Brazilian restaurants, as well as by eating at high-end French, Italian, and contemporary American restaurants. I also like to grab salads and wraps at health food bars, try baked goods at small bakeries, and sample juices at juice bars. Tastes, textures, and stimulating ideas are out there.

I try to order sensibly in restaurants. Make healthful choices the next few times you eat out and see how you feel afterward. You don't need heavy sauces and deep-fried foods to take pleasure in a meal. You will want such indulgences sometimes, but not always. If you want dessert, share. Restaurants are used to this nowadays and happily supply a table with extra spoons or forks for just one or two desserts. You won't feel the least bit deprived. I never do, and in fact I cherish the very act of sharing.

If you make an effort to recognize which flavors and textures please you and your family and then choose recipes that reflect these preferences, you will come to enjoy cooking even more than you do now. At the same time you will set examples for your children, who will grow up with taste memories nurtured in your kitchen. That's what I call a far-reaching kitchen life!

PART
TWO

HOMEMADE SNACKS, SANDWICHES, AND BEVERAGES

We are a nation of snackers, and to meet our demands, food companies have come up with an impressive array of tempting snack foods. I love these treats as much as the next guy, yet I try to limit my indulgence. But I still need snacks, and so does your family. That's why I included this chapter, which is full of great ideas for creating snacks at home.

When you make your own snacks, not only do you know exactly what goes into them, but you can adjust the spice or sweet meter to your family's level.

For instance, when I want something with a "wow" in the heat department, I make the Habanero and Garlic Popcorn (page 89) and take the time to locate fiery habanero chilies instead of the easier to find and milder jalapeños. When I want something sweet and crunchy, nothing beats the Spiced Honey-Glazed Nuts (page 88).

I have a few recipes here for sandwiches that can serve as light meals or after-school snacks for hungry teenagers. Some rely on meat that you buy at the deli counter while others call for the meat remaining from recipes found in Chapter 11, Meat Main Courses. Either way, they can be made in a jiffy!

Finally, you'll love the iced tea, fruit cooler, smoothie, and shake at the end of the chapter. In the summertime I consume gallons of iced tea and love to experiment with different types of tea. The recipe here is for iced green tea! Try it—it's refreshing and so good for you, too.

These recipes are totally fun and delicious, and very easy to make. Include them in your repertoire and enjoy your kitchen life!

recipes

Asian Snack Mix

Spiced Honey-Glazed Nuts

Habanero and Garlic Popcorn

Fruit-and-Nut Bagel Spread

Smoked Salmon and Scallion Spread

Make-Ahead Salsa

Quick Lemon Hummus

Smoked Turkey, Apple, and Cheddar Quesadillas

Barbecued Ribs and Slaw Sandwiches

Hot Italian Beef Open-faced Sandwich

Soft Beef Tacos

Three-Citrus Iced Green Tea

Tropical Fruit Cooler with Ginger Syrup

Peach-Banana Smoothie

High-Protein Shake

This is everything a snack should be: sweet, salty, crunchy, and spicy, all at the same time. Homemade soy glazed almonds hold everything together. The wasabi-coated peas explode with flavor. If you haven't tried them, go for it!

ASIAN SNACK MIX

1 cup (4 ounces) whole natural almonds

¼ cup reduced-sodium soy sauce

1 teaspoon sugar

1 cup (6 ounces) coarsely chopped dried pineapple

1 cup (4 ounces) wasabi-coated peas

One 3-ounce can chow mein noodles

1 Mix the almonds, soy sauce, and sugar in a medium nonstick skillet. Bring to a boil over high heat. Cook, stirring often, until the soy sauce has completely evaporated, about 3 minutes. Spread the almonds on a nonstick baking sheet or cake pan and cool completely. Break the almonds apart.

2 Toss the almonds, pineapple, peas, and noodles in a large bowl. (The snack mix can be stored in an airtight container at room temperature for up to 1 week.)

MAKES ABOUT 4½ CUPS

ASK ART

Is there really any difference from one soy sauce to another?

Yes, there is a difference from brand to brand and from one type to another. Many of the most inexpensive brands are not made in the authentic method and because of this don't have the body and depth of flavor of the "real thing." Luckily, traditional soy sauce is barely more expensive than cheaper sauces and provides better flavor. Look for Chinese or Japanese soy sauces. They may be light, medium, or dark. Light soy sauce is not fermented as long as dark soy sauce, which has added molasses and tastes very rich and sweet. I use medium soy sauce, which is by far the most commonly available grade and meets my every need. Lately I have been sticking to low-sodium or reduced-sodium sauces, which provide excellent flavor. Tamari is soy sauce made without wheat, and for those with wheat allergies, it works just as well as soy sauce.

These are similar to the spiced pecans in my first book, *Back to the Table*, but are a bit sweeter and spicier. Nuts are great snacks because they fill you up and are chock-full of healthful oils. It's nice to have a jar of these on hand for entertaining, but it is nearly impossible to keep from snacking on the entire batch yourself!

SPICED HONEY-GLAZED NUTS

4 cups assorted unsalted roasted mixed nuts

⅓ cup honey

⅓ cup light corn syrup

½ cup sugar

1 tablespoon salt

1 ½ teaspoons ground cumin

1 ½ teaspoons chili powder

½ teaspoon ground hot red (cayenne) pepper

1 **Position a rack** in the center of the oven and preheat the oven to 350°F.

2 **Spread the nuts** on a large rimmed baking sheet. Bake just until the nuts are warm to the touch, about 3 minutes. Remove the baking sheet from the oven. Drizzle the nuts with the honey and corn syrup, and mix well. Continue baking, stirring often with an oiled spatula (the nuts on the edges of the baking sheet will cook more quickly than the ones in the center), until the liquid has evaporated into a glaze, 10 to 12 minutes.

3 **Mix the sugar,** salt, cumin, chili powder, and red pepper in a large bowl. Add the nuts and mix well to coat them with the spiced sugar. Transfer to a clean baking sheet and let cool, breaking apart any nuts that stick together. The nuts will crisp as they cool. (The nuts can be stored in an airtight container at room temperature for up to 1 week.)

MAKES ABOUT 4 CUPS

The phrase "hot and spicy" doesn't begin to describe this irresistible snack. Frying releases the tantalizing flavors of the zesty habanero chili and pungent garlic cloves, infusing the oil and then transferring their glory to the popcorn itself. The fluffy kernels are so tasty that you may find yourself passing up the butter. If they served this stuff in movie theaters, who knows how the Oscars would turn out?

HABANERO AND GARLIC POPCORN

¼ cup olive or vegetable oil

1 habanero or jalapeño chili (habaneros are spicier and will give the popcorn a hotter, deeper flavor), seeds and ribs removed, and cut into ½-inch pieces

2 garlic cloves, crushed under a knife and peeled

½ cup popcorn kernels

Salt for serving

Melted butter, optional

1 **Place the oil,** chili, and garlic in a moderately large saucepan and place over medium heat. Tilt the saucepan so that the oil collects in a corner. Heat until the garlic is golden brown and the chili is very tender, about 3 minutes. Using a slotted spoon, scoop out and discard the chili and garlic.

2 **Add the popcorn** to the saucepan and cover. Increase the heat to high. Cook, shaking the saucepan often, until the kernels have stopped popping. Pour the popcorn into a large bowl. Sprinkle with salt and drizzle with the melted butter, if using. Serve hot.

MAKES ABOUT 12 CUPS

Make this creamy, not-too-sweet spread on a weekend morning and watch it disappear! Be sure to use whipped cream cheese so that the chilled spread can be slathered straight from the refrigerator on bagels, English muffins, toast, or whatever suits your family's fancy. Substitute other dried fruits for the cranberries, from cherries to raisins, and pecans, hazelnuts, or almonds happily pinch-hit for the walnuts.

FRUIT-AND-NUT BAGEL SPREAD

½ cup dried cranberries

One 12-ounce container whipped cream cheese

⅓ cup walnuts, toasted (see page 251) and chopped

2 tablespoons confectioners' sugar

Grated zest of ½ orange

⅛ teaspoon ground cinnamon

1 **Place the dried cranberries** in a small bowl and add enough hot water to cover. Let stand to plump the cranberries, about 20 minutes. Drain and pat dry with paper towels.

2 **Using a rubber** spatula, mash the cranberries, cream cheese, walnuts, confectioners' sugar, orange zest, and cinnamon in a medium bowl. (The spread can be stored, covered and refrigerated, for up to 3 days.) Use chilled or let stand at room temperature for about 30 minutes to lose its chill.

MAKES ABOUT 2 CUPS

ost supermarkets carry sliced smoked salmon in the refrigerated section. Piled high on bagels with a amount of cream cheese, it can be spectacular but perhaps I like to mix the salmon with whipped cream cheese, scallions, and dill to make a more modest alternative to the classic method that still delivers a lovely flavor punch. If there's any left after breakfast or brunch, mix it with sour cream for an incredible dip for potato chips.

SMOKED SALMON AND SCALLION SPREAD

One 12-ounce container whipped cream cheese

3 ounces smoked salmon (a moderately priced variety such as lox), chopped into ¼-inch dice

1 scallion, white and green parts, finely chopped

1 tablespoon chopped fresh dill or 1½ teaspoons dill seed

Freshly ground pepper to taste

1 **Using a rubber spatula,** mash the cream cheese, smoked salmon, scallion, dill, and a generous grind of pepper in a medium bowl. (The spread can be prepared, covered, and refrigerated for up to 3 days.) Use chilled.

MAKES ABOUT 1½ CUPS

SMOKED SALMON DIP: Mix ¾ cup Smoked Salmon and Scallion Spread with ½ cup sour cream. Serve with sturdy potato chips.

S alsa is much, much more than a dip. Spoon it over burgers and meat loaf, stir it into sautéed vegetables or rice, and use it as a condiment for Mexican-style dishes. Sure, you can buy jars of salsa to stash in the pantry—and these are terrific to have on hand—but frozen homemade salsa allows you to have more leeway with spiciness and added ingredients.

MAKE-AHEAD SALSA

1 tablespoon olive oil, preferably extra-virgin

1 medium onion, chopped

1 jalapeño chili, seeds and ribs discarded, and finely chopped

2 garlic cloves, finely chopped

One 28-ounce can diced tomatoes in juice, drained

One 15-ounce can crushed tomatoes in thick puree

½ teaspoon pure ground chili powder, such as chipotle or ancho (see Note), optional

1   **Heat the oil** in a medium saucepan over medium heat. Add the onion and cook, stirring often, until golden, about 5 minutes. Stir in the jalapeño and garlic, and cook until the garlic is fragrant, about 1 minute. Stir in the diced tomatoes, crushed tomatoes, and ground chili powder, if using.

2   **Reduce the heat** to medium-low and simmer, stirring often, until the salsa is slightly thickened, about 30 minutes. Cool completely. Transfer the salsa to 1- or 2-cup covered containers. (The salsa can be refrigerated for up to 3 days or frozen for up to 3 months. Defrost the frozen salsa before using.)

MAKES ABOUT 4 CUPS

VARIATION: If you want more chili heat, stir in pure ground chili powder (see Note below). For some variety, for every cup of salsa stir in ½ cup thawed frozen corn kernels or rinsed canned beans (black, pinto, or red) or 1 ripe avocado, peeled, pitted, and chopped.

NOTE: Unlike chili powder, which includes other ingredients such as cumin or oregano for seasoning a pot of chili, pure ground chili powder is unadulterated ground chilies (some people call them chili peppers). The variety of chili dictates the powder's heat. Chipotles are very, very hot, whereas anchos are milder and sweeter. Pure ground chili powders are available at Latino and specialty food markets, and by mail order from Penzeys Spices (*www.penzeys.com*, 1-800-741-7787, and at their retail shops, concentrated in the Midwest).

ummus is most commonly thought of as a dip, but it's so much more. Use it as a sandwich spread (try it with cucumbers, sprouts, and sliced tomatoes on whole wheat bread) or as a sauce for grilled lamb. It's pretty great with firm white fish such as cod. My fast version is made with canned garbanzo beans and, as an easy-to-find substitute for the traditional tahini (which is sesame seed paste), smooth peanut butter.

QUICK LEMON HUMMUS

One 15- to 19-ounce can garbanzo beans (chickpeas), drained and liquid reserved

3 tablespoons creamy peanut butter

Grated zest of 1 lemon

3 tablespoons fresh lemon juice

½ teaspoon ground cumin

1 garlic clove, crushed through a press

¼ cup olive oil, preferably extra-virgin

Salt and ground hot red (cayenne) pepper to taste

Combine the garbanzo beans, peanut butter, lemon zest and juice, cumin, and garlic in a food processor. With the machine running, add the oil. Add enough of the reserved bean liquid to make a smooth, fluffy puree. Season with salt and red pepper. (The hummus can be prepared, covered, and refrigerated up to 5 days ahead.)

MAKES ABOUT 1½ CUPS

Knowing how to make a proper quesadilla opens up all kinds of possibilities for meals and snacking. You need flour tortillas (which have become a refrigerator staple in many households); some kind of melting cheese; and meat, chicken, or seafood. In my kitchen that means I have the basics on hand all the time. Here is one of my favorite combinations that adds sliced tart apples to the essentials. It is really great with homemade smoked turkey, such as the Kitchen Workhorse Smoked Turkey Breast with Cranberry Mustard (page 194), but you can use turkey from the delicatessen and still get a great quesadilla.

SMOKED TURKEY, APPLE, AND CHEDDAR QUESADILLAS

2 flour tortillas

½ cup (2 ounces) shredded cheddar cheese

½ cup smoked turkey, chopped

½ Granny Smith apple, peeled and thinly sliced

Make-Ahead Salsa (page 92) or store-bought salsa for serving, optional

1 **Heat large skillet** over medium heat until the surface is hot. Place a tortilla in the skillet and cook until the underside is warm, about 20 seconds. Flip the tortilla over. Sprinkle the surface with half of the cheese, the turkey, the apple, and then the remaining cheese. Top with the second tortilla.

2 **Cook until** the underside is toasted, about 1½ minutes. Flip the quesadilla and cook until the second side is toasted, about 1½ minutes more.

3 **Transfer the quesadilla** to a cutting board and cut into 6 wedges. Serve hot with the salsa, if desired.

MAKES 1 QUESADILLA (6 WEDGES)

What are flour tortillas, and where can I find them?

Flour tortillas are larger and lighter colored than corn tortillas and, of course, are made from wheat. They're sold in every supermarket alongside corn tortillas in a refrigerated bin and are pliable enough for wraps, quesadillas, and other stacked and rolled preparations. If yours are stubborn, warm them in a dry skillet and they will soften.

What's the best cheese for grilled cheese sandwiches, quesadillas, and cheeseburgers?

It's a matter of personal taste, but I recommend a good melting cheese such as cheddar, Monterey Jack, provolone, fontina, or Muenster. These are firm (not hard) cheeses that slice easily.

If you bake a large batch of Barbecued Orange-Maple Country Ribs (page 162), you are likely to have extras. Here's a fine way to make a bonus meal: a chopped rib sandwich topped with a tangy coleslaw.

BARBECUED RIBS AND SLAW SANDWICHES

SIMPLE SLAW

1 tablespoon cider vinegar

1 teaspoon sugar

¼ cup vegetable oil

½ pound (half of a 1-pound bag) coleslaw mix, about 3 cups

1 scallion, white and green parts, chopped

Salt and freshly ground pepper to taste

2 large Barbecued Orange-Maple Country Ribs (page 162), bones removed and meat chopped into ½-inch dice

4 soft sandwich rolls, toasted

1 **To make the slaw,** whisk the vinegar and sugar in a medium bowl, then gradually whisk in the oil. Add the coleslaw mix and scallion, and mix well. Season with salt and pepper. Cover and let stand at room temperature for at least 30 minutes and up to 2 hours.

2 **Place the chopped rib** meat in a microwave-safe medium bowl and cover with plastic wrap. Microwave at 50 percent (medium) power until the meat is heated through, about 2 minutes. Or place the ribs and 2 tablespoons water in a small saucepan, cover, and cook over medium-low heat, stirring often, until the ribs are heated through, about 5 minutes.

3 **For each sandwich,** heap the meat on the bottom half of a roll. Top with about ½ cup of the slaw and then the top of the roll. Serve immediately.

MAKES 4 SERVINGS

In **Philadelphia** (and maybe some other places, too), you can get a mouth-watering sandwich like this at the best home-style diners. It all starts with the Kitchen Workhorse Italian Pot Roast on page 144.

HOT ITALIAN BEEF OPEN-FACED SANDWICH

2 or 3 thin slices and ½ cup sauce from Kitchen Workhorse Italian Pot Roast (page 144)

1 large slice crusty Italian bread

⅓ cup (about 1½ ounces) shredded mozzarella cheese

1 **Place the pot** roast slices and sauce in a microwave-safe medium bowl and cover. Microwave on 50 percent (medium) power until the meat is hot, about 2 minutes. Or place the pot roast and sauce in a small saucepan and cook over medium heat, stirring often, until hot, about 5 minutes.

2 **Place the bread** on a toaster oven rack. Overlap the pot roast slices on the bread and sprinkle with the cheese. Toast until the cheese melts, about 1 minute.

3 **Transfer the bread** to a plate and top with the hot sauce. Serve immediately.

MAKES 1 SANDWICH

Because the Kitchen Workhorse Chunky Beef Chili (page 150) is on the thick side, it is just about perfect for filling warmed corn tortillas for some very fine soft tacos.

SOFT BEEF TACOS

8 corn tortillas, warmed

2 cups Kitchen Workhorse Chunky Beef Chili (page 150), heated

1 1/3 cups packed shredded iceberg lettuce

1/4 cup finely grated Romano cheese

For each taco, place 2 tortillas on a plate, slightly overlapping them to make a double thickness. Spoon 1/2 cup of the chili onto the tortillas. Top with 1/3 cup of the lettuce and 1 tablespoon of the cheese. Roll up the tortilla. Repeat with the remaining ingredients. Serve immediately.

MAKES 4 TACOS

Just like familiar black tea, green tea is wonderfully refreshing when chilled and served over ice. The flavor of green tea is famously refined, and a trio of citrus fruits gives it a lift. It is quite tart, so you may want to serve fast-dissolving sugar or a low-calorie sweetener on the side. If you're a child of the South like me, you'll want to sweeten the tea from the get-go while it is still warm in the steeping pot. We know how to make good iced tea south of the Mason-Dixon Line!

THREE-CITRUS ICED GREEN TEA

8 bags green tea

2 seedless oranges

2 lemons

2 limes

Superfine sugar or low-calorie sweetener on taste

Fresh mint for garnish

1 **Bring 2 quarts** of water to a boil in a large stainless-steel pot. Remove from the heat and add the tea bags. Let steep for 20 minutes.

2 **Slice 1 orange,** 1 lemon, and 1 lime into thin rounds. Squeeze and strain the juice from the remaining orange, lemon, and lime. Stir the citrus juices into the brewed tea. Pour the tea into a pitcher and stir in the orange, lemon, and lime juice and the citrus slices. Refrigerate the tea until chilled, at least 2 hours.

3 **Serve the tea** over ice, garnished with a mint sprig.

MAKES 8 SERVINGS

It's a simple matter to chop fresh ginger and simmer it with sugar and water into a syrup that can perk up your beverages. You'll find yourself adding it to hot and iced tea, sparkling water, and other drinks. This exotically flavored cooler combines it with tropical fruit nectar (found in the Latino section of the supermarket) and soda pop for a very tasty refreshment.

TROPICAL FRUIT COOLER WITH GINGER SYRUP

GINGER SYRUP

1 cup chopped fresh ginger (no need to peel)

1 cup sugar

2/3 cup canned tropical fruit nectar, such as mango or guava

2/3 cup lemon-lime or grapefruit soda, or sparkling water

Ice cubes, as needed

1 **To make the ginger syrup,** bring the ginger, sugar, and 1 cup water to a boil in a small saucepan over medium heat, stirring until the sugar dissolves. Boil without stirring for 2 minutes. Remove from the heat and let cool. Strain the syrup through a sieve into a covered jar, pressing hard on the solids. (The syrup can be stored, covered and refrigerated, for up to 2 weeks.)

2 **To make the cooler,** stir the nectar, soda, and 1 tablespoon of syrup in a tall glass. Add ice cubes and serve chilled.

MAKES 1 SERVING

Because this slushy, satisfying drink can be served anytime during the day (as a low-fat, on-the-go breakfast, a light lunch; a between-meal snack; and so on), I like to make a blenderful in the morning and store it in the freezer. It won't freeze solid for a few hours, and even if it does, it can be reblended with a splash of milk. I love it with peaches, but frozen strawberries, blueberries, blackberries, or even melon are just as tasty.

PEACH-BANANA SMOOTHIE

½ cup skim or reduced-fat milk

1 cup nonfat plain or vanilla-flavored yogurt

1 tablespoon honey, or more to taste

2 cups (8 ounces) frozen sliced peaches or other frozen fruit

1 ripe banana, sliced

1 tablespoon bran, optional

In the order given, place the milk, yogurt, honey, peaches, banana, and bran, if using, in a blender and process until smooth. (The smoothies can be prepared up to 8 hours ahead, then covered and stored in the freezer.) Serve chilled.

MAKES 2 SERVINGS

igh-protein diets make much use of the nutritional powerhouse peanut butter. Protein powder, which is available at every natural food grocery and many supermarkets, boosts the protein level, but even without it, you will still have a very hearty liquid meal.

HIGH-PROTEIN SHAKE

½ cup skim or reduced-fat milk, as needed

2 scoops (about ⅔ cup) frozen vanilla yogurt

¼ cup chunky or smooth peanut butter

1 ripe banana, sliced

2 tablespoons vanilla soy protein powder

½ teaspoon vanilla extract

2 ice cubes

In the order given, place the milk, yogurt, peanut butter, banana, protein powder, vanilla, and ice cubes in a blender and process until smooth. Serve chilled in a large glass.

MAKES 1 SERVING

ASK ART

What is protein powder? Where do I buy it?

Sold in health-food stores and some supermarkets, protein powders are designed to add protein to uncooked preparations such as smoothies and shakes. The most common powders may be soy- or whey-based; they come in different flavors, with vanilla and chocolate being the most popular. As they have become more popular, the taste and texture of protein powders have been improved. They are sold in individual packets or, more commonly, in large canisters.

SOUPS FOR SUPPER

When making soup, you are restricted only by the size of the soup pot and your own creativity. If you have freezer room, make quantities and freeze the extra in one-quart containers for tempting, comforting meals later in the month.

These soups are big and bold enough to be the main course at any family lunch or dinner. Add a green salad, and you're off! A loaf of good French bread is another tempting addition—excellent for dunking in the hot soup—but with the trend these days to restrict carbohydrates, you may decide to skip it.

I use chicken broth in my soups and suggest you find a kind you like and then stick with it. Chicken broth varies from brand to brand, and you may be unpleasantly surprised if you switch to an unfamiliar one. The cans keep for a year or more, so stock up on your chosen brand.

The soups included here are cooked in large saucepans. I like to use a six-quart saucepan with straight sides, but you can use a larger pot if you like. Stockpots with ten- or twelve-quart capacities are good choices if you plan to double the recipes. These are also the pots for making your own stock.

Serve soup piping hot, right from the pot. Soups taste delicious reheated and so are good choices for advance planning. If they thicken, add a little more broth or even water to thin them out.

If you want to freeze the soup, let it cool on the countertop and then chill it in the refrigerator before ladling it into freezer containers. Don't let it sit at room temperature longer than necessary, but don't put hot soup directly in the freezer. Your freezer will have to work overtime to chill it, and that's not good for the other food already in there.

Almost all kids like soup, and this collection is designed to please them. They will love the Quick Vegetable Soup (page 105), the Macaroni and Cheese Soup (page 109), the Sausage and Potato Soup (page 112), and the Cream of Tomato Soup with (or perhaps without) Shrimp (page 116).

Your kitchen life will be marvelously rewarding when the soup's on!

recipes

Quick Vegetable Soup

Smoked Turkey and White Bean Soup

Cabbage and Bacon Soup

Macaroni and Cheese Soup

Curried Carrot Soup

Cauliflower and Parmesan Soup

Sausage and Potato Soup

Spicy Black Bean Soup

Roasted Chicken Soup

Cream of Tomato Soup with Shrimp

Vegetarian soups can be difficult to prepare because not all of us have access to good homemade vegetable stock. In this easy soup, tomato-vegetable juice makes a good stand-in for a simmered stock. And the recipe also proves that, used in the right way, frozen vegetables can be a real boon to the busy cook.

QUICK VEGETABLE SOUP

1 tablespoon olive oil

1 medium onion, chopped

1 garlic clove, minced

One 32-ounce bottle tomato-vegetable juice, such as V8

One 16-ounce package frozen mixed vegetables, preferably an Italian-style mixture with cauliflower, green beans, carrots, and zucchini

¼ cup pasta for soup, such as ditalini or orzo

1 tablespoon Kitchen Workhorse Pesto (page 226) or store-bought pesto, or ½ teaspoon dried basil

Salt and freshly ground black pepper to taste

Freshly grated Parmesan cheese for serving

1 **Bring a medium saucepan** of lightly salted water to a boil.

2 **Meanwhile,** heat the oil in a large saucepan over medium heat. Add the onion and cook, stirring occasionally, until softened, about 3 minutes. Add the garlic and cook until it is fragrant, about 1 minute. Stir in the tomato-vegetable juice and bring to a simmer. Reduce the heat to low and simmer for 10 minutes. Stir in the vegetables and cook until they are heated through, about 5 minutes.

3 **While the soup is simmering,** add the pasta to the boiling water. Cook according to the package instructions until the pasta is barely tender, keeping in mind that it will cook further in the soup. Drain the pasta. Stir the pasta and pesto into the soup. Cook until the pasta is completely tender, about 5 minutes. Season the soup with salt and pepper.

4 **Serve hot,** sprinkling each serving with the Parmesan.

MAKES 6 SERVINGS

S moked turkey parts have all the flavor of smoked ham but fewer calories and less fat. Turkey wings, among the many available cuts, are the meatiest and easiest to use, and believe it or not, they are easy to find in the supermarket. Simmered with vegetables, they make a smoky base for a smooth, satisfying bean soup, and as they cook, their meat loosens on the bone so that it's easy to remove.

SMOKED TURKEY AND WHITE BEAN SOUP

1 tablespoon olive oil

1 medium onion, chopped

1 medium carrot, cut into ½-inch dice

1 medium celery rib with leaves, cut into ½-inch dice

1 garlic clove, crushed under a knife and peeled

1¾ pounds smoked turkey wings, broken or cut apart at the joints

1 teaspoon dried rosemary

1 bay leaf

Three 15- to 19-ounce cans white beans (cannellini), drained and rinsed

Salt and freshly ground pepper to taste

1 **Heat the oil** in a large saucepan over medium-low heat. Add the onion, carrot, celery, and garlic, and cover. Cook, stirring occasionally, until the vegetables soften, about 5 minutes. Add the smoked turkey wings, rosemary, and bay leaf to the pot. Pour in enough cold water to barely cover the wings, about 2 quarts. Bring to a boil, uncovered, over high heat. Return the heat to medium-low and simmer until the turkey meat is tender and can be removed easily from the bones, about 1 hour.

2 **Transfer the turkey** wings to a cutting board. Remove the meat, discarding the skin and bones. Cut the meat into bite-sized pieces and set aside.

3 **Add the beans** to the pot and return the liquid to a boil over medium-high heat. Return the heat to medium-low and simmer the soup for 5 minutes. Remove the bay leaf.

4 Transfer the soup in batches to a blender and process until smooth. Pour the pureed soup into a large bowl. (If you have an immersible hand blender, you can puree the soup right in the pot.) Return the pureed soup to the pot and add the reserved turkey. Reheat over medium heat, stirring often, until it is simmering. Season with salt and pepper. Serve hot.

MAKES 6 TO 8 SERVINGS

ASK ART

What is the best way to puree soups?

If you have a blender, you will have great success making smooth pureed soups. You can also use a handheld immersion blender—an electric appliance with a single rotating blade that goes directly in the pot of soup and gets to work—for lusciously smooth soup. Most home cooks have blenders, and the best way to puree soup is to fill the container about two-thirds full (no more!). Hold the lid slightly askew, and start at a low speed. As the hot soup blends, it releases steam, which will build up and jettison the lid if it is on tight. You can also cover the top of the blender with an absorbent kitchen towel instead of the lid and accomplish the same thing. Don't use a food processor; the soup will rise in the bowl and overflow through the center where the blade rests.

I f this substantial soup can't warm you up on a chilly day, nothing can. To make the soup meatier, add sautéed slices of your favorite smoked sausage, such as pork or turkey kielbasa or even spicy andouille.

CABBAGE AND BACON SOUP

6 bacon slices, cut into 1-inch-long pieces

1 large onion, chopped

2 medium carrots, cut into ½-inch dice

2 garlic cloves, minced

1 medium head cabbage (2 pounds), cored and sliced into ½-inch-wide strips

1 quart reduced-sodium chicken broth

1 teaspoon dried thyme

Salt and freshly ground black pepper to taste

1 **Place the bacon** in a large saucepan and cook over medium heat until it is crisp, about 8 minutes. Using a slotted spoon, transfer the bacon to paper towels to drain. Pour out all but 2 tablespoons of fat from the pot and return to the heat.

2 **Add the onion** and carrots, and cook, stirring often, until the onion is golden, about 5 minutes. Add the garlic and stir until it is fragrant, about 1 minute. Stir in the cabbage. Add the broth, 2 cups water, and the thyme, and bring to a boil over high heat.

3 **Reduce the heat** to medium-low and cover the pot, leaving the lid slightly ajar. Simmer until the cabbage is very tender, about 45 minutes. During the last 5 minutes, stir in the reserved bacon. Season with salt and pepper. Serve hot.

MAKES 6 TO 8 SERVINGS

If there is a more kid-friendly soup, I don't know it. And the fact that this can be made in a jiffy makes it even better. A pasteurized process cheese product (such as Velveeta) makes the smoothest soup going, and youngsters appreciate its mildness. For a sharper flavor, sprinkle shredded cheddar cheese over each serving.

MACARONI AND CHEESE SOUP

1 cup elbow macaroni

2 cups reduced-sodium chicken broth

One 14½-ounce can tomatoes with onions and green peppers, drained

½ pound pasteurized process cheese product, such as Velveeta, cubed

Salt and freshly ground pepper to taste

Hot red pepper sauce to taste

½ cup (2 ounces) shredded sharp cheddar cheese for serving, optional

1 **Bring a medium saucepan** of lightly salted water to a boil over high heat. Add the macaroni and cook until tender, about 9 minutes. Drain well.

2 **Meanwhile,** bring the broth and tomatoes to a simmer in a medium saucepan over medium heat. Gradually whisk in the cheese product until melted. Stir in the macaroni and heat through. Season the soup with salt and pepper and then the hot sauce. Serve hot, topping each serving with cheddar cheese, if desired.

MAKES 4 GENEROUS SERVINGS

What does it mean when a recipe calls for shredded cheese?

ASK ART

Shreds of cheese are fatter than the tiny slivers we know as grated cheese. Shred cheese in a food processor fitted with the shredding blade (one of the blades that sits high in the bowl) for fast work. You can also use the big-holed side of a box grater. In a pinch, buy packaged shredded cheese at the supermarket.

Curry adds an exotic edge to this brightly colored soup. When cooking with curry powder, always sauté it briefly, as I do here. This step warms the oils in the spices and intensifies the flavor. (For more on curry powder, see page 223.) While there are many kinds of curry powder, Madras-style is the most common and the version you will find at most supermarkets. For a creamier soup, use the yogurt or coconut milk option.

CURRIED CARROT SOUP

1 tablespoon olive oil

1 medium onion, chopped

1 celery rib, chopped

1 garlic clove, chopped

2 pounds carrots, scrubbed but unpeeled, cut into ½-inch-thick rounds

1 tablespoon Madras-style curry powder

1 teaspoon ground ginger

5 cups reduced-sodium chicken broth

1 cup plain nonfat yogurt or light coconut milk, optional

Salt and freshly ground pepper to taste

1 **Heat the oil** in a large saucepan over medium heat. Add the onion, celery, and garlic, and cover. Cook, stirring occasionally, until the onion is golden, about 5 minutes. Add the carrots and stir well. Stir in the curry powder and ginger, and cook, stirring almost constantly, for 30 seconds.

2 **Add the broth** and bring to a boil over high heat. Reduce the heat to medium-low and partially cover the pot. Simmer until the carrots are very tender, about 30 minutes.

3 **Transfer the soup** in batches to a blender and process until smooth. Pour the pureed soup into a large bowl. (If you have an immersible hand blender, you can puree the soup right in the pot.) Return the pureed soup to the pot. If desired, add the yogurt or coconut milk and stir over low heat just until the soup is very hot; do not simmer. Season the soup with salt and pepper. Serve hot.

MAKES 6 TO 8 SERVINGS

Cauliflower is a delicious choice for soup. If you wish, substitute an equal amount of broccoli (a close cousin), using both the florets and peeled stems.

CAULIFLOWER AND PARMESAN SOUP

1 tablespoon olive oil

1 medium onion, chopped

1 celery rib, chopped

1 garlic clove, minced

1 head cauliflower (2¼ pounds), trimmed and cut into florets

1 quart reduced-sodium chicken broth

½ cup freshly grated Parmesan cheese

Salt and freshly ground pepper to taste

1 Heat the oil in a large saucepan over medium heat. Add the onion, celery, and garlic, and cover. Cook, stirring occasionally, until the vegetables soften, about 3 minutes.

2 Add the cauliflower and stock, and bring to a boil over high heat. Reduce the heat to medium-low and simmer, partially covered, until the cauliflower is very tender, about 30 minutes. Stir in the Parmesan.

3 Transfer the soup in batches to a blender and process until smooth. Pour the pureed soup into a large bowl. (If you have an immersible hand blender, you can puree the soup right in the pot.) Season the soup with salt and pepper. Serve hot.

MAKES 6 TO 8 SERVINGS

Can I use garlic powder instead of fresh garlic? What about jarred garlic?

ASK ART

Fresh garlic is easily available, stores well at room temperature, and is easy to chop or mince, so I nearly always use it. But by all means you can use garlic powder instead and still get good flavor. Garlic powder is made by grinding up dehydrated garlic flakes, and ¼ teaspoon is the equivalent of 1 medium-sized clove of garlic. I also like to use chopped fresh garlic packed in oil, and I keep a jar of this handy ingredient in my refrigerator. Garlic salt is garlic powder mixed with salt. I don't particularly like using it; it's better to use fresh or powdered garlic and add salt separately.

This is another chunky, hearty warmer-upper. For a change of pace and for a creamier soup, I sometimes stir 1 cup of shredded sharp cheddar cheese into it. Use any kind of sausage you like. (I prefer a cooked poultry sausage such as Amy's or Aidell's.) There are various flavors of chicken or turkey sausage, from apple (especially good with the cheese option) to mushroom to sun-dried tomato, so have fun choosing your favorite.

SAUSAGE AND POTATO SOUP

2 tablespoons olive oil

One 13-ounce package cooked chicken sausage, cut into ½-inch rounds

1 large onion, chopped

2 medium carrots, cut into ½-inch dice

2 celery ribs, cut into ½-inch dice

4 cups reduced-sodium chicken broth

1 pound Yukon Gold or red-skinned potatoes, scrubbed but not peeled and cut into ¾-inch pieces

½ teaspoon dried thyme

Salt and freshly ground pepper to taste

1 **Heat the oil** in a large saucepan over medium heat. Add the sausage and cook, stirring occasionally, until it is lightly browned. Add the onion, carrots, and celery, and cover. Cook, stirring occasionally, until the vegetables soften, about 5 minutes.

2 **Add the broth,** potatoes, and thyme, and bring to a boil over high heat. Reduce the heat to medium-low and partially cover the pot. Simmer until the potatoes are tender, about 30 minutes. Season with salt and pepper. Serve hot.

MAKES 6 TO 8 SERVINGS

What can I use in place of Yukon Gold potatoes?

ASK ART Chefs and home cooks are enjoying a long-standing love affair with Yukon Golds, thin-skinned, golden-fleshed, buttery potatoes that became popular about ten years ago. These are easy to find in nearly every supermarket, but if you can't, use red-skinned, white-skinned, or new potatoes instead of Yukon Golds. I don't suggest substituting russet (Idaho) baking potatoes for Yukon Golds. These have their own delicious culinary uses but not as stand-ins for boiling potatoes.

Two types of pepper, sweet red bell and fiery jalapeño, conspire to give this rib-sticking soup a mild kick. Speaking of kicks, dry sherry is a traditional flavoring for black bean soup, but you can skip it and still have a great soup. Except for the chicken broth, this soup doesn't have any meat in it. If it strikes your fancy, add some sautéed spicy sausage (a Mexican chorizo would be perfect) or crumbled bacon once the soup has been pureed.

SPICY BLACK BEAN SOUP

2 tablespoons olive oil

1 medium onion, chopped

1 red bell pepper, ribs and seeds discarded, chopped

1 jalapeño, ribs and seeds discarded, chopped

2 garlic cloves, minced

Three 15- to 19-ounce cans black beans, drained and rinsed

1 quart reduced-sodium chicken broth

1/3 cup dry sherry, optional

Salt and freshly ground pepper to taste

Make-Ahead Salsa (page 92) or store-bought salsa, sour cream, and chopped fresh cilantro for garnish

1 **Heat the oil** in a large saucepan over medium heat. Add the onion, bell pepper, and jalapeño. Cook, stirring occasionally, until the vegetables soften, about 3 minutes. Add the garlic and stir until it gives off its aroma, about 1 minute.

2 **Stir in the beans** and broth. Bring to a simmer over high heat. Reduce the heat to medium-low and partially cover the pot. Simmer for 30 minutes. During the last 5 minutes, stir in the sherry, if using.

3 **Transfer the soup** in batches to a blender and process until smooth. Pour the pureed soup into a large bowl. (If you have an immersible hand blender, you can puree the soup right in the pot.) Season the soup with salt and pepper.

4 **Serve the soup** hot. Pass bowls of salsa, sour cream, and cilantro so each person can add whatever toppings he or she likes.

MAKES 6 SERVINGS

For an especially rich soup with lots of meaty flavor, roast the chicken first. This is an interesting twist on the traditional method where the chicken is first browned in the pot, if at all, and then cooked in the liquid. Dark-meat chicken thighs stand up to the roasting and simmering without drying out, something that cannot be said of chicken breasts. They are full of good flavor and cost less, too.

ROASTED CHICKEN SOUP

6 chicken thighs with skin and bone (about 2⅓ pounds)

1 medium onion, chopped

1 medium carrot, cut into ½-inch dice

1 medium celery rib with leaves, leaves chopped and rib cut into ½-inch dice

¼ teaspoon dried thyme

1 small bay leaf

Salt and freshly ground pepper to taste

Chopped fresh parsley for garnish

1 **Position a rack** in the top third of the oven and preheat the oven to 400°F. Place the chicken thighs in a roasting pan.

2 **Roast the chicken** until the skin is golden brown, about 30 minutes. Pour off and discard all but 2 tablespoons of fat. Scatter the onion, carrot, and celery around the chicken and stir to coat with the fat in the pan. Return to the oven and roast, stirring occasionally, until the vegetables soften, about 15 minutes.

3 **Transfer the chicken** and vegetables to a large saucepan. Place the roasting pan over medium heat and heat until sizzling. Add 1 cup water to the pan. Scrape up the browned bits in the pan with a wooden spatula and pour the liquid into the saucepan. Add enough cold water to barely cover the chicken, about 1½ quarts. Bring to a boil over high heat, skimming off any foam that rises to the surface. Add the thyme and bay leaf. Season lightly with salt and pepper.

4 **Reduce the heat** to low and partially cover the pot. Simmer for 30 minutes. Remove the chicken and transfer to a cutting board. Keep the soup simmering. Cool the chicken until easy to handle, about 20 minutes. Discard the skin and bones, and cut the meat into bite-sized pieces. Return the meat to the soup.

5 **Remove the soup** from the heat and let stand for 5 minutes. Skim off any fat on the surface and discard the bay leaf. Season the soup again with salt and pepper. Serve hot, sprinkling each serving with parsley.

MAKES 6 SERVINGS

This is an upscale version of the popular classic, but it is still comforting and homey. The shrimp makes it special, and the simple step of simmering the shrimp shells in the stock provides another layer of flavor. Truth be told, if you use plain chicken broth and peeled shrimp, few people will be the wiser—the soup is that good.

CREAM OF TOMATO SOUP WITH SHRIMP

¾ pound (25 to 31 count per pound) medium unshelled shrimp

2 cups reduced-sodium chicken broth

5 tablespoons (½ stick plus 1 tablespoon) unsalted butter, divided

1 medium celery rib, finely chopped

½ cup chopped shallots

1 garlic clove, minced

⅓ cup all-purpose flour

One 28-ounce can diced tomatoes in juice

2 cups half-and-half

1 teaspoon chopped fresh marjoram or oregano, or ½ teaspoon dried marjoram

Salt and freshly ground black pepper to taste

1 **Peel and devein** the shrimp, reserving the shells. Combine the shells and broth in a small saucepan and bring to a simmer over medium heat. Reduce the heat to low, cover and simmer for 15 minutes. Strain the soup, reserving the broth. You should have 2 cups; add water as needed.

2 **Meanwhile,** melt 4 tablespoons butter in a large saucepan over medium heat. Add the celery and cook, stirring occasionally, until it begins to soften, about 2 minutes. Add the shallots and garlic, and cook, stirring often, until the shallots soften, about 2 minutes.

3 **Add the flour** and stir well. Add the tomatoes with their juice. Stir in the reserved broth, half-and-half, and marjoram, and stir well. Bring to a boil, stirring often. Reduce the heat to medium-low. Simmer, uncovered, until the soup is lightly thickened, about 30 minutes. Season the soup with salt and pepper.

4 **Just before serving,** melt the remaining tablespoon of butter in a large skillet over medium-high heat. Add the shrimp and cook, stirring often, just until they turn opaque. Season with salt and pepper. Stir the shrimp into the soup and serve hot.

MAKES 4 TO 6 SERVINGS

TEN

SALAD FOR SUPPER

I call this chapter Salad for Supper because, with only two exceptions, that is precisely what these recipes are: greens and other vegetables with added protein, such as chicken, beef, tuna, shrimp, salmon, and cheese. They are meals in themselves, suitable for lunch or dinner, and sure to please everyone in the family.

Salads are great for using anything you have left from other meals, as I suggest in the Roast Pork on Boston Lettuce Salad with Asian Pears (page 124) and the Taverna Pasta Salad with Roast Lamb (page 132).

They are also easy-to-prepare dishes that turn an ordinary salmon steak or roast chicken into an endlessly creative meal. Use my ideas for added ingredients but feel free to add your own favorites.

A tossed green salad has a place at nearly every meal. The fresh-dressed greens add verve to the other dishes, and you can pack the salad bowl with crunchy sliced carrots, cucumbers, onions, and radishes as well as tomatoes, green beans, avocados, or whatever vegetables strike your fancy. What a good way to get your kids to eat their vegetables!

Because of this I have a recipe for a standard balsamic vinaigrette, which I call a house dressing. Its formula will become commonplace in your kitchen and eliminate the need for an assortment of bottled dressings, which while very good can become expensive (especially if, like me, you let them languish on the refrigerator door). Don't get me wrong: I love some bottled dressings much of the time and will never abandon them. I also appreciate dried dressings such as Good Seasons, which you can use for bold flavoring.

When you buy greens, make sure they look fresh and crisp rather than limp and tired. Bagged greens are a boon to the busy cook, but don't think they are clean. Wash them. If you invest in a good salad spinner, assembling a green salad will be effortless. Plus, washing and spinning greens is a good job for the kids. Getting the family involved in meal preparation is one of the best ways I know to improve your kitchen life.

recipes

Balsamic Vinaigrette "House Dressing"

Chopped Grilled Vegetable Salad

Romaine Hearts with "Caesar" Dressing

Roast Chicken Waldorf Salad with Pecans and Rosemary

Roast Pork on Boston Lettuce Salad with Asian Pears

Greek Shrimp and Tomato Salad

Grilled Shrimp Salad with Avocado Dressing

Salmon Steaks with Citrus Couscous Salad

Grilled Tuna with Mediterranean Bean Salad

Taverna Pasta Salad with Roast Lamb

E very family needs a house dressing that can be made in a jiffy and used for tossing with salad greens. Now that everyone buys balsamic vinegar, a vinaigrette made with the heady stuff is one of the most popular dressings around—and for good reason. It's versatile and tasty, with a touch of sweetness. I use a blender, which produces a thicker vinaigrette than you might expect. Allow 2 to 3 tablespoons of dressing per serving. A cup should easily be enough for six to eight servings of mixed greens.

BALSAMIC VINAIGRETTE "HOUSE DRESSING"

3 tablespoons balsamic vinegar

1 tablespoon red wine vinegar

1 teaspoon Dijon mustard

1 garlic clove, crushed through a press

¾ cup olive oil, preferably extra-virgin

Salt and freshly ground pepper to taste

Combine the balsamic and red wine vinegars, mustard, and garlic in a blender. With the machine running, gradually add the oil through the opening in the lid to process into a thick dressing. Season with salt and pepper. (The dressing can be made up to 1 week ahead, stored in a covered container, and refrigerated. Stir well before using.)

MAKES ABOUT 1 CUP

Prepared salad dressing is a well-known marinade for fish, but it does wonders for grilled vegetables, too. Use whatever vegetables you like. This is my favorite combination when summer's bounty produces wonderful eggplant and squash. If you can't find them all or don't like one or the other, just one or two veggies will still work. The tofu adds valuable protein. Don't be afraid of it—it really fills out the salad.

CHOPPED GRILLED VEGETABLE SALAD

1 medium eggplant, cut crosswise into ½-inch-thick rounds

1 teaspoon salt

1 medium zucchini, cut lengthwise

1 medium yellow squash, cut lengthwise

1 red bell pepper, seeds and ribs removed, and cut lengthwise into quarters

½ pound thick asparagus spears

One 0.7-ounce package all-natural Italian salad dressing mix, such as Good Seasons, prepared according to package directions with vinegar, oil, and water

One 6-ounce package Mediterranean-style mixed greens (such as Romaine lettuce, radicchio, and curly endive)

One 8-ounce package firm barbecue-flavored tofu, cut into strips

½ cup (2 ounces) shredded sharp cheddar cheese

⅓ cup sliced almonds, toasted (see page 251)

1 **Place the eggplant in** a colander and toss with the salt. Let stand in the sink to drain off the excess bitter juices, about 1 hour. Rinse well and pat dry with paper towels.

2 **Mix the eggplant,** zucchini, yellow squash, red pepper, and asparagus with ½ cup of the prepared salad dressing, reserving the remaining dressing. Let stand while preparing the grill.

3 **Build a charcoal fire** in an outdoor grill and let it burn until the coals are covered with white ash. In a gas grill, preheat the grill on high.

4 **Lightly oil the grill.** Place the vegetables on the grill, arranging the asparagus perpendicular to the grate so the spears don't fall through. Cover and grill,

turning the vegetables occasionally, until they are crisp-tender, an average of 10 minutes. As the vegetables become tender—the asparagus may take only 5 minutes, and the eggplant may take 12 minutes—transfer them to a large bowl. When all the vegetables are cooked, let them cool. Using kitchen scissors, snip the vegetables into bite-sized pieces.

5   **Toss the salad** greens with the reserved salad dressing. Add the tofu and chopped vegetables and toss well. Sprinkle with the cheddar and almonds, and serve immediately.

MAKES 6 TO 8 SERVINGS

Authentic Caesar dressing is made with coddled eggs, which are not cooked enough to dispel concerns about the harmful salmonella bacterium. I use a base of store-bought mayonnaise to supply the egg and oil component and then add other Caesar essentials such as lemon juice, garlic, and Worcestershire sauce. Crisp and sturdy Romaine lettuce hearts are the greens of choice for this thick and creamy dressing. To transform this into a complete meal, serve it topped with grilled chicken or shrimp, just as they do in restaurants.

ROMAINE HEARTS WITH "CAESAR" DRESSING

¾ cup light or regular mayonnaise

3 tablespoons fresh lemon juice

1 teaspoon Worcestershire sauce

1 garlic clove, crushed through a press

Freshly ground pepper to taste

Two 6-ounce Romaine lettuce hearts, torn into bite-sized pieces

½ cup freshly grated Parmesan cheese

1 **Mix the mayonnaise,** lemon juice, Worcestershire sauce, and garlic in a small bowl. Season generously with pepper. (For a thinner dressing, dilute with a tablespoon or two of water.)

2 **Toss the lettuce** and dressing well in a large bowl. Add the Parmesan and toss again. Serve immediately.

MAKES 6 SERVINGS

ASK ART

Do I need to wash salad greens sold in bags?

Yes! Studies show that these greens need washing just as much as those sold as loose heads of lettuce. Soak the greens in cold water, then shake or spin dry. I always wash my greens twice to remove all grit and dirt.

There are many versions of this lunchroom classic. While most suffer from blandness, mine gets its oomph from roasted chicken breasts, rosemary, and toasted pecans. Roasting the chicken gives it a firmer texture and a meatier flavor than the traditional poached method, but you can use any leftover chicken you have on hand, even grilled chicken. This makes a pretty darned good chicken salad sandwich on toasted wheat bread, too.

ROAST CHICKEN WALDORF SALAD WITH PECANS AND ROSEMARY

Three 7-ounce chicken breasts with skin and bone

Salt and freshly ground pepper to taste

1/2 cup regular or light mayonnaise

1/3 cup pecans, toasted (see page 251) and chopped

1 Granny Smith apple, peeled, cored, and cut into 1/2-inch dice

1 celery rib, cut into 1/2-inch dice

1 scallion, white and green parts, finely chopped

1 teaspoon chopped fresh rosemary

1 head Boston or butter lettuce, torn into individual leaves

1 **Position a rack** in the upper third of the oven and preheat the oven to 400°F.

2 **Season the chicken** breasts with salt and pepper and place in a small roasting pan. Roast until the chicken is golden brown and an instant-read thermometer inserted in the thickest part of the breast reads 170°F, about 40 minutes. Cool completely. Discard the skin and bones, and cut the meat into bite-sized pieces. You should have 2 cups of chopped chicken.

3 **Combine the chicken,** mayonnaise, pecans, apple, celery, scallion, and rosemary in a medium bowl. Season with salt and pepper. Cover and refrigerate until chilled, at least 1 hour and up to 1 day.

4 **For each serving,** make a bed of lettuce leaves on a plate. Mound the salad on the lettuce and serve immediately.

MAKES 4 TO 6 SERVINGS

This recipe was designed to use slices of leftover Kitchen Workhorse Roast Pork Tenderloin with Asian Glaze (page 154), but you can use freshly sautéed pork tenderloin slices or any other poultry or meat with Asian seasoning. The meat will have better texture and flavor if it is not ice-cold from the refrigerator, so let it sit for about thirty minutes before serving. Without the meat it is a refreshing salad on its own, with Asian pears adding an exotic touch.

ROAST PORK ON BOSTON LETTUCE SALAD WITH ASIAN PEARS

2 tablespoons rice vinegar

1 teaspoon sugar

2 tablespoons vegetable oil

1 large head Boston lettuce, washed, dried, and torn into bite-sized pieces

6 scallions, white and green parts, trimmed and thinly sliced on the diagonal

¼ cup chopped fresh cilantro

1 Asian pear or Granny Smith apple, unpeeled, cored, and cut into thin wedges

Salt and freshly ground pepper to taste

12 slices Kitchen Workhorse Roast Pork Tenderloin with Asian Glaze (page 154), at room temperature

1 Whisk the vinegar and sugar in a large bowl, then gradually whisk in the oil. Add the lettuce, scallions, cilantro, and Asian pear, and toss well. Season with salt and pepper.

2 Serve on 4 dinner plates, topping each salad with 3 slices of pork.

MAKES 4 SERVINGS

n the interest of saving time, make this with cooked shrimp from the supermarket seafood counter. If you have time, home-cooked shrimp will provide more flavor. Serve the salad immediately after making it or the cucumber will give off its juices and dilute the dressing. If you want to make the salad well ahead of time (it's a nice picnic salad), salt the diced cucumber and tomatoes beforehand to remove some juices. Sprinkle the vegetables with about 1/2 teaspoon of salt and let drain in a colander for an hour or so. If you do this, take care when seasoning the salad because the vegetables will already be salted.

GREEK SHRIMP AND TOMATO SALAD

1 pound (21 to 25 count per pound) large shrimp

1 1/2 tablespoons red wine vinegar

1/2 teaspoon dried oregano

1 garlic clove, crushed through a press

1/3 cup olive oil, preferably extra-virgin

4 large tomatoes, seeded and cut into 3/4-inch dice

1 cucumber, peeled, seeded, and cut into 1/2-inch dice

1/2 cup crumbled feta cheese

Salt and freshly ground pepper to taste

1 cup store-bought croutons

1 Bring a medium saucepan of lightly salted water to a boil over high heat. Add the shrimp and cook just until opaque, about 3 minutes (the water does not have to come back to a boil). Drain and rinse under cold water. Peel and devein the shrimp.

2 Combine the vinegar, oregano, and garlic in a medium bowl. Whisk in the oil. Add the shrimp, tomatoes, cucumber, and feta cheese, and mix. Season with salt and pepper. (The salad can be made up to 1 hour ahead, covered, and refrigerated.)

3 Just before serving, top with the croutons.

MAKES 4 TO 6 SERVINGS

When I want a lot of different herbs and spices in a dish, rather than measuring out ½ teaspoon of this and that, I grab an envelope of salad dressing mix. Here I use it as a seasoning for grilled shrimp, which you could broil just as easily. This avocado dressing is one of my most requested recipes, and it could become one of yours, too.

GRILLED SHRIMP SALAD WITH AVOCADO DRESSING

AVOCADO DRESSING

2 ripe avocados, peeled, pitted, and coarsely chopped

2 tablespoons red wine vinegar

2 tablespoons fresh lemon juice

1 cup olive oil

Salt and freshly ground pepper to taste

GRILLED SHRIMP

2 pounds (21 to 25 count per pound) large shrimp, peeled and deveined

One 0.7-ounce package all-natural Italian salad dressing mix, such as Good Seasons

¼ cup fresh lemon juice

¼ cup olive oil, preferably extra-virgin

Three 6-ounce Romaine lettuce hearts, torn into bite-sized pieces

1 pint cherry or grape tomatoes

2 scallions, white and green parts, chopped

1   **To make the dressing,** puree the avocados, vinegar, and lemon juice in a food processor. With the machine running, add the oil. Season with salt and pepper. (The dressing can be prepared up to 3 days ahead, covered tightly, and refrigerated. Stir well before using. If the dressing is too thick, dilute with a tablespoon or two of water.)

2   **Mix the shrimp,** salad dressing mix, lemon juice, and oil in a zippered plastic bag. Let marinate at room temperature while preparing the outdoor grill.

3   **Build a charcoal** fire in an outdoor grill and let burn until the coals are covered with white ash and are medium-hot (you should be able to hold your hand over the grill grate for about 3 seconds). In a gas grill, preheat the grill on high, then reduce the heat to medium.

4   **Lightly oil the grill.** Arrange the shrimp on the grill or in a grill basket and cook, turning once, until they are opaque and firm, about 5 minutes. Transfer the shrimp to a platter and let cool.

5   **To serve, mix** together the shrimp, lettuce, cherry tomatoes, and scallions. Serve in bowls and pass the dressing on the side.

MAKES 6 TO 8 SERVINGS

erved cool or at room temperature, this is a refreshing supper for a warm summer evening, but it is equally delicious served warm. It's up to you. Like all pasta salads, the couscous will soak up more flavors if it is dressed while it is warm. Adjust the seasonings before serving.

SALMON STEAKS WITH CITRUS COUSCOUS SALAD

SALMON

Four 8- to 10-ounce salmon steaks

1 tablespoon olive oil

Salt and freshly ground pepper to taste

COUSCOUS SALAD

2 juice oranges

1 cup reduced-sodium chicken broth

½ teaspoon salt, plus more to taste

1 cup plain couscous

1 tablespoon white or red wine vinegar

2 tablespoons olive oil, preferably extra-virgin

4 scallions, chopped

1 cucumber, peeled, seeded, and cut into ¼-inch-thick half-moons

½ cup chopped (½-inch dice) red bell pepper

1 tablespoon chopped fresh mint

Freshly ground pepper to taste

1 **Oil the broiler** rack. Position the rack 6 inches from the heat source and preheat the broiler. Brush both sides of the salmon with the oil and season with salt and pepper. Broil the salmon, turning once, about 8 minutes, until it looks opaque and has a slightly rosy center when pierced with the tip of a knife. Transfer to a plate. Let cool until tepid, then cover and refrigerate until chilled, about 2 hours.

2 **To make the salad,** zest one of the oranges, and squeeze the juice from both. You should have about ½ cup of juice.

3 **Bring the broth,** orange juice, and ½ teaspoon salt to a boil in a medium saucepan over high heat. Stir in the couscous and cover. Remove from the heat and let stand until the couscous has absorbed the liquid, about 5 minutes. Transfer to a large bowl, fluff with a fork, and cool slightly, about 10 minutes.

4 Whisk the vinegar, oil, and orange zest together in a small bowl and stir into the couscous, breaking up any lumps as you stir. Cool completely. Stir in the scallions, cucumber, red pepper, and mint. Season with salt and pepper. Cover and refrigerate until chilled, at least 1 hour. Season again with salt and pepper before serving.

5 Remove the skin and bones from the salmon and break the salmon into large flakes. To serve, spoon the couscous salad into bowls and top with the salmon. Serve chilled.

MAKES 4 TO 6 SERVINGS

ASK ART

Some recipes call for extra-virgin olive oil and others for just olive oil. Is there a difference? And does it really matter which I use?

Not all olive oils are the same. Extra-virgin olive oil is pressed from the olives without heat or chemicals; it has a full, fruity flavor and may look greener than other oils. This makes it better for uncooked preparations such as salad dressings. It's also usually more expensive than plain olive oil, which is my choice for sautéing and other cooking. Taste the olive oil you buy and make your own decision. You won't go wrong.

A double dose of beans, garbanzo and white cannellini, makes this an especially tasty bean salad. Keep the seasonings for the grilled tuna simple so that the combination can blend without clashing. If you don't want to grill the tuna, sear it in a hot nonstick skillet over medium-high heat for about 2½ minutes per side.

GRILLED TUNA WITH MEDITERRANEAN BEAN SALAD

WHITE BEAN SALAD

1 tablespoon red wine vinegar

1 garlic clove, crushed through a press

¼ cup olive oil, preferably extra-virgin

One 15- to 19-ounce can white beans (cannellini), drained and rinsed

One 15- to 19-ounce can garbanzo beans (chickpeas), drained and rinsed

1 pint cherry tomatoes, cut in half lengthwise

¼ cup coarsely chopped fresh basil

Salt and freshly ground pepper to taste

Four 6-ounce tuna steaks

2 tablespoons olive oil

Salt and freshly ground pepper to taste

1 To make the salad, place the vinegar and garlic in a medium bowl and whisk in the oil. Add the white beans, garbanzos, tomatoes, and basil, and mix. Season with salt and pepper. Let the salad stand for about 1 hour to blend the flavors.

2 Build a charcoal fire in an outdoor grill and let burn until the coals are covered with white ash. In a gas grill, preheat the grill on high.

3 Lightly oil the grill. Brush both sides of the tuna with oil and season with salt and pepper. Grill the tuna, turning once, until browned on both sides, about 5 minutes for rare tuna.

4 To serve, place a tuna steak on each of 4 dinner plates. Spoon equal portions of the bean salad to the side of each steak and serve immediately.

MAKES 4 SERVINGS

Is there any trick to selecting canned beans?

ASK ART

Canned beans are among the best canned products, and I always keep a few cans of white, black, and red kidney beans in my pantry. Choose a brand you trust. This may be a question of trial and error. Try different brands. Once you find one you like, save the label or jot the name down in your journal. The best beans are firm and unbroken and don't taste salty or metallic.

This wonderful pasta salad is what you can make when you have leftovers of Roast Leg of Lamb with Pesto (page 167). I first enjoyed it at a lunch at Kraft International Food Corporation in Chicago, where they made it with chicken. And it can be served hot or cold. No matter how you decide to make it, it's sensational.

TAVERNA PASTA SALAD WITH ROAST LAMB

2 cups dried penne

2 cups bite-sized Roast Leg of Lamb with Pesto (page 167), about 12 ounces

½ cup prepared Italian dressing, such as Good Seasons

½ cup crumbled feta cheese

⅓ cup thinly sliced basil leaves

¼ cup sun-dried tomatoes, preferably not oil-packed

¼ cup chopped red onion

1 **Bring a large** pot of lightly salted water to a boil over high heat. Add the penne and cook until tender, about 9 minutes. Drain and rinse under cold water until cool. Drain well.

2 **Mix the penne,** lamb, Italian dressing, feta cheese, basil, sun-dried tomatoes, and onion. Cover and refrigerate until chilled, about 1 hour. Serve chilled.

MAKES 4 TO 6 SERVINGS

ELEVEN

MEAT MAIN COURSES

B eef, pork, and lamb. I love them all, from homey pot roast (the ultimate comfort food) to quick and easy glazed pork chops. I don't suggest that you and your family eat meat every night of the week, but when you're in the mood, these recipes will fit the bill for easy, appealing, friendly dishes. Some are for large cuts of meat, which means you will have enough for several meals (a concept I love!). You might want to buy large cuts at price clubs and freeze them—which is a great money- and time-saver. For more on freezing, read Chapter 2, Getting Organized.

To save time, roast the vegetables alongside the meat. This is how Grandma used to cook, and it still works today. It's easy and truly delicious because the complementary flavors mingle in the finished dish while each ingredient maintains its own identity. For examples, look at the recipes for Kitchen Workhorse Roast Pork Loin with Sweet Potatoes and Apples (page 158) and Peppered Roast Eye of Round with Pesto Vegetables (page 146)—and be sure to use a good-sized roasting pan. I suggest one that measures about 16 × 13 inches.

Several of these recipes call for cooking the meat on top of the stove. Use generously sized pans for cooking. If the meat is crowded in the pan, it will steam instead of brown nicely. When I call for a large skillet, I usually mean one with a 12-inch diameter. Both sautés and stir-fries require a lot of room to cook.

In general, buy heavy cookware. It doesn't have to be the best, but since you will have it for years to come, why not invest in good pots and pans that conduct heat evenly? Read Chapter 6, Different Ways of Cooking, for more on cookware.

recipes

Beef and Tomatoes in Black Bean Sauce

Skirt Steaks with Red Wine Butter Sauce

Braised Round Steak with Mushrooms

Steak Hoisin with Stir-fried Broccoli Slaw

Kitchen Workhorse Italian Pot Roast

Peppered Roast Eye of Round with Pesto Vegetables

Java Beef Stew

Kitchen Workhorse Chunky Beef Chili

Mini Meat Loaves with Really Good Gravy

Kitchen Workhorse Roast Pork Tenderloin with Asian Glaze

Pork Pot Roast with Dried Cranberries

Kitchen Workhorse Roast Pork Loin with Sweet Potatoes and Apples

Pork Tenderloin with Mushroom Marsala Sauce

Barbecued Orange-Maple Country Ribs

Bacon, Spinach, and Cheddar Frittata

Sesame Pork Chops

Roast Leg of Lamb with Pesto

Lamb Chops with Asparagus, Tomatoes, and Feta

Fragrant Lamb Chops with Tomatoes and Cinnamon

This is a fine example of old-fashioned but still wonderful Chinese cooking, the kind you might have ordered at a Cantonese restaurant before fiery Szechuan cuisine took off. Serve it with steamed rice or with a stir-fry of green beans and garlic.

BEEF AND TOMATOES IN BLACK BEAN SAUCE

1 ½ pounds top round steak, trimmed and cut crosswise into ½-inch-thick strips

2 teaspoons cornstarch

Salt and freshly ground black pepper to taste

3 tablespoons vegetable oil

3 scallions, green and white parts, chopped

2 garlic cloves, finely chopped

6 ripe plum (Roma) tomatoes, seeds removed and cut lengthwise into quarters

3 tablespoons Chinese black bean sauce

1 teaspoon sugar

Hot cooked rice for serving

1 **Place the steak** strips in a small bowl. Sprinkle with the cornstarch, salt, and pepper, and toss well.

2 **Heat 2 tablespoons** vegetable oil in a large skillet over medium-high heat. Add the beef and cook, stirring almost constantly, until it is browned, about 3 minutes. Transfer to a plate.

3 **Add the remaining** 1 tablespoon oil to the skillet and heat. Add the scallions and garlic, and stir until the garlic is fragrant, about 1 minute. Add the tomatoes and cook, stirring almost constantly, until they begin to soften, about 2 minutes. Stir in ½ cup water, the bean sauce, sugar, and reserved beef. Bring to a boil and scrape up any browned bits in the skillet with a wooden spatula.

4 **Spoon over the rice** and serve immediately.

MAKES 4 TO 6 SERVINGS

How do you seed a tomato? And why should I bother?

Tomato seeds can be annoying in some sauces and smooth-textured preparations. While you don't have to seed tomatoes all the time, now and then it makes a difference. The easiest way is to slice a raw tomato in half through the equator. Hold each half over the sink or a bowl and gently squeeze and shake the fruit to dislodge the seeds. You can give them some help by poking them with your fingers. Don't get upset if some seeds remain. They won't hurt anything.

Skirt steak, which somewhat resembles a meaty accordion and packs plenty of beefy flavor, has become the darling cut at many restaurants. While it looks a little like flank steak and comes from the same general area on the beef, there are differences. The main difference is that skirt steak should be cut with, and not against, the grain. Panfrying the steak results in plenty of drippings that can be turned into a savory sauce, such as this one created from red wine and butter. Be forewarned that this method produces a fair amount of smoke, so be sure to have the kitchen fan on full blast.

SKIRT STEAKS WITH RED WINE BUTTER SAUCE

1²/₃ pounds skirt steak, cut into 4 equal portions

Salt and freshly ground pepper to taste

1 tablespoon vegetable oil

1 cup hearty red wine, such as Zinfandel or Shiraz

⅓ cup finely chopped shallots

1 garlic clove, finely chopped

6 tablespoons unsalted butter, cut into tablespoons and chilled

Chopped parsley for serving

1 **Season the steaks** with salt and pepper. Heat the oil in a large, heavy skillet over high heat until the oil is very hot but not smoking. Add the steaks and cook until the undersides are well browned, about 3 minutes. Reduce the heat to medium. Turn and cook until the other sides are browned and the steaks feel somewhat soft when pressed in the center, about 4 minutes more for medium-rare steaks. (Do not cook skirt steak more than medium-rare, or it will toughen.) Transfer the steaks to 4 dinner plates.

2 **Pour out the fat** in the skillet. Add the red wine, shallots, and garlic, and bring to a boil over high heat. Boil until the wine has reduced by half, about 3 minutes. Reduce the heat to very low. Whisk in the butter, 1 tablespoon at a time, to slightly thicken the sauce. Season with salt and pepper.

3 **Pour the sauce** over the steaks and sprinkle with parsley. Serve immediately.

MAKES 4 SERVINGS

What are shallots, and why are they so useful in cooking?

Members of the onion family, shallots are one of my favorite secrets. These small bulbs—which kind of look like an overblown clove of garlic with light brown skin—provide subtle flavor. When you don't want a strong oniony taste, reach for a shallot. Once you get in the habit, you will love them as much as I do!

ound steak makes a great family meal for those evenings when you can let
dinner simmer for about an hour. This dish was originally made with steaks
that were tenderized by a pounding process called swissing. The Swiss also use
lots of mushrooms in their cooking, which is true of our dish. This updated version
relies on earthy dried porcini mushrooms along with fresh, full-flavored cremini
mushrooms, but toss in more familiar white mushrooms and eliminate the dried
porcini if it's easier. Serve over hot egg noodles.

BRAISED ROUND STEAK
WITH MUSHROOMS

1 ounce (about ½ cup) dried porcini
mushrooms

1½ pounds top round steak, trimmed of
excess fat

Salt and freshly ground black pepper to
taste

3 tablespoons olive oil, divided

½ cup all-purpose flour

10 ounces fresh cremini (baby
portobello) mushrooms, sliced

2 scallions, white and green parts,
chopped

½ cup reduced-sodium beef broth or
additional water

½ cup whole or reduced-fat sour cream

2 teaspoons Dijon mustard

1 **Place the dried mushrooms** in a small glass bowl and add 1 cup water.
Microwave on 100 percent (high) power until the liquid boils. Set aside for
10 minutes. (If you don't have a microwave oven, cover the mushrooms with
1 cup boiling water and let stand until the mushrooms soften, about 20
minutes.) Lift the mushrooms out of the liquid and chop coarsely. Set the
soaking liquid aside.

2 **Pound the round steak** with a meat mallet (preferably the pointed side if it has
one) or a rolling pin until the meat is about ¼ inch thick. Cut the steak into 6
serving portions. Season the steaks with salt and pepper.

3 **Heat 2 tablespoons** oil in a large skillet over medium-high heat. Spread the
flour in a shallow dish. Coat each steak with the flour, shaking off the excess
flour, and add to the skillet. Add the steaks to the skillet in batches and cook,
turning once, until browned on both sides, about 5 minutes. Transfer the
steaks to a plate.

4 **Heat the remaining** 1 tablespoon oil in the skillet. Add the fresh mushrooms and cook, stirring often, until they begin to brown, about 6 minutes. Stir in the white part of the scallions and about half of the greens, reserving the remaining scallion greens for garnish. Cook until wilted, about 1 minute. Add the soaked mushrooms and broth. Carefully pour the mushroom soaking liquid into the skillet, leaving the grit at the bottom of the bowl. (If you are not using dried mushrooms, add a scant cup of water instead.) Return the steaks to the skillet. Reduce the heat to medium-low, cover, and simmer until the steaks are tender, about 45 minutes.

5 **Transfer the steaks** to a platter. Stir the sour cream and mustard into the cooking liquid and heat through but do not boil. Season with salt and pepper. Pour over the steaks and sprinkle with the reserved scallion greens. Serve hot.

MAKES 6 SERVINGS

ere's another recipe that makes good use of the Asian condiments I have in my pantry. Hoisin sauce—thick, sweet, and savory—is the base for a quick marinade and a sauce for the stir-fried vegetables. Sesame oil adds its delicious distinctive flavor to the mix. If you have the chance, make the marinade before you go to work and refrigerate the steak in it all day. Frankly, the marinade is so flavorful, just a brief soak is sufficient, so if time doesn't permit this advance planning, don't neglect this dish! And the broccoli slaw is truly delicious with this. Look for it alongside the other bags of coleslaw mix in the supermarket.

A few things to remember to keep flank steak juicy and tender: Don't cook it more than medium-rare, let it stand for a few minutes before slicing, and cut it across the grain into thin slices.

STEAK HOISIN WITH STIR-FRIED BROCCOLI SLAW

SAUCE

¼ cup hoisin sauce

Grated zest of 1 orange

¼ cup fresh orange juice

1 tablespoon shredded fresh ginger (use the large holes on a box grater)

2 teaspoons dark Asian sesame oil

¼ teaspoon crushed hot red pepper flakes

1½ pounds flank steak

1 tablespoon vegetable oil

1 tablespoon shredded fresh ginger (use the large holes on a box grater)

1 garlic clove, minced

One 12-ounce package broccoli slaw

1 **To make the sauce,** whisk the hoisin sauce, orange zest and juice, ginger, sesame oil, and red pepper in a small bowl to combine.

2 **Place the steak** in a zippered plastic bag and add ⅓ cup of the sauce. Close the bag and toss the steak in the sauce to coat. Cover and reserve the remaining sauce. Refrigerate the marinating steak and the reserved sauce for at least 20 minutes or up to 10 hours.

3 **Oil the broiler** rack. Position it about 4 inches from the heat source and preheat the broiler.

4 Remove the steak from the marinade. Broil the steak, turning once, until the steak is medium-rare, about 3 minutes on each side. Transfer to a carving board. Tent with aluminum foil and let stand for 3 to 5 minutes before carving.

5 Meanwhile, heat the vegetable oil in a large skillet over high heat. Add the ginger and garlic, and stir until they give off their fragrance, about 15 seconds. Add the broccoli slaw and stir-fry until heated through, about 3 minutes. Add the reserved sauce and mix well. Remove from the heat.

6 Holding a sharp knife at a 45-degree angle and cutting across the grain, thinly slice the steak. Heap the vegetables on a platter and top with the sliced steak.

MAKES 4 SERVINGS

Making pot roast takes time, but very little of *your* time. It's just a matter of letting the roast simmer its way to tenderness. With this recipe you will get the meat and a terrific tomato sauce. Leftovers cry out to be transformed into pasta sauce or a sandwich for another meal. For a quick way to chop the tomatoes, use kitchen shears to snip them into pieces right in the can.

ITALIAN POT ROAST

spin-off recipes
Penne with Pot Roast Sauce (page 220)
Hot Italian Beef Open-faced Sandwich (page 97)

2 tablespoons olive oil, or more if needed

One 3¾-pound bottom round beef roast

Salt and freshly ground pepper to taste

1 large onion, chopped

1 medium carrot, cut into ½-inch dice

1 medium celery rib, cut into ½-inch dice

2 garlic cloves

¾ cup dry red wine, such as Zinfandel or Shiraz

One 28-ounce can tomatoes in thick puree, chopped

1 teaspoon dried oregano

1 teaspoon dried basil

1 **Heat the oil** in a Dutch oven over medium-high heat. Season the roast with salt and pepper. Add to the pot and cook, turning occasionally, until the roast is browned on all sides, about 8 minutes. Transfer the roast to a plate.

2 **Heat more oil** in the pot if needed. Add the onion, carrot, and celery, and cook, stirring often, until the vegetables soften, about 5 minutes. Add the garlic and cook until fragrant, about 1 minute. Add the wine and bring to a boil. Add the tomatoes and their puree, oregano, and basil. Return the roast to the pot and bring the sauce to a boil. Reduce the heat to low and cover the pot. Simmer, occasionally turning the roast in the sauce, until the meat is fork-tender, about 2 hours.

3 Transfer the meat to a platter. Remove the pot from the heat and let stand for 5 minutes. Skim off any fat that rises to the surface of the sauce. Carve the meat and pour the sauce on top. Serve hot.

MAKES 6 TO 8 SERVINGS

What's the best kind of cutting board?

ASK ART

The choice is yours—either wood or plastic. I use both kinds. While wooden cutting boards were in disrepute a decade ago, their honor has been restored. In fact, there is some evidence that bacteria lodged in the tiny cracks and crevices of wooden boards are far less likely to resurface than the bacteria lodged in plastic boards. The best advice I can give you is to keep your cutting boards clean and dry, whether they are made of wood or plastic. Wash them with hot soapy water between uses and let them air-dry.

E ye of round slices like a dream and therefore is a popular cut for roasting. It is extremely lean and so must be roasted at a moderate temperature to avoid drying out. For the same reason it should not be cooked beyond medium-rare. To let the beef flavor shine through, I give the roast a simple rub of salt and pepper. I like to use the four-peppercorn blend available at many supermarkets, which includes black, white, pink, and green peppercorns. Because it just doesn't make sense not to roast some vegetables alongside, I like to prepare this zesty mix of eggplant, red peppers, potatoes, and onion—perfect with the understated beef.

PEPPERED ROAST EYE OF ROUND WITH PESTO VEGETABLES

1 medium eggplant, cut into 1-inch chunks

2 teaspoons salt, divided, plus more to taste

1½ teaspoons four-peppercorn blend, or 1 teaspoon black peppercorns, coarsely crushed in a mortar or under a heavy saucepan

2½ pounds beef eye of round

4 tablespoons olive oil, preferably extra-virgin, divided

1 pound Yukon Gold potatoes, peeled and cut into 1-inch cubes

1 large red bell pepper, seeds and ribs discarded, and cut into 1½-inch chunks

1 large onion, cut into 1½-inch chunks

Freshly ground pepper to taste

2 tablespoons Kitchen Workhorse Pesto (page 226) or use store-bought pesto

1 **About 1 hour** before cooking, place the eggplant in a colander and toss with 1 teaspoon salt. Let stand over a bowl for 1 hour to drain off the bitter juices. Rinse well and pat dry with paper towels.

2 **Position a rack** in the center of the oven and preheat the oven to 325°F. Lightly oil a large (preferably 18 × 14-inch) roasting pan.

3 **Mix the peppercorn** blend and remaining 1 teaspoon salt in a small bowl. Rub all over the beef. Heat 1 tablespoon oil in a large skillet over medium-high heat. Add the roast and cook, turning occasionally, until browned on all sides, about 8 minutes.

4 **Mix the eggplant,** potatoes, red pepper, and onion in a large bowl. Add the remaining 3 tablespoons oil and mix well. Season with salt and pepper. Spread the vegetables in the roasting pan and place the beef on top.

5 **Roast, occasionally stirring** the vegetables, until an instant-read thermometer inserted in the center of the roast reads 130°F for medium-rare meat. Transfer the meat to a carving board and let stand for 10 minutes.

6 **Increase the oven** temperature to 450°F and roast the vegetables until the tips are lightly browned, about 10 minutes. Stir in the pesto. Transfer the vegetables to a serving bowl.

7 **Slice the beef** thinly across the grain and serve hot with the vegetables.

MAKES 6 TO 8 SERVINGS

Can I defrost meat in the microwave?

ASK ART

Try to avoid the microwave but instead defrost meat in the refrigerator—never on the countertop. This means planning ahead and taking the frozen meat from the freezer twelve or even twenty-four hours ahead of time. Put the wrapped meat in a shallow dish to catch leaks as it defrosts. Once it is partially thawed, you can hasten its progress in the microwave on a low setting, but this is not my favorite way to go. If you don't watch carefully, the meat will cook a little in the microwave. (Be sure to wipe the microwave clean with warm soap and water if the meat's juices leak onto the turntable.)

Who would have thought that a cup of coffee could add so much flavor to a simple beef stew? This is actually an old chuck wagon trick from the cowboy days when coffee was far easier to come by than beef broth. It turns out that the deep, roasted coffee flavor works perfectly with the beef.

JAVA BEEF STEW

3 pounds beef chuck, cut into 1½-inch chunks

Salt and freshly ground pepper to taste

2 tablespoons olive oil, as needed

2 medium onions, chopped

4 garlic cloves, chopped

2 cups hearty red wine, such as Zinfandel or Shiraz

1 cup strong brewed coffee (but not espresso)

1 teaspoon dried thyme

1 bay leaf

2 medium carrots, cut into ¾-inch-thick rounds

2 medium parsnips, peeled and cut into ¾-inch-thick rounds

⅓ cup unsalted butter, softened

⅓ cup all-purpose flour

1 **Season the beef** with salt and pepper. Heat the oil in a large saucepan or Dutch oven over medium-high heat. Add the beef to the pot in batches without crowding, adding more oil as needed. Cook, turning occasionally, until browned, about 8 minutes. Transfer the beef to a platter.

2 **Add more oil** to the pot if needed. Add the onions and cook, stirring occasionally, until golden, about 6 minutes. Add the garlic and cook until it is fragrant, about 1 minute.

3 **Add the wine** and coffee, and bring to a boil. Scrape up the browned bits in the pot with a wooden spatula. Return the beef to the pot and add the thyme and bay leaf. Bring to a boil, reduce the heat to low, and cover the pot. Simmer until the beef is almost tender, about 1½ hours. Stir the carrots and parsnips into the pot. Continue cooking until the carrots and beef are tender, about 30 minutes.

4 **Mash the butter** and flour together with a rubber spatula in a medium bowl. Whisk in about 1 cup of the cooking liquid to make a smooth paste. Whisk this mixture into the pot. Simmer until the stew has thickened and lost any raw flour taste, about 5 minutes. Season with salt and pepper. Serve hot.

MAKES 6 TO 8 SERVINGS

Get out your biggest pot for this blue-ribbon chili. Don't be put off by the chocolate in the recipe; many a chili master uses it as a secret ingredient. A bowl of chili is a beautiful thing, but so are the soft tacos and casseroles that can be made from the leftovers.

CHUNKY BEEF CHILI

spin-off recipes
Soft Beef Tacos (page 98)
Chili Shepherd's Pie with Buttermilk Potato Topping (page 245)
Chili and Macaroni Casserole (page 246)

2 tablespoons olive oil

6 pounds beef chuck, cut into 1½-inch chunks

Salt and freshly ground pepper to taste

2 medium onions, chopped

2 green bell peppers, seeds and ribs discarded, and chopped

2 jalapeños, seeds and ribs discarded, and finely chopped

6 garlic cloves, finely chopped

2 tablespoons chili powder

1 tablespoon ground cumin

1 tablespoon dried oregano

One 14½-ounce can diced tomatoes in juice

One 14½-ounce can reduced-sodium beef broth

One 12-ounce bottle lager beer, or 1½ cups additional beef broth

¼ cup yellow cornmeal

1 ounce unsweetened chocolate, finely chopped

Sour cream, shredded sharp cheddar cheese, and chopped scallions for serving

1 **Heat the oil** in a very large Dutch oven over high heat. Season the beef with salt and pepper. Add the beef to the pot in batches without crowding. Cook, stirring occasionally, until browned, about 5 minutes. Using a slotted spoon, transfer the beef to a platter.

2 **Add the onions,** bell peppers, and jalapeños to the pot and cook, stirring often, until the vegetables soften, about 5 minutes. Add the garlic and cook until fragrant, about 1 minute. Sprinkle with the chili powder and cumin, and stir

well. Return the beef and any juices on the platter to the pot. Stir in the tomatoes and their juice, beef broth, and beer, and bring to a boil. Reduce the heat to medium-low and cover the pot. Simmer until the meat is tender, about 2 hours.

3 **Remove the chili** from the heat and let stand for 5 minutes. Skim off any fat that rises to the surface. Transfer 1 cup of the cooking liquid to a small bowl. Add the cornmeal and whisk to make a thin paste. Stir the cornmeal into the pot along with the chocolate. Cook just until the sauce thickens slightly, about 5 minutes.

4 **Serve hot with sour cream,** cheddar, and scallions passed on the side.

MAKES 8 TO 10 SERVINGS

CHUNKY BEEF CHILI WITH BEANS: **Add two 15- to 19-ounce cans of pinto beans, drained and rinsed, to the chili during the last 15 minutes of cooking.**

Do you recommend canned broth rather than bouillon cubes?

ASK ART

Yes. I use canned chicken broth freely in my recipes and like the results. I am more selective when it comes to canned beef and vegetable broth. Beef broth is strong tasting and is best used in recipes with lots of other ingredients to balance its flavor. I avoid bouillon cubes completely because they are far saltier and their flavors are not as pleasing as canned broth. Chefs and many home cooks prefer homemade stock, made from bones, aromatic vegetables, and fresh seasonings, and these truly are superior in flavor to canned broth. If you have time, make your own stock, but if not (and, let's face it, most of us don't have the time), use canned broth or the high-quality frozen broth sold in some gourmet shops.

Broth comes in cans that hold about 14 ounces. This is just shy of 2 cups, which is 16 ounces. Instead of opening a fresh can, simply add water to make 2 cups to satisfy a recipe. The flavor will hardly be diluted. In fact, I have added as much as a cup of water to 14 ounces of broth before the flavor has been drastically affected.

Meat loaf remains a stalwart dinner favorite, but many home cooks overlook it because it needs more than an hour to cook. To speed up the cooking time, form the meat mixture into individual mounds; they're done in half the time. For a really great-tasting meat loaf, look for the combination of ground beef, pork, and veal that many supermarkets carry; it may be called "meat loaf mix." And why not make gravy out of the pan drippings to spoon over a side of your favorite mashed potatoes?

MINI MEAT LOAVES WITH REALLY GOOD GRAVY

1 1/3 pounds meat loaf mix (beef, pork, and veal)

1/3 cup plus 2 tablespoons catsup, divided

1/3 cup dried bread crumbs

1 large egg, beaten

1 tablespoon Dijon mustard

2 teaspoons Worcestershire sauce

1 teaspoon salt

1/2 teaspoon freshly ground pepper

GRAVY

3 tablespoons unsalted butter

1/4 cup all-purpose flour

2 cups canned reduced-sodium beef broth

Salt and freshly ground black pepper to taste

1 **Position a rack** in the center of the oven and preheat the oven to 350°F. Lightly oil a 13 × 9-inch metal baking dish.

2 **Combine the meat** loaf mix, 1/3 cup catsup, bread crumbs, egg, mustard, Worcestershire sauce, salt, and pepper in a large bowl (your hands work best). In the baking dish, shape the meat mixture into six 3-inch-wide mounds. Poke your finger into the middle of each mound to make a hole.

3 **Bake until an** instant-read thermometer inserted in a meat loaf reads 165°F, about 40 minutes. During the last 5 minutes of baking, spread the remaining 2 tablespoons catsup over the tops of the meat loaves. Transfer them to a platter and tent with aluminum foil to keep warm.

4 **Tilt the baking** dish and spoon out the clear fat, leaving 1 tablespoon juice in the pan. Place over 2 burners on medium heat. Add the butter and melt it. Sprinkle with the flour and whisk well. Whisk in the broth and bring to a simmer. Reduce the heat to low and simmer, whisking often, until the gravy is smooth and thick, about 3 minutes. Season with salt and pepper.

5 **Serve the meat** loaves hot with the gravy passed on the side.

MAKES 6 SERVINGS

Pork tenderloin can be found in every supermarket, usually packed two tenderloins to a package. That's a fair amount of meat for one meal, so you might as well face the music and roast both tenderloins. Use the sliced cooked meat in other dishes later in the week. What a perfect opportunity for an unexpected extra meal! With this simple wet rub of Asian ingredients, the pork will be ready for the oven in no time.

ROAST PORK TENDERLOIN WITH ASIAN GLAZE

spin-off recipes

Soba Noodles in Miso Broth with Roast Pork and Vegetables (page 228)

Roast Pork on Boston Lettuce Salad with Asian Pears (page 124)

2 tablespoons soy sauce

2 tablespoons light brown sugar

1 tablespoon peeled and minced fresh ginger

2 teaspoons dark Asian sesame oil

2 garlic cloves, crushed through a press

¼ teaspoon crushed hot red pepper flakes

2 pork tenderloins, trimmed of excess fat and any thin silver skin

1 scallion, white and green parts, thinly sliced for garnish

1 **Position a rack** in the center of the oven and preheat the oven to 400°F. Line a small roasting pan with aluminum foil and lightly oil the foil. This is important because the glaze has a high sugar content and will scorch during roasting.

2 **Meanwhile, combine the soy sauce,** brown sugar, ginger, sesame oil, garlic, and red pepper in a self-sealing plastic bag and mix to dissolve the sugar. Add the pork tenderloins and close the bag. Toss the meat in the bag to coat it with the marinade. Let stand at room temperature while the oven heats.

3   **Remove the pork** tenderloins from the marinade and place in the roasting pan. Drizzle about half of the marinade over the pork. Pour the remaining marinade into a small saucepan and add 2 tablespoons water; set aside.

4   **Roast for 15** minutes. Baste the pork with the marinade in the roasting pan. Continue roasting until an instant-read thermometer inserted in the center of the meat reads 150–155°F, about 25 minutes more. The marinade will eventually thicken and scorch, but the foil will protect the pan, so don't worry. Transfer the pork to a cutting board and let stand for 5 minutes.

5   **While the pork** is resting, bring the reserved marinade in the saucepan to a boil over high heat. Cut the roast pork crosswise on a slight diagonal into thin slices and arrange the overlapping slices on a platter. Drizzle the hot marinade over the pork, sprinkle with the scallion, and serve immediately.

MAKES 8 TO 10 SERVINGS

When you say pot roast, most people think of beef, but why not apply the concept to pork? You'll get exceptionally moist and juicy pork—something that is getting hard to find these days as pork gets leaner and leaner. Be sure to use a center-cut pork loin, not the smaller pork tenderloin.

PORK POT ROAST WITH DRIED CRANBERRIES

1 tablespoon olive oil

One 3½-pound boneless pork loin roast, patted dry with paper towels

Salt and freshly ground black pepper

2 tablespoons unsalted butter, divided

1 small onion, chopped

¾ cup dry white wine, such as Sauvignon Blanc or Pinot Grigio

1¾ cups chicken broth, homemade, or use canned low-sodium

1 tablespoon dried rosemary

1 teaspoon ground sage

½ cup dried cranberries

1 tablespoon all-purpose flour

½ teaspoon sugar

1 Heat the oil in a Dutch oven over medium-high heat. Season the pork roast with ¾ teaspoon salt and ½ teaspoon pepper. Add the pork roast to the pot and cook, turning occasionally, until browned on all sides, about 8 minutes. Transfer the pork to a platter.

2 Discard the fat in the pot. Add 1 tablespoon butter and melt. Add the onion and cook, stirring often, until golden, about 5 minutes. Stir in the wine, scraping up the browned bits in the bottom of the pot. Add the broth, rosemary, and sage. Return the pork to the pot and bring to a boil. Reduce the heat to medium-low and cover. Cook at a brisk simmer until a meat thermometer inserted in the center of the roast reads 150°F, about 1¼ hours. During the last 10 minutes, add the cranberries to the pot. Transfer the meat to a platter.

3 Mash the flour and the remaining 1 tablespoon butter in a small bowl to make a thick paste. Whisk about ½ cup of the cooking liquid into the bowl to thin the paste, then whisk this into the simmering liquid in the pot. Simmer the

sauce until thick and smooth and no raw flour taste remains, about 5 minutes. Season the sauce with the sugar, salt, and pepper.

4 **Slice the meat** and layer the slices on a platter. Spoon the sauce over the meat and serve hot.

MAKES 8 SERVINGS

PORK POT ROAST WITH BABY CARROTS AND DRIED CRANBERRIES: For a one-dish meal that needs only mashed potatoes or another starchy side dish, add 1 pound of baby-cut carrots to the pot about 15 minutes before the pork is finished. The carrots will cook along with the pork.

While this herb-rubbed pork roasts, the aroma is downright irresistible. This recipe calls for the large roast that you are likely to find at a warehouse shopping club, and unless you serve it to a big group, you will have leftovers for other dishes—always good news! You will need a big roasting pan to hold the pork, sweet potatoes, and apples; a 17 × 14-inch pan is ideal. Pork loin tends to be quite lean, and an overnight brine to add moisture is a good idea. But if you are short on time, skip this step. If you do, be especially careful not to cook the pork above 155°F, or it could be drier than you like. If you don't brine the pork, add 1½ teaspoons salt to the herb rub.

ROAST PORK LOIN WITH SWEET POTATOES AND APPLES

related recipe

Pork Tenderloin with Mushroom Marsala Sauce, page 160

½ cup iodized table salt, plus more for the yams and sauce

½ cup packed light brown sugar

One 7-pound double-loin boneless pork roast, tied

1½ teaspoons dried sage

1½ teaspoons crumbled dried rosemary

1½ teaspoons dried thyme

1 teaspoon fennel seed, crushed in a mortar or under a heavy saucepan

Freshly ground black pepper

2 pounds orange-fleshed (Louisiana) yams, peeled and cut lengthwise in half and then into 1-inch chunks (look for elongated, not chubby, yams)

2 pounds Granny Smith apples, peeled, cored, and cut lengthwise into quarters

5 tablespoons (½ stick plus 1 tablespoon) unsalted butter

⅓ cup all-purpose flour

2 cups reduced-sodium chicken broth

One 12-ounce bottle hard apple cider (see Note)

1 Combine 1 gallon water with the ½ cup salt and the brown sugar in a large nonreactive pot (stainless steel, not uncoated aluminum). Stir to dissolve the salt. Add the pork roast and soak for 6 to 12 hours (8 hours is ideal, but there is some flexibility).

2 **Position a rack** in the center of the oven and preheat the oven to 450°F.

3 **Combine the sage,** rosemary, thyme, fennel, and 1 teaspoon pepper in a small bowl. Remove the pork from the brine and pat dry with paper towels. Rub the herb mixture all over the pork. Place the pork on a meat rack in a large roasting pan.

4 **Roast the pork** for 15 minutes. Reduce the heat to 350°F and roast for 45 minutes more. Scatter the yams around the pork, mix well with the fat in the pan, and season with salt and pepper. Roast for 45 minutes. Mix in the apples. Continue roasting until an instant-read thermometer inserted in the center of the pork reads 155°F, about 45 minutes more (2½ hours total roasting time). Transfer the roast to a carving board and let stand for 15 minutes before carving.

5 **If the yams** aren't tender when the pork is done, return the oven temperature to 450°F and cook, stirring often, until they can be pierced with the tip of a knife. Otherwise, use a slotted spoon to transfer the yams and apples to a heatproof serving bowl. Cover with aluminum foil and keep warm in the turned-off oven.

6 **Place the roasting** pan on 2 burners over medium heat. Add the butter and melt. Sprinkle with the flour and whisk until smooth. Whisk in the broth and cider, and bring to a boil, stirring up the browned bits in the pan with the whisk. Reduce the heat to medium-low and cook, whisking often, until the sauce is slightly thickened, about 5 minutes. Season with salt and pepper.

7 **Remove the strings** and slice the roast crosswise. Serve the pork immediately with the yams and apples, and pass the sauce on the side.

MAKES 10 TO 12 SERVINGS

> NOTE: **Hard apple cider is available in six-packs of 12-ounce bottles, and there are many good domestic brands. If you prefer, use 1 cup semidry white wine (such as Riesling or Gewürztraminer) and ½ cup apple juice instead. For an alcohol-free version, use 1 cup apple cider and an additional ½ cup chicken broth. They are all good!**

There are two ways to make this quick dinner. The first, as written here, calls for pork tenderloin, and it is a winner. But if you have leftover slices of roast pork loin, follow the variation that follows. In either case, use dry marsala, not the sweet variety, which should be reserved for desserts and after-dinner drinks.

PORK TENDERLOIN WITH MUSHROOM MARSALA SAUCE

1 1/3 pounds pork tenderloin, trimmed of excess fat and thin silver skin

Salt and freshly ground pepper to taste

1/4 cup all-purpose flour

2 tablespoons olive oil, as needed

3 tablespoons unsalted butter, divided

10 ounces brown cremini (baby portobello) mushrooms, sliced

1/4 cup finely chopped shallots

1/2 teaspoon dried sage

1/2 teaspoon crumbled dried rosemary

1/2 cup dry marsala

1 cup reduced-sodium beef broth

1 **Cut the pork** tenderloin crosswise into 1/2-inch-thick slices. Lightly pound the slices with a meat pounder or rolling pin until they are about 1/3 inch thick. Season the pork with salt and pepper.

2 **Place the flour** in a shallow bowl. Heat the oil in a large skillet over medium-high heat. Dip the pork slices in the flour to coat and shake off the excess flour. Add to the skillet and cook, turning once, just until browned on both sides, about 3 minutes. Transfer the pork to a plate.

3 **Wipe out the skillet** with paper towels. Heat 2 tablespoons butter over medium heat. Add the mushrooms and cook, stirring often, until they give off their juice and it evaporates, about 6 minutes. Add the shallots, sage, and rosemary and cook until the shallots soften, about 1 minute. Add the marsala and broth, and bring to a boil. Return the pork to the skillet and cook, turning the pork, until the liquid is slightly thickened, about 2 minutes. Remove from the heat and stir in the remaining 1 tablespoon butter. Season with salt and pepper. Serve hot.

MAKES 4 TO 6 SERVINGS

ROAST PORK LOIN WITH MUSHROOM MARSALA SAUCE: Have ready 12 slices of Kitchen Workhorse Roast Pork Loin (page 158). Omit the step of sautéing the floured pork tenderloin. Sauté the mushrooms and shallots. Sprinkle the mushroom mixture with 2 teaspoons flour and mix well. Add the herbs, marsala, and broth, and bring to a boil. Add the pork slices to the sauce and cook just until the pork is heated through, about 2 minutes.

Again, here is a recipe that makes a lot for the bonus of extra meals. Country pork ribs have a lot of meat, all the better to cut off and turn into sandwiches for a lunch or supper entrée. You can certainly use this sweet and spicy marinade/sauce for spareribs or baby back ribs, which are deliciously succulent if a little less meaty. And for the final glazing, if you have a hankering for a smoky flavor, fire up the outdoor grill and let the coals burn to medium heat or set the gas grill to medium. Add hickory chips to get a good head of smoke and grill the ribs, brushing with the sauce, for about 10 minutes.

BARBECUED ORANGE-MAPLE COUNTRY RIBS

Zest of 2 large oranges

1 cup fresh orange juice

¾ cup maple-flavored pancake syrup (see Note)

¼ cup Worcestershire sauce

1 tablespoon Asian chili paste with garlic

7 pounds country pork ribs

Salt to taste

¼ cup catsup

2 teaspoons cornstarch dissolved in 2 tablespoons water

1   **Mix the orange** zest and juice, pancake syrup, Worcestershire sauce, and chili paste in a large bowl. Divide the ribs between two 1-gallon zippered plastic bags. Pour half of the marinade into each bag and close. Marinate the ribs in the refrigerator for at least 2 hours or overnight.

2   **Position a rack** in the center of the oven and preheat the oven to 350°F.

3   **Remove the ribs** from the marinade and arrange in a roasting pan large enough to hold them without crowding (you can divide them between two pans if you wish). Reserve the marinade. Lightly season the ribs with salt and cover the pan with aluminum foil.

4   **Bake the ribs** for 1¼ hours. Remove the foil and turn the ribs. Continue baking until the ribs are tender, about 1 hour more.

5   Meanwhile, combine the reserved marinade and catsup in a medium saucepan. Cook over high heat until the marinade is reduced to 1 cup, about 10 minutes. Stir the dissolved cornstarch into the marinade to thicken it and turn it into a glaze for the ribs. Set the glaze aside.

6   When the ribs are tender, increase the oven temperature to 400°F. Brush the ribs generously with the glaze. Bake until the glaze on the ribs bubbles, about 15 minutes. Serve hot.

MAKES 8 TO 10 SERVINGS

NOTE: Maple-flavored pancake syrup, which has a stronger flavor than pure maple syrup, works best in this recipe. If you want to use pure maple syrup, look for the Grade B variety, which has the richest maple flavor. Reserve the mellow Grade A maple syrup for pancakes and waffles, where its mild sweetness can be fully appreciated.

BARBECUED ORANGE-MAPLE BABY BACK RIBS: Substitute baby back ribs for the country ribs. Divide the marinated ribs between 2 roasting pans or large rimmed baking sheets and cover with foil. Bake for 30 minutes, uncover, and bake about 30 minutes more, until tender. Glaze as directed.

BARBECUED ORANGE-MAPLE SPARERIBS: Substitute spareribs for the country ribs. Divide the marinated ribs between 2 roasting pans or large rimmed baking sheets and cover with foil. Bake for 1 hour, uncover, and bake about 45 minutes more, until tender. Glaze as directed.

The all-American flavors of bacon, spinach, and cheddar work well in the Italian guise of a frittata. Save the bacon fat for making Bacon-Buttermilk Corn Bread (page 258).

BACON, SPINACH, AND CHEDDAR FRITTATA

5 slices bacon

1 tablespoon extra-virgin olive oil

1 small onion, chopped

8 large eggs

¾ teaspoon salt

¼ teaspoon hot red pepper sauce

One 10-ounce box frozen chopped spinach, thawed and squeezed well to remove excess moisture

¾ cup (3 ounces) shredded sharp cheddar cheese

1 **Position the broiler** rack 6 inches from the heat source and preheat the broiler.

2 **Place the bacon** in a large skillet. Cook over medium heat until the bacon is browned and crisp, about 10 minutes. Transfer the bacon to paper towels to drain and cool. Discard the bacon fat or save it for another use. Coarsely chop the bacon.

3 **Heat the oil** in a medium nonstick skillet over medium heat. Add the onion and cook, stirring occasionally, until golden, about 5 minutes.

4 **Meanwhile, beat the eggs,** salt, and red pepper sauce well in a medium bowl. Stir in the spinach and bacon, and mix well to break up the spinach.

5 **Pour into the skillet** with the onions and cook until the edges begin to set. Using a rubber spatula, lift up an edge of the frittata, and tilt the skillet so the uncooked eggs run underneath the frittata. Continue cooking, occasionally lifting the frittata and tilting the skillet, until the top is almost set, 4 to 5 minutes. Sprinkle the top of the frittata with the cheddar.

6 **Broil the frittata** until the top is puffed and the cheddar has melted, about 1 minute. Place a plate over the top of the skillet and invert the frittata onto the plate. Cut into wedges and serve hot or cooled to room temperature.

MAKES 6 SERVINGS

Can I freeze bacon?

Sure. Keep it in its original packaging, or if you want to divide it into smaller portions, wrap it well in plastic wrap and then put it in a plastic freezer bag. Freeze it for up to two months. Let it defrost in the refrigerator. I like to freeze small amounts of bacon so that it's available when I want to cook with it. Bacon keeps in the fridge for about two weeks.

The flavor of pork is enhanced by a bit of sweetness, and these pork chops are a perfect example. For the juiciest results use thick-cut pork chops, which you might have to buy at a butcher shop. For the typical chops found in supermarkets, which tend to be thinly cut, reduce the simmering time to 10 minutes. Transfer the chops to a platter and boil the cooking liquid for a minute or so in the uncovered skillet until it thickens into a glaze. Serve the chops with a stir-fry of broccoli and cauliflower along with steamed rice if you wish.

SESAME PORK CHOPS

1 tablespoon sesame seeds

1 tablespoon vegetable oil

4 center-cut pork loin chops on the bone, about 1 inch thick (10 to 12 ounces each)

Salt and freshly ground black pepper to taste

½ cup reduced-sodium chicken broth

2 tablespoons rice vinegar

2 teaspoons light brown sugar

2 teaspoons Dijon mustard

2 teaspoons dark Asian sesame oil

¼ teaspoon crushed hot red pepper flakes

1 **Heat a large** skillet over medium-high heat. Add the sesame seeds and cook, stirring often, until they are lightly toasted. Transfer the seeds to a small plate and set aside.

2 **Add the vegetable** oil to the skillet. Season the pork chops with salt and pepper. Add the chops to the skillet and cook, turning once, until browned on both sides, about 5 minutes. Pour off any fat in the skillet. Transfer the chops to a platter.

3 **Add the broth,** vinegar, brown sugar, mustard, sesame oil, and red pepper to the skillet. Stir to combine and bring to a boil. Return the chops to the skillet and sprinkle with the sesame seeds. Reduce the heat to medium-low and cover. Simmer about 20 minutes, until the chops show just the barest hint of pink when pierced at the bone with the tip of a knife and the cooking liquid has been reduced to a glaze. Transfer the chops to a platter and pour the sauce on top of them. Serve hot.

MAKES 4 SERVINGS

It's not that boneless leg of lamb is tricky, it's just that knowledge is power. At most price clubs and markets you can be sure that the leg of lamb will be untrimmed. There will be plenty of thick fat on the surface that needs to be removed. If necessary, discard any netting and then trim off that fat with a thin knife. A 5-pound boneless leg of lamb could lose a pound of fat in the trimming. Next, do not worry about butterflying the lamb (slicing the thick areas almost all the way through and opening them up to flatten the roast), because you actually have more control if the lamb retains its lumpy shape. It's easier to determine the internal temperature with an instant-read thermometer (stick it in a thick section) and easier to carve. That said (whew!), you will get a heck of a lot of flavor from the few ingredients that this recipe requires.

ROAST LEG OF LAMB WITH PESTO

One 5-pound boneless leg of lamb, trimmed of excess fat and sinew (about 3¾ pounds after trimming)

Salt and freshly ground pepper to taste

⅓ cup Kitchen Workhorse Pesto (page 226) or store-bought pesto

1 **Position a rack** in the center of the oven and preheat the oven to 425°F. Lightly oil a rimmed baking sheet.

2 **Season the lamb** with salt and pepper and place it on a baking sheet (it will have 2 large lumps of meat separated by a thinner area).

3 **Roast the lamb** until an instant-read thermometer inserted in the thickest part of the lamb reads 125°F, about 30 minutes. Spread the pesto over the lamb and continue roasting until the thermometer reads 130°F for medium-rare lamb, about 5 minutes.

4 **Transfer the lamb** to a carving board and let stand for 5 minutes. Cut across the grain into thin slices and serve hot.

MAKES 6 TO 8 SERVINGS

The uncomplicated mixture of Worcestershire sauce and olive oil makes the perfect marinade for lamb chops. Most of the time I broil my lamb chops in the oven, but if your gas grill is handy, fire it up. Grilled lamb chops, cooked directly over the heat, will take a little longer, about eight minutes for medium-rare. The asparagus, tomato, and feta cheese sauté is a sufficient side dish, but add some steamed new potatoes if you wish.

LAMB CHOPS WITH ASPARAGUS, TOMATOES, AND FETA

2 tablespoons Worcestershire sauce

3 tablespoons extra-virgin olive oil, divided

Freshly ground black pepper

Eight 4-ounce center-cut loin lamb chops (about 1 inch thick)

1 pound asparagus, tough ends discarded and cut into 1-inch lengths

1 pint grape tomatoes, cut in half

½ teaspoon dried oregano

½ cup crumbled feta cheese

Salt to taste

1 **Position the broiler** rack 6 inches from the heat source and preheat the broiler.

2 **Meanwhile, mix the Worcestershire** sauce, 2 tablespoons oil, and ½ teaspoon pepper in a zippered plastic bag. Add the lamb, close the bag, and shake to coat with the marinade. Set aside while cooking the asparagus. (If you have the time, you can refrigerate the lamb for up to 4 hours, keeping in mind that this marinade is strong and a longer marinating period won't have any real benefit.)

3 **Pour enough lightly** salted cold water to come ½ inch up the sides of a large skillet and bring to a boil over high heat. Add the asparagus and cook just until it is crisp-tender, about 3 minutes. Drain and rinse under cold water. Set aside.

4 **Lightly oil the broiler pan.** Broil the lamb chops, turning once, until they are browned but still feel somewhat soft when pressed in the center, about 6 minutes for medium-rare.

5   **While the lamb chops** are cooking, prepare the asparagus sauté. Heat the remaining 1 tablespoon oil in a large skillet over medium heat. Add the asparagus and cook, stirring often, until it is beginning to get hot, about 2 minutes. Add the tomatoes and oregano, and cook until the vegetables are heated through, about 3 minutes. Add the feta and mix well. Remove from the heat and season with salt and pepper.

6   **Spoon equal portions** of the asparagus sauté onto 4 dinner plates and top each plate with 2 lamb chops. Serve immediately.

MAKES 4 SERVINGS

What's the difference between grilling and broiling?

ASK ART Grilled foods are cooked from below, and broiled foods are cooked from above. I use a broiler far more often than the grill, mainly because it's more accessible. Grills have more intense heat, and if they are fired by charcoal, the heat is less reliable. If you are a skilled grill chef, feel free to translate my broiling recipes to the grill.

Shoulder lamb chops are an economical cut—a fact that usually indicates the meat is naturally tough. True enough in this case! These chops are often broiled, but they really benefit from braising. This aromatic blend of golden onions, heady garlic, acidic tomatoes, and fragrant cinnamon brings exotic flavors and aromas to the dinner table. Couscous is the best side dish here.

FRAGRANT LAMB CHOPS WITH TOMATOES AND CINNAMON

2 tablespoons olive oil, divided

Four 8-ounce shoulder lamb chops

Salt and freshly ground black pepper to taste

3 medium onions, chopped

3 garlic cloves, minced

1 teaspoon ground cinnamon

One 28-ounce can chopped tomatoes in juice

1 **Heat 1 tablespoon** oil in a large skillet over medium-high heat. Season the lamb chops with salt and pepper, add to the skillet, and cook, turning once, until browned on both sides, about 5 minutes. Transfer the chops to a platter.

2 **Add the remaining** 1 tablespoon oil to the skillet and heat. Add the onions and reduce the heat to medium. Cook, stirring often, until the edges of the onions begin to brown, about 6 minutes. Add the garlic and cook until it is fragrant, about 1 minute. Stir in the cinnamon and tomatoes with their juice.

3 **Return the lamb** chops to the skillet and bring the sauce to a simmer. Reduce the heat to medium-low. Cover and simmer until the lamb chops are almost tender, about 30 minutes. Uncover and cook until the sauce thickens, about 15 minutes more. Serve hot.

MAKES 4 SERVINGS

TWELVE

PERFECT POULTRY

Just about everyone loves chicken, and I am no exception. I like to cook turkey, too, and have also included a sweet little recipe for Cornish hens, which are little birds that make a big statement.

Chicken can be roasted, sautéed, pan-cooked, broiled, grilled, and baked, and because it marries well with so many different flavors, from mild to sweet to spicy, recipe ideas are endless. I leap around in this chapter, from elegant Bacon-Wrapped Chicken Breasts with Gorgonzola and Walnut Stuffing (page

175) to fast and fun Asian Chicken Wrap with Hoisin Sauce (page 192). And why not? I have a great time cooking all of these!

Many of the recipes are for boneless and skinless chicken breasts, which are incredibly popular these days for busy home cooks. I love them. They're fast to cook and healthful to boot. Take a little care with them. They need to be thoroughly cooked, of course, without being overcooked. Don't cut into boneless breasts because they really can't afford to lose any juices. Instead, test for doneness by pressing gently on the thick middle of the breast. If it feels firm and springs back, the chicken is done.

I adore chicken thighs and drumsticks (legs), partly because they can withstand longer cooking than breasts without drying out and they have so much flavor. If you haven't tried thighs or drumsticks lately, get busy! You'll love my recipes for Sicilian Chicken Thighs with Penne and Mozzarella (page 186), Grilled Jerk Chicken Thighs with Pineapple-Cilantro Salad (page 188), and Chicken Drumsticks with Lemon-Pepper Marinade (page 191). All easy, all terrific.

recipes

Butterflied Roast Chicken with Herbs and Garlic Oil

Bacon-Wrapped Chicken Breasts with Gorgonzola and Walnut Stuffing

Honey-Mustard Chicken Breasts

Chicken Breasts in Orange Sauce

Parmesan and Sesame Chicken Breasts on Spicy Garlic Spinach

Chicken Breasts Piccata

Chicken Breasts with Yukon Gold Potatoes, Spinach, and Fontina Gratin

Chicken Breasts Primavera

Chicken and Peas Risotto

Sicilian Chicken Thighs with Penne and Mozzarella

Grilled Jerk Chicken Thighs with Pineapple-Cilantro Salad

Cajun Chicken Wings

Chicken Drumsticks with Lemon-Pepper Marinade

Asian Chicken Wrap with Hoisin Sauce

Curry-Crusted Cornish Hens with Roasted Peppers

Kitchen Workhorse Smoked Turkey Breast with Cranberry Mustard

When you and your family are in the mood for comforting roast chicken but don't have much time, I have a solution. Cut the whole bird down the backbone and open it up like a book—called "butterflied" chicken. It roasts in about half the time and tastes just as good. Olive oil infused with garlic lends fragrant flavor, and you don't need to worry about garlic cloves scorching in the hot oven. Roast the vegetables with the chicken for a convenient side dish. Add a green salad, and the meal is complete.

BUTTERFLIED ROAST CHICKEN WITH HERBS AND GARLIC OIL

⅓ cup extra-virgin olive oil

3 garlic cloves, crushed under a knife and peeled

1½ teaspoons crumbled dried rosemary

1 teaspoon dried thyme

4 medium carrots, cut in half lengthwise and cut into 2-inch lengths

4 medium red-skinned potatoes (1½ pounds), scrubbed but unpeeled and cut into 6 wedges

1 large onion, unpeeled and cut into quarters lengthwise

Salt and freshly ground black pepper to taste

One 4½-pound chicken

1 Position an oven rack in the center of the oven and preheat the oven to 425°F. Lightly oil a large roasting pan.

2 Heat the oil and garlic in a small saucepan over low heat until small bubbles form around the garlic, about 5 minutes. Remove from the heat and let stand while preparing the remaining ingredients. Then, using a slotted spoon, remove the garlic from the oil and discard.

3 Mix the rosemary and thyme in a small bowl. You will have 2½ teaspoons of mixed herbs. Toss the carrots, potatoes, and onion with 3 tablespoons garlic oil and 1½ teaspoons mixed herbs. Season with salt and pepper. Spread on the roasting pan.

4 Using poultry shears, kitchen scissors, or a large knife, cut down one side of the chicken's backbone. Spread the chicken open, skin side up, and press down on the chicken at the breastbone to give the chicken a relatively even

thickness. Place the chicken, skin side up, on the vegetables. Brush the remaining garlic oil all over the chicken. Season with salt and pepper and sprinkle with the remaining 1 teaspoon mixed herbs.

5 **Roast, occasionally stirring** the vegetables, until an instant-read thermometer inserted in the chicken breast reads 170°F, about 1 hour.

6 **Transfer the chicken** to a carving board. Keep the vegetables warm in the turned-off oven. Let the chicken stand for 10 minutes. Carve the chicken and serve with the vegetables.

MAKES 4 SERVINGS

How should I handle raw poultry?

ASK ART

Leave poultry in its store wrapping, and if it is leaking, overwrap it with plastic wrap or waxed paper. Refrigerate or freeze poultry as soon as you get it home from the market and never let it sit out at room temperature for longer than twenty to thirty minutes before cooking it. Most home cooks know that chicken and other poultry can harbor salmonella bacteria, which makes some people ill, particularly the elderly, the very young, and anyone with immune deficiencies. Salmonella is rendered harmless once the meat is properly cooked. The safest way to handle raw poultry is to keep it segregated from other food to avoid cross-contamination. Wash the cutting board, the knife, and your hands with hot, soapy water as soon as you finish working with the poultry. Set it aside in a bowl so that it won't touch or leak onto other food until you are ready to cook it.

This is an outrageously sinful dish fit for company, although it is actually easy enough for a special weeknight treat. Choose large, plump chicken breasts—the smaller ones won't be meaty enough to make the pocket for stuffing. Domestic Gorgonzola, which is firm enough to crumble, is perfect, or use any blue cheese with a sturdy texture. And while the bacon gives the breasts a professional look and indulgent flavor, it can be omitted. But try it this way the first time and go to the gym the next day!

BACON-WRAPPED CHICKEN BREASTS WITH GORGONZOLA AND WALNUT STUFFING

½ cup crumbled Gorgonzola cheese

⅓ cup walnuts, toasted (see page 251) and finely chopped

1 tablespoon dried plain bread crumbs

1 tablespoon chopped fresh sage, plus sprigs of sage for serving

Freshly ground pepper to taste

Four 7- to 8-ounce skinless and boneless chicken breasts (do not pound to uniform thickness)

Salt to taste

4 bacon slices

1 tablespoon vegetable oil

1 **Position a rack** in the top third of the oven and preheat the oven to 350°F.

2 **Mash the Gorgonzola,** walnuts, bread crumbs, and sage in a small bowl until combined. Season with pepper. Mold the cheese mixture into 4 finger-shaped logs.

3 **Using a sharp,** thin-bladed knife, cut a deep pocket into the thickest side of each breast, being careful not to cut through to the top, bottom, or other side of the breast. (If you do cut through, the hole can be patched by wrapping the bacon strip over it.) Season the chicken lightly with salt and pepper. One at a time, stuff each breast with a cheese log. With the smooth side of the breast facing up, wrap a bacon strip around each breast in a spiral, beginning at a point under the breast to hold the bacon in place while it cooks. If necessary, use a wooden toothpick to secure the bacon.

4 **Heat the oil** in a large nonstick skillet over medium-high heat. Place the chicken, smooth sides up, in the skillet. Cook until the undersides are browned, about 2 minutes. Turn carefully and brown the other sides. Turn right side up. Holding the breasts back with a large spatula, tilt the skillet to pour off a good amount of the bacon fat (don't worry about getting rid of it all). Loosely cover the skillet with foil. Cook until the chicken feels firm when pressed in the center, about 20 minutes. Discard the foil.

5 **Position the broiler** rack about 6 inches from the heat source and preheat the broiler. Place the skillet under the broiler and broil until the bacon crisps, about 2 minutes. Serve immediately.

MAKES 4 SERVINGS

What does it mean when a recipe says to use "fresh bread crumbs"?

ASK ART These are made from fresh slices of bread or a couple of store-bought dinner rolls. You'll get the best texture using day-old bread slices (or rolls) or those you leave on the countertop for several hours to dry out a little bit. Put them in the blender or food processor and zap them into coarse crumbs. It works! A slice of bread makes about ½ cup of crumbs. Some recipes in this book call for dry bread crumbs, which you buy in a store. Some are seasoned, some are plain. Buy the right kind for the recipe.

Honey and mustard have become popular partners over the years, and here they work their magic on boneless chicken breasts. It's hard to fit four chicken breasts in most skillets, but I do so because it works so well to fry the breasts first to set the crusts and then bake them for a final crisping. This is truly a family-friendly recipe!

HONEY-MUSTARD CHICKEN BREASTS

Nonstick vegetable oil spray for the pan

Four 6-ounce boneless and skinless chicken breasts, trimmed and lightly pounded to uniform thickness

Salt and freshly ground pepper to taste

2 tablespoons Dijon mustard, preferably whole grain

2 tablespoons honey

2 1/2 cups fresh bread crumbs

4 tablespoons olive oil, divided

1 **Position a rack** in the center of the oven and preheat the oven to 400°F. Coat a baking sheet with vegetable oil spray.

2 **Season the chicken** with salt and pepper. Combine the mustard and honey in a shallow dish. Spread the bread crumbs in another dish. Dip each breast in the mustard to coat on both sides. Dip both sides of each breast in the crumbs, patting them to make them adhere. Set aside on a plate.

3 **Heat 2 tablespoons** oil in a large skillet over medium heat until the oil is very hot but not smoking. Add 2 chicken breasts and cook until the undersides are golden brown, about 2 minutes. Turn and brown the other sides, about 2 minutes more. Transfer to the baking sheet. Repeat with the remaining 2 tablespoons oil and breasts.

4 **Bake the breasts** on the baking sheet until they feel firm when pressed in the centers, about 10 minutes. Serve hot.

MAKES 4 SERVINGS

onsider these tender chicken breasts poached in a tangy orange sauce as a jumping-off point to your own culinary creativity. The technique sounds more difficult than it is, so give it a try. Here are some ideas for giving this your own twist: Add a teaspoon of chopped fresh tarragon or rosemary to the scallion tops. Or substitute a tablespoon of finely chopped shallot for the white part of the scallion, and top each serving with chopped parsley or chives instead of the scallion greens. For an elegant garnish use a zester to remove thin strips of zest from the orange before grating the remaining zest for the sauce. And consider using leftovers for the Roast Chicken Waldorf Salad with Pecans and Rosemary on page 123.

CHICKEN BREASTS IN ORANGE SAUCE

1 scallion, trimmed

2 tablespoons unsalted butter, divided

Four 6-ounce boneless and skinless chicken breasts, trimmed and lightly pounded to uniform thickness

Salt and freshly ground black pepper to taste

1 garlic clove, crushed through a press

Grated zest of ½ orange

½ cup fresh orange juice

½ cup canned reduced-sodium chicken broth

1 Finely chop the white part of the scallion. Cut the green top of the scallion crosswise into thin rounds and set aside for the garnish.

2 Melt 1 tablespoon butter in a large nonstick skillet over medium-high heat. Season the chicken breasts with salt and pepper. Add the chicken to the skillet and cook, turning once, until lightly browned on both sides, about 4 minutes. Transfer the chicken to a plate.

3 Add the white part of the scallion and the garlic to the skillet and stir just until the scallion wilts, about 1 minute. Add the orange zest and juice and the broth. Return the chicken to the skillet and bring the liquid to a boil. Reduce the heat to medium-low, cover, and cook until the chicken feels firm when pressed in the thickest part, about 12 minutes.

4   Using a slotted spatula, transfer the chicken to a platter and tent with aluminum foil to keep warm. Increase the heat to high and bring the liquid to a rapid boil. Cook until the liquid has been reduced by half, about 3 minutes. Remove the skillet from the heat. Add the remaining 1 tablespoon butter to the skillet and whisk it into the liquid. Season with salt and pepper.

5   Serve each chicken breast on a dinner plate. Top with a spoonful of the sauce and sprinkle with the scallion greens. Serve immediately.

MAKES 4 SERVINGS

How do I pound a chicken breast?

ASK ART

Nothing to it! Lay the boneless and skinless breast on a work surface and cover it with plastic wrap (or not). Using the flat side of a small, heavy skillet or the smooth side of a meat mallet, gently pound the meat. Work in small areas, moving over the meat until it's quite uniform. The meat will cook more evenly after it's pounded, and if you plan to roll it around a filling, it will work much better.

s there anyone who doesn't appreciate a tender chicken breast with a crisp, tasty crust? This is a cross between two of my favorite cooking styles, old-fashioned southern and Asian. The breasts will remind you a little of fried chicken, but the spinach is totally Eastern Hemisphere cuisine. And if you don't feel like having spinach, serve this chicken with another favorite vegetable. Kids love this chicken because of the crunchy crust.

PARMESAN AND SESAME CHICKEN BREASTS ON SPICY GARLIC SPINACH

Four 6-ounce skinless and boneless chicken breasts, trimmed and lightly pounded to uniform thickness

Salt and freshly ground pepper

1 large egg

⅓ cup all-purpose flour

3 tablespoons freshly grated Parmesan cheese

3 tablespoons sesame seeds

3 tablespoons vegetable oil

Spicy Garlic Spinach (page 270)

Lemon wedges for serving

1 **Season the chicken** breasts with salt and pepper. Line a baking sheet or plate with waxed paper. Beat the egg in a wide, shallow dish or bowl just large enough to hold a chicken breast. Mix the flour, cheese, sesame seeds, ½ teaspoon salt, and ½ teaspoon pepper in another dish of a similar size. Dip each chicken breast on both sides in the egg and then roll in the flour to coat it completely. Place on the waxed-paper-lined baking sheet.

2 **Heat the oil** in a large skillet over medium-high heat until the oil is very hot but not smoking. Add the chicken (it should sizzle when it hits the pan) and reduce the heat to medium. Cook, occasionally turning the breasts, until the crust is golden brown and the chicken feels firm when pressed in the center, about 12 minutes. Adjust the heat as needed so the chicken cooks steadily but does not burn. Transfer to a carving board.

3 **To serve,** spoon one-fourth of the spinach onto a dinner plate. Cut a breast crosswise into ½-inch strips. Slip the knife under the chicken and transfer to the plate, fanning out the slices. Repeat with the remaining chicken and spinach. Serve immediately with the lemon wedges.

MAKES 4 SERVINGS

n Italian, *piccata* is another word for *scallopini*, which is a word that describes a thin slice of meat. The flavor of this restaurant favorite is piquant with its lemon, wine, and capers, so it wouldn't be surprising if the name came from the Italian *piccante*. No matter what the semantics are, this is a great recipe that will make you feel as if you are eating out when you're at home.

CHICKEN BREASTS PICCATA

1 large lemon

Four 6-ounce boneless and skinless chicken breasts, trimmed and lightly pounded to uniform thickness

Salt and freshly ground pepper to taste

1/3 cup all-purpose flour

2 tablespoons olive oil

1/2 cup dry white wine, such as Sauvignon Blanc or Pinot Grigio

1/2 cup reduced-sodium chicken broth

2 tablespoons bottled capers, rinsed and drained

2 tablespoons unsalted butter

2 tablespoons chopped fresh parsley (for garnish)

1 **Slice off** and discard one end of the lemon. Cut 4 thin slices from the lemon and set aside for garnish. Squeeze the juice from the remaining lemon. You should have about 2 tablespoons lemon juice.

2 **Season the chicken** breasts with salt and pepper. Place the flour in a shallow dish and coat the chicken on both sides with the flour. Transfer the chicken to a plate.

3 **Heat the oil** in a large skillet until it is very hot but not smoking. Add the chicken to the skillet and reduce the heat to medium. Cook, turning occasionally, until the chicken is browned and feels firm when pressed in the center, about 12 minutes. Transfer the chicken to a platter and tent with aluminum foil to keep warm.

4 **Wipe out the** skillet with paper towels. Return to the stove and increase the heat to high. Add the wine and bring to a boil. Add the broth and capers, and return to a boil. Cook until the liquid has been reduced by one-fourth, about 2 minutes. Remove the skillet from the heat. Add the butter and whisk until it melts and slightly thickens the sauce.

5 **Pour the sauce** over the chicken and sprinkle with the parsley. Serve hot.

MAKES 4 SERVINGS

This one-dish meal needs only a big green salad to round it out, since it already sports chicken, potatoes, tomatoes, spinach, and cheese. You can use regular Italian or Danish fontina, but if you can find it, try the superior Fontina d'Aosta for its complex flavor and mushroom-like aroma.

CHICKEN BREASTS WITH YUKON GOLD POTATOES, SPINACH, AND FONTINA GRATIN

4 tablespoons olive oil, divided

5 Yukon Gold potatoes (about 2¼ pounds), peeled and cut into ⅛-inch-thick slices

1 small onion, finely chopped

Salt and freshly ground pepper to taste

1¼ cups (about 5 ounces) shredded fontina cheese, preferably Fontina d'Aosta

One 10-ounce package frozen chopped spinach, thawed and squeezed to remove excess water

1 cup Kitchen Workhouse Marinara Sauce (page 234) or store-bought marinara sauce

Four 6-ounce boneless and skinless chicken breasts, trimmed and lightly pounded to uniform thickness

1 **Position a rack** in the center of the oven and preheat the oven to 350°F. Lightly oil an 11 × 8½-inch baking dish.

2 **Heat 3 tablespoons** oil in a large nonstick skillet over medium-high heat. Add the potatoes and cook, stirring often and separating the slices as needed, until most of the potatoes are lightly browned, about 7 minutes. Sprinkle with the onion and cover. Cook, stirring occasionally, until the potatoes are almost tender, about 7 minutes more. Season with salt and pepper.

3 **Spread half of** the potatoes in the baking dish. Sprinkle with half of the fontina cheese. Scatter the spinach on top. Spread the remaining potatoes on the spinach. Pour and spread the marinara sauce over the potatoes.

4 **Wipe out the** skillet with paper towels. Add the remaining 1 tablespoon oil to the skillet and heat over medium heat. Season the chicken with salt and pepper. Add to the skillet and cook until the underside is browned, about 2 minutes. Turn and brown the other side, about 2 minutes more. Arrange the chicken on the potatoes. Sprinkle with the remaining fontina cheese.

5   **Bake until the** potatoes are tender and the chicken feels firm when pressed in
    the center, about 20 minutes. Let stand for 5 minutes, then serve.

MAKES 4 SERVINGS

It's a simple matter to add cooked vegetables to marinara sauce and instantly enhance chicken breasts. I often use mushrooms and artichoke hearts, but there is no reason that you can't use steamed broccoli florets, asparagus spears, or peas. Serve with rice or orzo (rice-shaped pasta) to soak up the fantastic sauce.

CHICKEN BREASTS PRIMAVERA

Four 6-ounce boneless and skinless chicken breasts, trimmed and lightly pounded to uniform thickness

Salt and freshly ground pepper to taste

2 tablespoons extra-virgin olive oil

10 ounces white or brown mushrooms, sliced

1 quart Kitchen Workhouse Marinara Sauce (page 234) or store-bought marinara sauce

One 9-ounce box frozen artichoke hearts, thawed

½ cup reduced-sodium chicken broth

Crushed hot red pepper flakes to taste

2 tablespoons chopped fresh parsley for garnish

1   **Season the chicken** breasts with salt and pepper.

2   **Heat the oil** in a large skillet over medium-high heat. Add the chicken breasts
    and cook until the underside is browned, about 2 minutes. Turn and brown
    the other side, about 2 minutes more. Transfer to a plate.

3   **Add the mushrooms** to the skillet and cook, scraping up the browned bits in
    the bottom of the skillet with a wooden spatula, until the mushroom juices
    evaporate, about 10 minutes. Add the marinara sauce, artichokes, and broth,
    and bring to a boil. Return the chicken to the sauce and reduce the heat to
    medium-low. Cover and simmer until the chicken feels firm when pressed in
    the center, about 5 minutes. Season the sauce with salt and red pepper.

4   **Serve immediately, sprinkling** each serving with chopped parsley.

MAKES 4 SERVINGS

I love old-fashioned flavors, and one of my favorite combinations is chicken and rice, which brings back memories of my family's southern cooking. This is an updated version, turned into a creamy risotto.

CHICKEN AND PEAS RISOTTO

1 quart reduced-sodium chicken broth

1 tablespoon olive oil

Four 6-ounce boneless and skinless chicken breasts, cut into bite-sized pieces

Salt and freshly ground pepper to taste

2 tablespoons unsalted butter

1 medium onion, chopped

½ cup (diced ½ inch) red bell pepper

1½ cups rice for risotto, such as arborio

⅓ cup dry sherry, such as fino

1 cup frozen peas and baby onions, thawed

½ cup freshly grated Parmesan cheese

1 **Bring the broth** and 1 cup water to a boil in a medium saucepan. Reduce the heat to very low and keep warm while making the risotto.

2 **Heat the oil** in a large, heavy-bottomed saucepan over medium-high heat. Add the chicken and season with salt and pepper. Cook, stirring often, until the chicken is lightly browned and has lost its raw look, about 6 minutes. (It will be cooked further later.) Using a slotted spoon, transfer the chicken to a plate.

3 **Add the butter** to the pot and melt. Add the onion and red pepper, and cook, stirring often, until the vegetables soften, about 3 minutes. Add the rice and cook, stirring often, until it feels heavy in the spoon (do not brown), about 2 minutes. Add the sherry and cook until it has almost evaporated, about 1 minute.

4 **Add 1 cup** hot stock to the rice and cook, stirring almost constantly, until the rice absorbs almost all the stock, about 3 minutes. Add in another cup of stock and stir until it is almost absorbed. Repeat, keeping the risotto at a steady simmer and adding more stock as the rice absorbs it until you use all the stock and the rice is almost tender, about 25 minutes total. Add the reserved chicken with the peas and onions, and continue cooking until the

chicken is cooked through and the rice is tender, about 5 minutes more. If you run out of stock and the rice isn't tender, add hot water. Stir in the Parmesan. Season with salt and pepper. If you like your risotto on the loose side, add a bit more broth or water to reach the desired thickness.

5 Spoon into individual bowls and serve hot.

MAKES 4 TO 6 SERVINGS

What is the best way to defrost poultry?

ASK ART

Defrost poultry in the refrigerator—never on the countertop. This means planning ahead and taking the frozen chicken from the freezer twelve or even twenty-four hours ahead of time. Put the wrapped meat in a shallow dish to catch leaks as it defrosts. Once the poultry is partially thawed, you can hasten its progress in the microwave on a low setting, but this is not my favorite way to go. If you don't watch carefully, the poultry will cook a little in the microwave. (Be sure to wipe the microwave clean with warm soap and water if the poultry juices leak onto the turntable.)

Chicken thighs are great candidates for braising because they can be simmered longer than chicken breasts without drying out. Don't overlook them when you're shopping—and their lower price tag is an extra bonus! Here I simmer them in a zesty tomato sauce (leave out the capers and green olives if you wish), top them with mozzarella, and serve them with pasta. Toss a salad, and dinner is served. If you want to prepare this recipe for later use, freeze the chicken thighs in sauce and add to the penne just before serving.

SICILIAN CHICKEN THIGHS WITH PENNE AND MOZZARELLA

2 tablespoons olive oil, divided

6 chicken thighs

Salt and freshly ground black pepper to taste

1 medium yellow onion, chopped

1 medium red bell pepper, ribs and seeds removed and chopped

2 garlic cloves, chopped

1 teaspoon dried Italian herbs, or ½ teaspoon each dried basil and dried oregano

One 28-ounce can diced tomatoes in juice

⅓ cup pitted and coarsely chopped green olives

2 tablespoons drained and rinsed capers

8 ounces mozzarella, preferably fresh, cut into 6 slices

1 pound penne, cooked

1 Heat 1 tablespoon oil in a large skillet over medium-high heat. Add the chicken, season with salt and pepper, and cook, turning once, until browned on both sides, about 5 minutes. Transfer the chicken to a plate.

2 Heat the remaining 1 tablespoon oil in the skillet. Add the onion and red pepper, and cook, stirring often, until the onion softens, about 3 minutes. Stir in the garlic and Italian herbs, and stir until the garlic gives off its aroma, about 30 seconds. Stir in the tomatoes with their juice. Return the chicken to the skillet and bring the sauce to a boil. Reduce the heat to medium-low, cover, and simmer until the chicken shows no sign of pink when pierced in the thickest part, about 30 minutes. Stir in the olives and capers. Place 1 mozzarella slice on each thigh, cover, and cook just until the mozzarella melts, about 3 minutes.

3   **Meanwhile,** bring a large pot of lightly salted water to a boil over high heat. Add the penne and cook until barely tender, about 9 minutes. Drain well. Return the pasta to the pot and cover to keep warm.

4   **Using a slotted** spoon, transfer the mozzarella-topped chicken to a platter and tent with aluminum foil to keep warm. Increase the heat to high and boil the tomato sauce until slightly thickened, about 3 minutes. Stir the tomato sauce into the penne.

5   **Place the penne** in bowls and top with a chicken thigh. Serve hot.

MAKES 4 TO 6 SERVINGS

Jerk has moved pretty quickly from an unusual Caribbean seasoning to one of America's favorite ways to add flavor to grilled meats and poultry. You can even find super fiery habanero or Scotch bonnet chilies in supermarkets (and if you can't, use a jalapeño). If you want to use the jerk seasoning for a whole, cut-up chicken, double the recipe and grill the chicken parts for about 1 hour. You can also broil or roast the chicken in the oven, but grilling adds the smokiness that makes jerk special. The pineapple salad is a refreshing balance to the spicy chicken. While I like to buy a whole pineapple and pare and core it myself, feel free to buy the precut fresh rings sold in many produce departments.

GRILLED JERK CHICKEN THIGHS WITH PINEAPPLE-CILANTRO SALAD

PINEAPPLE SALAD

3 cups (diced ¾ inch) ripe pineapple (about ½ pineapple)

2 tablespoons chopped fresh cilantro

1 tablespoon rice vinegar

1 tablespoon honey

1 tablespoon olive oil

JERK CHICKEN THIGHS

2 garlic cloves, peeled

1 habanero or Scotch bonnet chili, seeds and ribs removed (see Note)

6 scallions, trimmed and coarsely chopped

1 tablespoon light brown sugar

1 teaspoon ground allspice

1 teaspoon dried thyme

½ teaspoon salt

2 tablespoons vegetable oil

8 chicken thighs, skin removed

1 To make the salad, mix the pineapple, cilantro, vinegar, honey, and oil in a medium bowl. Cover and refrigerate until chilled, at least 1 hour and up to 4 hours.

2 To prepare the chicken, with the machine running, drop the garlic and chili through the feed tube of a food processor fitted with the metal chopping blade. Add the scallions, brown sugar, allspice, thyme, and salt. Process, occasionally stopping the machine to scrape down the sides of the bowl, until

the scallions are very finely chopped, about 2 minutes. Add the oil and process to make a thick paste. Pour the jerk seasoning into a zippered plastic bag.

3   Add the chicken and close the bag. Rub the chicken through the bag to coat it with the seasoning. Marinate for at least 30 minutes or up to 2 hours.

4   Meanwhile, build a charcoal fire in an outdoor grill and let it burn until the coals are covered with white ash. Lightly oil the grill. Place the chicken around but not over the coals. Cover the grill. To use a gas grill, preheat the grill on high. Turn one burner off and let the other burner(s) remain on high. Place the chicken on the off burner and close the cover.

5   Cook until the chicken shows no sign of pink when pierced at the bone with the tip of a knife, about 50 minutes. Transfer to a platter. Serve hot with the chilled pineapple salad.

MAKES 4 SERVINGS

NOTE: Habanero and Scotch bonnet chilies (which look similar but are actually different) are the hottest chilies around. I strongly recommend that you wear rubber gloves when handling them and be extra careful not to touch any tender spots on your body (especially your eyes and lips) if your hands come in contact with the peppers. A whole chili will make the jerk good and spicy, but if you are a tenderfoot, use only half a chili your first time and make a note in your journal if you think you can stand it hotter the next time.

The phrase "finger-lickin' good" could have been coined for these succulent, if clearly indulgent, chicken wings. They are a close relation to the famous Buffalo wings except that these are not deep-fried. Instead, they are roasted, and as they cook, the mayonnaise evaporates to leave behind a tasty crust. In fact, these wings are so moist and juicy, you can skip the blue cheese dip that is typically served with Buffalo wings.

CAJUN CHICKEN WINGS

Nonstick vegetable oil spray

5 pounds chicken wings, or 4 pounds chicken wing drumettes

1 cup mayonnaise

1 tablespoon salt-free Cajun seasoning, or mix ½ teaspoon each paprika,

dried thyme, dried basil, garlic powder, onion powder, and freshly ground pepper with ⅛ teaspoon ground red (cayenne) pepper

1 teaspoon salt

1 **Position a rack** in the center of the oven and preheat the oven to 450°F. Line a large baking sheet with aluminum foil and coat the foil with vegetable oil spray.

2 **Using a large** knife or a cleaver, cut the wings into 3 sections at the joints, discarding the wing tips. If you are using drumettes, they will not need any cutting.

3 **Mix the mayonnaise,** Cajun seasoning, and salt in a large bowl. Add the chicken wings and mix well to coat. Arrange the wings on the baking sheet.

4 **Bake for 15 minutes.** Turn the chicken wings over and continue baking until the wings are golden brown and tender, 15 to 20 minutes more. Serve hot with plenty of napkins and a bowl for the bones.

MAKES 6 SERVINGS

Sometimes the simplest combinations are the best. Take the trio of lemon, oregano, and pepper, items you probably have in the kitchen right now. Mix them up into a marinade for chicken drumsticks and let them do their thing. This marinade is just as good on other chicken parts, but since kids love drumsticks, I concentrate on them in this recipe. Roasting is a great way to cook these, but if you want to set up the outdoor grill, go ahead.

CHICKEN DRUMSTICKS WITH LEMON-PEPPER MARINADE

¼ cup olive oil, preferably extra-virgin

Grated zest of 1 lemon

¼ cup fresh lemon juice

2 teaspoons dried oregano

½ teaspoon salt

½ teaspoon coarsely ground black peppercorns (preferably whole peppercorns cracked in a mortar, but butcher-grind peppercorns will do)

8 chicken drumsticks

1 Mix the oil, lemon zest and juice, oregano, salt, and pepper in a self-sealing plastic bag. Add the drumsticks, close the bag, and turn the bag to coat the drumsticks with the marinade. Refrigerate for at least 30 minutes or up to 2 hours.

2 Position a rack in the center of the oven and preheat the oven to 400°F.

3 Arrange the drumsticks so they do not touch each other on the baking sheet. Pour the marinade on top and roast for 30 minutes. Turn the drumsticks and roast until they show no sign of pink when pierced at the bone with the tip of a sharp knife, about 25 minutes.

MAKES 4 SERVINGS

Take-out moo-shu chicken has numerous ingredients, with some being exotic (dried lily buds, anyone?). This streamlined version delivers much of the flavor with supermarket ingredients and turns the moo-shu into a wrap.

ASIAN CHICKEN WRAP WITH HOISIN SAUCE

CHICKEN

2 tablespoons soy sauce

1 tablespoon dry sherry

1 teaspoon cornstarch

Two 6-ounce boneless and skinless chicken breasts, cut into long ½-inch-thick strips

1 tablespoon vegetable oil

VEGETABLES

1 tablespoon vegetable oil

1½ cups sliced button mushrooms

2 scallions, white and green parts, chopped

1 garlic clove, finely chopped

Half of a 1-pound bag (about 3 cups) coleslaw mix

3 tablespoons reduced-sodium chicken broth or water

1 tablespoon soy sauce

2 teaspoons hoisin sauce

4 flour tortillas, heated

1 **For the chicken,** mix the soy sauce, sherry, and cornstarch in a small bowl. Add the chicken strips and mix to thoroughly coat the chicken. Heat the oil in a large skillet over high heat. Add the chicken and cook, stirring almost constantly, until it turns white, about 3½ minutes. Transfer to a plate.

2 **For the vegetables,** heat the oil in the same skillet over high heat. Add the mushrooms and cook, stirring often, until they give off their juices and begin to brown, about 3 minutes. Stir in the scallions and garlic, and cook until the garlic is fragrant, about 30 seconds. Stir in the coleslaw mix, broth, and soy sauce. Add the chicken. Cook, stirring often, until the coleslaw is wilted and heated through, about 3 minutes. Stir in the hoisin sauce.

3 **For each wrap,** place one-fourth of the chicken mixture on a tortilla and roll up. Serve hot.

MAKES 4 SERVINGS

ornish game hens provide the flavor of chicken in a small, compact package. When they are rubbed with curry butter and baked on a bed of sweet peppers, they make a colorful and flavorful dish. The combination of three differently colored bell peppers looks terrific, but use whatever mix you can get. Just don't include green bell peppers, because they turn a little bitter when roasted.

CURRY-CRUSTED CORNISH HENS WITH ROASTED PEPPERS

3 bell peppers, preferably 1 red, 1 yellow, and 1 orange, seeds and ribs discarded and cut into ½-inch-wide strips

1 large onion, cut into ½-inch-wide half-moons

1 tablespoon vegetable oil

Salt and freshly ground pepper

2 Cornish hens (about 1 pound each)

3 tablespoons unsalted butter, softened

1 tablespoon Madras-style curry powder

1 garlic clove, minced

1 **Position a rack** in the center of the oven and preheat the oven to 400°F.

2 **Toss the bell** peppers, onion, and oil in a 13 × 9-inch baking dish. Season with salt and pepper. Roast for 10 minutes.

3 **Meanwhile,** using kitchen shears or a heavy knife, cut each hen in half lengthwise down one side of the backbone and through the breast cartilage. Season the hens with salt. Mash the butter and curry together in a small bowl. Spread the butter over the skin sides of the hens.

4 **Remove the baking** dish from the oven and stir the vegetables. Arrange the hens skin sides up on top of the peppers. Continue roasting, stirring the peppers occasionally, until an instant-read thermometer inserted in the thick part of the breast reads 170°F, about 35 minutes. During the last 5 minutes, stir the garlic into the vegetables.

5 **Transfer the hens** to a platter, tent with aluminum foil, and let stand for 5 minutes. If the peppers aren't quite tender, continue roasting for a few minutes.

6 **Using a slotted spoon,** spoon the vegetables around the hens. Serve hot.

MAKES 4 SERVINGS

For a holiday main course, smoked turkey is gaining ground on the familiar roasted version. Turkey breasts are much more manageable than a whole bird, and they are suitable for weekend meals. Brining helps solve the age-old problem of a dry turkey breast, but because the breasts are small, they require only a few hours' soaking. You might as well smoke two breast halves (most butchers sell whole breasts that average 5½ pounds) and use the leftovers in smoke-kissed sandwiches and salads. You can substitute smoked turkey for an extra burst of flavor in just about any casserole that uses cooked boneless chicken breasts. Without question this takes some time and tending to, but it's fun and easy. And the final result? Sublime!

SMOKED TURKEY BREAST WITH CRANBERRY MUSTARD

spin-off recipes
Smoked Turkey, Apple, and Cheddar Quesadillas (page 94)

TURKEY	CRANBERRY MUSTARD
½ cup iodized table salt	1 cup whole berry cranberry sauce
½ cup light brown sugar	3 tablespoons whole-grain Dijon mustard
One 5½-pound whole turkey breast, cut in half lengthwise (see Note)	
2 cups hickory or mesquite chips, soaked in water for at least 30 minutes	

1 **About 5 hours** before smoking the turkey, combine 1 gallon water, the salt, and brown sugar in a large bowl and stir to dissolve the salt. Add the turkey breast halves and cover. Refrigerate for 4 hours.

2 **Build a charcoal** fire on one side of an outdoor grill, using about 3 pounds of charcoal briquettes. Let burn until the coals are covered with white ash. Place

a disposable aluminum foil pan on the empty side of the grill and add 3 cups water to the pan. Lightly oil the grill. Toss a handful of drained chips on the coals.

3 **To use a gas grill,** preheat the grill on high. Turn one burner off and let the other burner(s) remain on high. Place a disposable aluminum foil pan on the empty side of the grill and add 3 cups water to the pan. Lightly oil the grill. Place about 1 cup drained chips on a 12-inch square of aluminum foil and crimp the foil to contain the chips, leaving the top open. Place the foil packet directly on the heat source, allowing the chips to smolder and smoke before adding the turkey to the grill.

4 **Place the turkey breast** halves on the rack directly above the foil pan and cover the grill. If your grill does not have a thermometer in the lid, stick a deep-frying thermometer through the vent to gauge the temperature in the grill. Grill until an instant-read thermometer inserted in the thickest part of a breast reads 170°F, about 2 hours. Every 40 minutes or so, add a few briquettes and a handful of chips to the coals (or to the foil packet in the gas grill) to maintain an average temperature of 350°F.

5 **To make the mustard,** mix the cranberry sauce and mustard in a small bowl.

6 **Transfer the breasts** to a carving board and let stand for 10 minutes before carving. Cut into thin slices and serve hot with the cranberry mustard.

MAKES 10 TO 12 SERVINGS

NOTE: You can sometimes find 2½-pound turkey breast halves with skin and bone at the supermarket. It is much more likely that you will come across a whole turkey breast that needs to be cut in half. Here's how to do it: Using a cleaver or a heavy knife, cut down one side of the backbone of the turkey. Then cut lengthwise through the breastbone to cut the breast in half. (If using a knife, hold the knife in position over the breast, then "hammer" the back of the knife with a meat pounder for extra cutting power. Do not hack at the bone, or you could chip the knife blade.) Cut down the other side of the backbone and discard it.

THIRTEEN

FROM THE SEA

We all want to put more fish on our table. It's so good for us! Over the years I have come to truly love fish. I admit it took a while to think of fish as readily as I do chicken or beef when I plan supper, but now that I have, I couldn't be happier. Learning how to cook fish correctly opens up a world of possibilities.

Fish is low in fat and high in protein. The omega-3 fatty acids in oily fish such as tuna and salmon are healthful polyunsaturated fats and are especially beneficial to our overall well-being. Many types of fish are mild and thus lend themselves to light sauces and coatings, as in my recipe for Striped Bass with Clam Sauce (page 210), while others can take some jazzing up, as in the recipe for Spicy Catfish on Succotash (page 200). Other, fuller-flavored fish can stand on their own or be treated gently, such as Salmon with Scallions, Tarragon, and Lemon (page 207). These fish also do well cooked with assertive ingredients.

The recipes I planned for this chapter take advantage of the types of fish sold in most supermarkets. I cook a lot of fillets because they are boned and thin, which makes them ready to go and quick to cook. Kids always profess to "hate" fish. Start them on the milder fish. Try The Best Fish Tacos on page 204 and see how they like them.

I also offer recipes for shrimp and clams, considered seafood and not really fish, but they all come from the water and so belong together. Shrimp is the number one choice of many shoppers. I suggest you buy them in the shell rather than peeled. Not only is this less expensive, but they also have more taste. When time is an issue, take advantage of peeled and cooked shrimp to tuck into salads and sandwiches.

Buy your family's fish from a reliable fishmonger or from a supermarket with an active fish counter. Fish has to be super fresh, so turnover is important. Don't hesitate to buy frozen fish. Much of it is flash frozen right on the boat and therefore maintains its good flavor and texture. Check it for signs of freezer burn, but otherwise it might be your best choice if you don't have access to a reliable supply of fresh fish.

I have only touched on the wide variety of fish in the sea (and lakes and rivers). Try any kind that catches your fancy and use my recipes as inspiration for some of your own.

recipes

The catfish you get today is quite different from the fish that were brought home years ago. Now it is farm-raised and has a much milder taste. In fact, I find spicing up catfish a bit does it good.

SPICY CATFISH ON SUCCOTASH

SUCCOTASH

1 tablespoon olive oil

1 small onion, chopped

2 cups frozen corn kernels, thawed

1 cup frozen lima beans, thawed

1 cup cherry or grape tomatoes

½ teaspoon dried thyme

Salt and freshly ground pepper to taste

Three 8-ounce catfish fillets, cut in half crosswise to make 6 portions

2 teaspoons Art's Cajun Seasoning (see page 201) or salt-free store-bought Cajun seasoning

½ teaspoon salt

1 tablespoon vegetable oil

1 **To make the succotash,** heat the oil in a large skillet over medium heat. Add the onion and cook, stirring occasionally, until golden, about 6 minutes. Add the corn and lima beans, cover, and cook, stirring often, until the vegetables are heated through, about 3 minutes. Add the tomatoes and thyme, and cook until the tomatoes are heated through, about 2 minutes. Season with salt and pepper. Transfer to a platter and cover with aluminum foil to keep warm.

2 **Season the catfish** on both sides with the Cajun seasoning and salt. Heat the oil in the skillet over medium-high heat. Add the catfish and cook until the underside turns opaque, about 3 minutes. Turn and cook until the catfish looks opaque when pierced in the center with the tip of a knife, 2 to 3 minutes more.

3 **Arrange the catfish** on the succotash and serve immediately.

MAKES 4 TO 6 SERVINGS

Art's Cajun Seasoning

There are plenty of brands of Cajun seasoning at the supermarket, but many of them are heavily salted. Besides, making your own gives you more control over the flavors. The base is paprika, which should be a high-quality brand from Hungary or Spain. If you wish, use the smoky Spanish paprika, pimentón de La Vera, available at specialty food shops. Here's how I make it:

Mix 2 tablespoons sweet paprika, 2 teaspoons dried basil, 2 teaspoons dried thyme, 1 teaspoon onion powder, 1 teaspoon garlic powder, 1 teaspoon ground black pepper, and ¼ teaspoon ground hot red (cayenne) pepper. Store in an airtight container in a cool, dark place for up to six months.

MAKES ABOUT ⅓ CUP

ASK ART

How can I work more fish into my family's diet?

Look through the recipes in this chapter and decide on some that fit the way you cook and eat. When it's cooked correctly—and my recipes have plenty of good tips—fish is totally wonderful. Broil or grill salmon and tuna steaks and shrimp kabobs. Add canned tuna to salads and casseroles. Pan-cook fillets. Put a sautéed fish fillet between a soft roll with lettuce, tomato, and really delicious tartar sauce, or wrap them in tortillas. Your kids will come to like fish when it's cooked right and served creatively.

aking fish fillets en papillote (that is, wrapped in an envelope-like package)
holds in flavor and moisture. This technique usually calls for parchment
paper, and while aluminum foil doesn't look as dramatic, it is easier to use. You
must rely on blind faith when cooking en papillote because it is not advisable to
open the packages to check for doneness. Be sure that your oven temperature is
accurate—you should have an oven thermometer anyway. For a lighter sauce,
substitute 1 teaspoon of dark Asian sesame oil for each tablespoon of butter in
the foil packages.

COD WITH CASHEWS BAKED IN FOIL ENVELOPES

1 tablespoon vegetable oil

1 red bell pepper, seeds and ribs
discarded and cut into long, ¼-inch-
wide strips

4 scallions, white and green parts,
chopped

1 tablespoon shredded fresh ginger (use
the large holes of a box grater)

1 garlic clove, finely chopped

4 ounces sugar snap peas

Salt and freshly ground pepper to taste

Four 6-ounce cod fillets

4 tablespoons soy sauce, divided

4 tablespoons unsalted butter, divided

½ cup unsalted roasted cashews, very
coarsely chopped

1 **Position a rack** in the center of the oven and preheat the oven to 400°F. Have
ready four 12-inch squares of aluminum foil. Lightly oil the dull sides of the
foil squares. Fold each square in half.

2 **Heat the oil** in a large skillet over medium-high heat. Add the red pepper and
cook, stirring often, just until it begins to soften, about 1 minute. Add the
scallions, ginger, and garlic, and stir until the garlic gives off its aroma, about
30 seconds. Remove from the heat, add the sugar snap peas, and stir just until
they are coated with the oil. Season the vegetables lightly with salt and pepper
(the soy sauce and ginger will provide salt and heat).

3 **Lightly season the cod** with salt and pepper. Open a foil square and place a
fillet on the bottom half. Top with one-fourth of the vegetables, 1 tablespoon

soy sauce, and 1 tablespoon butter, cut into a few pieces. Sprinkle with one-fourth of the chopped cashews. Fold the square over to enclose the fish and vegetables, and tightly crimp the edges closed. Place on a large baking sheet. Repeat with the remaining fish, vegetables, soy sauce, and butter.

4 **Bake for 15 minutes.** Remove from the oven and let stand for 5 minutes (this will complete the cooking of the fish).

5 **To serve,** place a foil packet on each dinner plate. Allow everyone to open each foil package by piercing it with the tip of a sharp dinner knife. You can spill the contents of the package onto each plate or eat directly out of the foil. Take care: The escaping steam can be very hot!

MAKES 4 SERVINGS

Why should I use an oven thermometer?

ASK ART Cooking food at the correct temperature is important, and the best way to know whether the oven is heating properly is with an oven thermometer. These inexpensive gadgets are sold in many supermarkets and hardware stores from coast to coast. If, after twenty minutes of preheating, the oven thermometer does not jibe with the set temperature, adjust the oven dial up or down to compensate. Easy.

Fish tacos have become a specialty of many a southern California restaurant, and some versions are pretty fancy. I make them here the way they were originally conceived—simple and tasty, with chunks of cod served on corn tortillas and offset with tangy slaw. It's easiest to serve the tortillas, fish, and slaw in separate containers at the table, allowing each person to make his or her own taco.

THE BEST FISH TACOS

LIME SLAW

3 tablespoons mayonnaise

Grated zest and juice of 1 lime

3 cups (half of a 16-ounce bag) coleslaw mix

2 scallions, white and green parts, chopped

2 tablespoons chopped fresh cilantro, optional

Salt and freshly ground pepper to taste

3 tablespoons olive oil

1 pound cod fillets, cut into 6 equal portions

1 teaspoon chili powder

Salt to taste

¼ cup all-purpose flour

12 corn tortillas, heated

1 **To make the** slaw, mix the mayonnaise and lime zest and juice in a medium bowl. Add the coleslaw mix, scallions, and cilantro, if using, and mix well. Season with salt and pepper. Let stand while making the fish for the tacos.

2 **Heat the oil** in a large skillet over medium heat until the oil is hot but not smoking. Season the cod all over with the chili powder and then the salt. Place the flour in a small bowl. Coat each piece of cod in the flour, shaking off the excess. Add to the skillet and cook, turning once, until golden brown, about 6 minutes. Transfer the cod to a plate.

3 **Place the tortillas** in a napkin-lined basket and close the napkin to keep the tortillas warm. Serve the tortillas, fish, and lime slaw at the table. To make each taco, place 2 tortillas, slightly overlapping, on the plate. (The juicy filling will likely soak through a single tortilla, so a double layer of tortillas is really necessary.) Top with 1 piece of fish and break it up with a fork. Top with a spoonful of the lime slaw and roll up the taco.

MAKES 6 TACOS

In Louisiana a popular method of cooking fish calls for spreading fillets with bright yellow ballpark mustard and flour before deep-frying them. It's darn good, but this version is a bit more refined, with smooth-tasting Dijon mustard meeting the crunch of cornmeal. And I don't deep-fry them but instead cook them in a skillet in hot oil. Mild flounder fillets benefit from this treatment, which perks up their flavor considerably.

FLOUNDER FILLETS WITH CORNMEAL-MUSTARD CRUST

Four 5- to 6-ounce flounder fillets

Salt and freshly ground pepper to taste

¼ cup Dijon mustard

⅓ cup all-purpose flour

⅓ cup yellow cornmeal, preferably stone-ground

Vegetable oil for frying

1 **Season the fillets** with salt and pepper. Place the mustard in a shallow dish. Mix the flour and cornmeal in another shallow dish. Line a baking sheet with waxed paper.

2 **Drag each fillet** through the mustard to coat it thinly on both sides. Dip in the flour, turning to coat. Place on the waxed paper and let stand for a few minutes to set the coating.

3 **Pour enough vegetable oil** into a large skillet to come ⅛ inch up the sides of the pan. Heat the oil over medium-high heat until very hot but not smoking. Add the fish fillets and cook until the undersides are crisp and golden brown, about 2 minutes. Turn and cook until the other sides are crisp, about 2 more minutes. Transfer to paper towels and drain very briefly (if allowed to stand too long, steam will collect and soften the crust). Serve immediately.

MAKES 4 SERVINGS

Nothing could be easier and faster than baking flounder fillets with just a handful of ingredients. If you're trying to work more fish into family meals, here's a great way to do so. Rolling up the flounder fillets makes them thicker and easier to cook. Spicy Garlic Spinach (page 270) would go nicely with these.

BAKED FLOUNDER WITH PESTO

⅓ cup mayonnaise

1 tablespoon Kitchen Workhorse Pesto (page 226) or store-bought pesto

Four 5- to 6-ounce flounder fillets

Salt and freshly ground pepper to taste

1 **Position a rack** in the top third of the oven and preheat the oven to 400°F. Lightly oil an 11½ × 8-inch baking dish.

2 **Mix the mayonnaise** and pesto in a small bowl. Season the flounder with salt and pepper. Starting at the small end, roll up each flounder fillet into a thick cylinder. Place in the baking dish. Slather the mayonnaise mixture on the top of each fillet.

3 **Bake until the mayonnaise** mixture is tinged with golden brown and the fish looks opaque when pierced in the center with the tip of a knife, about 15 minutes.

MAKES 4 SERVINGS

How long can I keep fresh fish before I cook it?

ASK ART I don't recommend keeping fish for more than a day. While it's best to prepare fish the day you buy it, never let more than twenty-four hours go by. When you store it, keep it as cold as you can. It's best to put the wrapped fish on top of cracked ice in a shallow dish and keep this in the coldest part of the refrigerator, which is usually the back of the shelf closest to the freezer compartment. Otherwise, keep it wrapped and stored in a cold spot in the refrigerator.

Serve this extraordinary salmon dish on a weekday and feel as though you are pampering your family. It's as good as a trip to a fancy French restaurant but couldn't be easier to make—or more delicious.

SALMON WITH SCALLIONS, TARRAGON, AND LEMON

9 scallions, trimmed

One 14½-ounce can reduced-sodium chicken broth

Grated zest of 1 lemon

2 tablespoons fresh lemon juice

Four 6-ounce skinless salmon fillets

Salt and freshly ground pepper to taste

1 teaspoon chopped fresh tarragon, or ½ teaspoon dried tarragon

½ cup heavy cream

1 tablespoon unsalted butter

1 Chop 1 scallion, white and green parts; leave the remaining scallions whole.

2 Bring the broth, lemon zest and juice, and chopped scallion to a boil in a large skillet over high heat. Boil until the broth has reduced by half, about 5 minutes.

3 Season the salmon with salt and pepper. Place the fillets in the broth and sprinkle with the tarragon. Top the salmon with the whole scallions. Reduce the heat to medium-low and cover the skillet. Simmer until the fillets have a slightly rosy center when pierced with the tip of a sharp knife, 7 to 9 minutes. Using a slotted spatula, transfer the salmon and whole scallions to a platter and cover with aluminum foil to keep warm.

4 Add the heavy cream to the skillet and bring to a boil over high heat. Cook, whisking occasionally, until the sauce has thickened and reduced by half, about 3 minutes. Remove from the heat and stir in the butter. Season with salt and pepper.

5 To serve, spoon equal amounts of the sauce onto 4 dinner plates. Top each with a salmon fillet and 2 scallions. Serve hot.

MAKES 4 SERVINGS

Packaged coleslaw mix is put to elegant use in this sophisticated but incredibly simple dish. American bistros (French ones, too) have long appreciated the combination of cabbage and salmon. If you haven't tried it, this recipe is a good opportunity.

SALMON ON CABBAGE AND DILL

1 tablespoon unsalted butter

One 1-pound bag coleslaw (chopped cabbage) mix

3 teaspoons chopped fresh dill, divided

Salt and freshly ground pepper to taste

¾ cup reduced-sodium chicken broth

Four 6-ounce skinless salmon fillets

3 tablespoons sour cream

½ teaspoon cornstarch

1 **Heat the butter** in a skillet over medium heat. Add the coleslaw and 2 teaspoons dill. Cook, stirring often, until the coleslaw wilts and is heated through, about 3 minutes. Season with salt and pepper. Transfer to a large platter and cover tightly with aluminum foil to keep warm.

2 **Wipe out the** skillet with paper towels. Add the broth and bring to a boil over medium heat. Season the salmon with salt and pepper and sprinkle the tops with the remaining 1 teaspoon dill. Add to the skillet and reduce the heat to medium-low. Cover and simmer until the fillets have a rosy center when pierced with the tip of a sharp knife, 7 to 9 minutes. Using a slotted spoon, transfer the salmon to the sautéed coleslaw and tent with foil.

3 **Whisk the sour** cream and cornstarch in a small bowl to dissolve the cornstarch. Whisk into the broth in the skillet and cook until the sauce returns to a simmer and thickens slightly. Season with salt and pepper.

4 **Pour the sauce** over the coleslaw and salmon, and serve immediately.

MAKES 4 SERVINGS

V inaigrette is perhaps the easiest sauce of all for fish fillets, and it needs no cooking. Because its flavor will be especially important to the end results, use a good extra-virgin olive oil. Many gourmet shops have tasting areas set up so you can compare and choose one you like. Serve the fish with some steamed new potatoes and green beans. The lemony olive vinaigrette will enhance the side dishes, too.

TILAPIA FILLETS WITH GREEN OLIVE VINAIGRETTE

GREEN OLIVE VINAIGRETTE

Grated zest of 1 lemon

1 tablespoon fresh lemon juice

1 small garlic clove, crushed through a press

1/8 teaspoon crushed hot red pepper flakes

1/3 cup olive oil, preferably high-quality extra-virgin

1/3 cup chopped pimiento-stuffed olives

Salt to taste

2 tablespoons olive oil

Four 6- to 7-ounce tilapia fillets

Salt and freshly ground pepper

1 **To make the vinaigrette,** whisk the lemon zest and juice with the garlic and red pepper in a small bowl. Gradually whisk in the oil. Stir in the olives. Season with salt. Let stand while cooking the fillets.

2 **Heat the oil** in a large skillet over medium heat until the oil is hot but not smoking. Season the fillets with salt and pepper. Add to the skillet and cook until the undersides are golden, about 3 minutes. Turn and cook until the other sides are golden and the fish looks opaque when pierced in the center with the tip of a knife, about 3 minutes more. Transfer each fish fillet to a dinner plate.

3 **Spoon an equal** amount of olives and vinaigrette over each fish fillet and serve immediately.

MAKES 4 SERVINGS

Here's another recipe that is so easy you can make it any night of the week, yet it is so elegant that it can be served for company as well. The meaty flavor of striped bass is perfectly suited to the sweet Manila or mahogany clams, but use any firm white fish fillets. The gorgeous small clams can be found at fish markets and many supermarkets, but if you can't get them, substitute 6 littleneck clams per person. For a bit of additional spice, season the fillets with Old Bay Seasoning instead of salt and pepper. Serve hot buttered pasta or rice on the side.

STRIPED BASS WITH CLAM SAUCE

1 teaspoon salt, plus more to taste

1½ pounds Manila or mahogany clams, or 24 littleneck clams

3 tablespoons olive oil, preferably extra-virgin, divided

Four 6-ounce skinless striped bass fillets

Freshly ground pepper to taste

2 garlic cloves, finely chopped

½ cup dry white wine, such as Pinot Grigio or Sauvignon Blanc

1 tablespoon fresh lemon juice

2 tablespoons chopped fresh parsley for garnish

1 **Stir 1 teaspoon** salt into 1 gallon cold water in a medium bowl. Add the clams and let stand for 1 hour to help the shellfish expel any grit. Drain well.

2 **Heat 2 tablespoons** oil in a large nonstick skillet over medium-high heat. Season the fish fillets with salt and pepper. Add to the skillet and cook until the undersides are lightly browned, about 2½ minutes. Turn and cook until the other sides are browned and the fillets are almost but not quite cooked through, about 2½ minutes more. Transfer each fillet to a deep bowl.

3 **Add the remaining** 1 tablespoon oil and the garlic to the skillet and stir over medium heat until the garlic is fragrant, about 1 minute. Add the wine and bring to a boil. Add the drained clams and cover. Cook, shaking the pan often, until the clams open, about 4 minutes. Discard any unopened clams. Stir the lemon juice into the cooking liquid. Season the sauce with salt and pepper carefully (the sauce could be quite salty from the clam juices).

4 **Spoon an equal** amount of clams and sauce over each fillet. Sprinkle with the parsley. Let stand for a couple of minutes before serving hot.

MAKES 4 SERVINGS

How important is it to buy the kind of fish a recipe calls for?

ASK ART

More important than the right fish is fresh fish. It should look and smell fresh—never filmy or fishy. If you recognize the difference between light-fleshed fish and oilier fish, you can make good decisions. The first category includes sole, flounder, cod, turbot, and catfish. The second includes salmon, tuna, bluefish, and swordfish. For most recipes, fish within these categories are interchangeable. Monkfish, snapper, and halibut are examples of fish that cross the line and pretty much can be used in any recipe.

S ave this roll-up-your-sleeves dish for very informal meals because there will be a lot of finger licking going on. Don't forget to provide bowls for the shrimp shells. If you have leftover shrimp, peel them to toss onto salad for another meal. Make a double batch of the Lime Slaw (an accompaniment to The Best Fish Tacos on page 204) to serve on the side.

ROASTED SHRIMP WITH LEMON-LIME DIPPING SAUCE

Grated zest of 1 lemon

1/4 cup fresh lemon juice

Grated zest of 1 lime

2 tablespoons fresh lime juice

2 tablespoons Worcestershire sauce

4 garlic cloves, finely chopped

1/2 teaspoon crushed hot red pepper flakes

2 pounds (21 to 25 count per pound) large shrimp, unpeeled

4 tablespoons unsalted butter, cut into 1/2-inch cubes

1 Position a rack in the top third of the oven and preheat the oven to 400°F.

2 Mix the lemon zest and juice, lime zest and juice, Worcestershire sauce, garlic, and red pepper in a large nonreactive (glass or stainless steel) bowl. Add the shrimp and mix well. Let stand while preheating the oven, but no longer than 20 minutes.

3 Spread the shrimp and marinade in a single layer in a 15 × 10-inch baking dish. Roast, occasionally stirring the shrimp, until they turn opaque and firm, about 12 minutes. Using a slotted spoon, transfer the shrimp to a large bowl and cover with foil to keep warm.

4 Whisk the butter a few pieces at a time into the baking dish to slightly thicken the marinade into a dipping sauce. Pour the sauce into small bowls.

5 Serve the shrimp with the sauce, letting the diners peel the shrimp as they go.

MAKES 4 TO 6 SERVINGS

FOURTEEN

NEW OLD-FASHIONED CASSEROLES AND PASTA DISHES

When I think of family meals, I think of casseroles. This may be a cliché, but let's face it: A warm, bubbling casserole invites us to the table for a casual, happy meal. Over the years the popularity of casseroles and pasta dishes has been linked to convenience foods that, while fabulous, are not necessarily recommended as a steady diet. I have lightened several of the recipes here to rely on fresh ingredients. I also use my share of convenience foods to keep these easy and accessible. After all, modern technology is wonderful!

When you make a casserole, prepare it in an attractive casserole dish because chances are the dish you use will end up on the table. It is equally important that the dish be heavy enough to hold in the heat—which explains why so many casserole dishes are ceramic, enamel-coated cast iron, or tempered glass. Most are sold with tight-fitting lids, which are handy for storage. I cook the casseroles here without lids because I like a browned, crusty top. While all casserole dishes are ovenproof, not all can be put on a flame. Make sure you know which of yours can be used on top of the stove. Finally, many casserole dishes can go from freezer to oven to dishwasher—but not all. Again, know your cookware to avoid disasters.

I rely on boneless chicken breasts and ground turkey for some dishes that traditionally have been made with beef, such as Turkey Meatballs and Linguine with Escarole Tomato Sauce (page 232). When you cook boneless chicken breasts for a casserole, cook them only until they lose their raw appearance; they will continue to cook in the oven.

Despite the current trend to reduce our intake of carbohydrates, families love pasta. And why not? It can be prepared in countless ways and with any number of favorite ingredients. Plus, it's easy on the weekly food budget. Don't stop eating pasta, just make dishes that combine it with lots of fresh veggies and lean meat and fish. When your kids clamor for spaghetti and marinara sauce, make it with whole wheat pasta so that they benefit from the fiber. Serve pasta with a big green salad and reserve the garlic bread for very special occasions.

Don't turn your back on casseroles and pasta dishes. Embrace them. They are the dishes that allow you to put a personal stamp on your cooking, feed your family easily, and make your kitchen life all the better.

recipes

Ultrathin capellini isn't known as angel-hair pasta for nothing! If it were any thinner, it would be impossible to work with. Keeping this in mind, toss it with only the lightest sauce, such as this vegetarian tomato sauce. For success the sauce must be made with the ripest in-season tomatoes, so wait until you find perfect specimens at the summer farmers' market or your own backyard garden.

CAPELLINI WITH SUMMER TOMATO-BASIL SAUCE

1/3 cup extra-virgin olive oil

4 garlic cloves, chopped

4 pounds ripe plum (Roma) tomatoes, seeded (see Note) and chopped into 1-inch chunks

1 cup packed fresh basil leaves, measured and then coarsely chopped

Salt and crushed hot red pepper flakes to taste

1 pound capellini (angel-hair pasta)

Freshly grated Parmesan cheese for serving

1 **Bring a large** pot of lightly salted water to a boil over high heat.

2 **Meanwhile,** combine the oil and garlic in a large skillet. Cook over medium heat, stirring often, just until the garlic softens, 3 to 4 minutes. Add the tomatoes and increase the heat to medium-high. Cook, stirring often, until the tomatoes soften and give off their juice, about 10 minutes. Stir in the basil and simmer for 2 minutes. Season with salt and red pepper. Transfer the sauce to a food processor and pulse until smooth (or keep it chunky if you prefer). Keep the sauce warm.

3 **Add the pasta** to the boiling water and cook just until barely tender, about 4 minutes. Drain well. Return the pasta to the pot, add the sauce, and toss lightly.

4 **Serve immediately in** deep bowls and pass the Parmesan on the side.

MAKES 4 TO 6 SERVINGS

NOTE: To seed plum tomatoes, dig out the stem indentation from each tomato and then cut in half lengthwise. Using your fingertip, poke out the clusters of seeds, but do not be concerned if you don't free every last seed. Regular, sphere-shaped tomatoes are seeded the same way, but cut each tomato in half crosswise through its "equator."

What is the quickest way to grate Parmesan cheese?

ASK ART

Grating your own Parmesan or other hard cheese gives you the best flavor. I find the fastest and easiest way to grate a good quantity is to cut the cheese into chunks and then pulse it in a food processor fitted with the metal blade until it is fine. If your grating attachment has very small holes, use it for grating cheese. For small amounts use a box grater, a rotary grater, or one of the handiest cooking tools to come along in years: a Microplaner. If none of these methods appeals to you, buy freshly grated cheese from the cheese counter of the supermarket or at a good cheese shop. It usually comes packed in plastic tubs.

ife without macaroni and cheese would be sad indeed, but unhappily the current emphasis on low-carb diets could make this dish disappear. What I offer here is a recipe that uses half of the pasta but has all the goodness and even more flavor. The trick is to substitute a tasty cheese-friendly vegetable such as cauliflower for some of the starchy carbs. If you are a cheddar fan, go right ahead and use it instead of Gruyère or Swiss cheese.

CAULIFLOWER AND PENNE GRATIN

Nonstick vegetable oil spray

1 head cauliflower (about 2¼ pounds), trimmed and cut into bite-sized florets

½ pound (about 3 cups) penne

5 tablespoons unsalted butter, divided

¼ cup all-purpose flour

3 cups milk, heated

2 cups (8 ounces) shredded Gruyère or Swiss cheese

Salt and freshly ground pepper to taste

¼ cup freshly grated Parmesan cheese

1 tablespoon dried bread crumbs

1 **Position a rack** in the center of the oven and preheat the oven to 350°F. Lightly coat the inside of a 2½- to 3-quart deep baking dish with the oil spray.

2 **Bring a large** pot of lightly salted water to a boil over high heat. Add the cauliflower and return to a boil. Cook just until the cauliflower is barely tender, about 3 minutes (it will cook further during baking, so do not overcook). Using a scoop or a large slotted spoon, transfer the cauliflower to a large bowl of very cold water to cool. Drain well.

3 **Add the penne** to the same pot of boiling water and cook just until barely tender (it will cook more in the oven), about 7 minutes. Drain well.

4 **Meanwhile,** melt 4 tablespoons butter in a medium heavy-bottomed saucepan over medium-low heat. Whisk in the flour and let the mixture bubble without browning for 2 minutes. Whisk in the hot milk and bring to a boil over medium heat, whisking often. Return the heat to medium-low and let the sauce simmer until it is slightly thickened and has no raw flour taste, about 5

minutes. Stir in the Gruyère cheese. Season with salt and pepper. Transfer to the baking dish. Mix the Parmesan cheese and bread crumbs, sprinkle over the pasta, and dot with the remaining 1 tablespoon butter.

5   **Bake until the** sauce is bubbling and the topping is golden brown, about 30 minutes. Let stand for 5 minutes, then serve hot.

MAKES 4 TO 6 SERVINGS

Many casseroles call for a white sauce. Do you have any tips for success?

ASK ART

You'll master making a basic white sauce very quickly. Many start with a roux, which is a mixture of flour and butter. For white sauce it is not allowed to brown but must cook for a few minutes to rid it of the raw taste of flour. You will find that if you heat the milk or other liquid for the sauce before you add it to the roux, the sauce will come to a boil faster and thicken and smooth out more easily. The sauce will never thicken if it doesn't boil.

Not all of my sauces use a roux; instead, I sprinkle flour over vegetables that have been sautéed in butter (or another fat). The flour is mixed well as the liquid is stirred into the pan, and everything comes together as a smooth, thick sauce. As you do when making a roux-based white sauce, heat the liquid first so that the sauce comes to a boil faster.

You will be glad that you have leftover Kitchen Workhorse Italian Pot Roast (page 144) when you taste this robust meat sauce. In fact, you may find yourself simmering a pot roast just to have some of the sauce and beef for pasta! Stretching dishes, as I do here, is a terrific way to cook and makes your kitchen life all the easier.

PENNE WITH POT ROAST SAUCE

2 cups coarsely chopped beef from Kitchen Workhorse Italian Pot Roast (page 144)

1 cup sauce from Kitchen Workhorse Italian Pot Roast (page 144)

One 15-ounce can crushed tomatoes

1 teaspoon dried basil

1 pound penne

Grated Parmesan cheese for serving

1 **Mix the beef,** sauce, tomatoes, and basil in a medium saucepan. Bring to a boil over medium-high heat, stirring often. Reduce the heat to medium-low and simmer until the flavors are well blended, about 30 minutes.

2 **Meanwhile,** bring a large pot of lightly salted water to a boil over high heat. Add the penne and cook just until the pasta is barely tender, about 9 minutes. Drain well and return to the pot.

3 **Add the sauce** to the pasta and mix well. Serve in deep bowls and pass the Parmesan on the side.

MAKES 4 TO 6 SERVINGS

In some parts of Italy, pasta is tossed with green beans, potatoes, and pesto to make a marvelously fresh-tasting dish. You can skip the potatoes and still have a great meal. In line with current dietary preferences, I've cut back on the pasta so that the green beans and pesto shine through.

PASTA VERDE WITH GREEN BEANS

¾ pound green beans, trimmed and cut into 1-inch lengths

½ pound (about 3 cups) bow tie pasta (also called farfalle)

¼ cup kitchen Workhorse Pesto (see page 226) or store-bought pesto

⅓ cup freshly grated Parmesan cheese, plus more for serving

Salt and freshly ground pepper to taste

1 Bring a large pot of lightly salted water to a boil over high heat. Add the green beans and cook until barely tender, about 5 minutes. Using a wire mesh scoop or a sieve, transfer the green beans to a bowl of ice water. Drain the green beans and set aside.

2 Add the pasta to the water and cook until it is barely tender, about 9 minutes. During the last minute or so of cooking, add the green beans so they can heat through. Scoop out about ⅓ cup of the cooking water from the pot, then drain.

3 Return the drained pasta and green beans to the pot. Add the pesto and ⅓ cup Parmesan, and toss well, adding enough of the cooking water to make a light-bodied sauce. Season with salt and pepper. Serve immediately with additional Parmesan passed on the side.

MAKES 4 SERVINGS

ASK ART

What does it mean when a container is "freezer and microwave safe"?

This means you can take the container filled with food from the freezer and put it directly in the microwave for defrosting and then reheating. A container made of metal or one utilizing aluminum foil should not go in the microwave.

Similar to Singapore noodles from the local Chinese takeout, this spicy dish is made with easy-to-find ingredients that are available at every supermarket. (In some states you may have to make a trip to the liquor store for the sherry. Sorry!)

CHINESE CURRIED NOODLES WITH CHICKEN AND VEGETABLES

½ pound thin egg noodles

3 tablespoons vegetable oil, divided

Two 6-ounce chicken breasts, cut into pieces about ½ inch wide and 2 inches long

⅔ cup reduced-sodium chicken broth

2 tablespoons soy sauce

1 tablespoon dry sherry

1 teaspoon cornstarch

1 red bell pepper, seeded and cut into strips about ¼ inch wide and 2 inches long

1 large carrot, peeled and cut into strips about ⅛ inch wide and 2 inches long

2 celery ribs, cut into strips about ⅛ inch wide and 2 inches long

2 scallions, white and green parts, chopped

1 tablespoon shredded fresh ginger (grated on the large holes of a box grater)

1 garlic clove, minced

2 teaspoons Madras-style curry powder

½ teaspoon sugar

1 **Bring a large pot** of lightly salted water to a boil over high heat. Add the noodles and cook until barely tender, about 5 minutes. Drain well and return to the pot.

2 **Meanwhile,** heat 1½ tablespoons oil in a large skillet over high heat. Add the chicken and cook, stirring often, until cooked through, about 4 minutes. Transfer the chicken to a plate.

3 **Mix the broth,** soy sauce, and sherry in a small bowl. Add the cornstarch and whisk until dissolved. Set aside.

4   **Heat the remaining** 1½ tablespoons oil in the skillet over high heat. Add the red pepper, carrot, and celery, and stir-fry until softened, about 2 minutes. Add the scallions, ginger, and garlic, and stir until they give off their fragrances, about 1 minute. Add the curry and sugar, and stir for 15 seconds.

5   **Stir the broth** mixture (the cornstarch will have sunk to the bottom). Add to the skillet, mix well, and bring to a boil. Add the chicken and cook just until it heats through, about 1 minute. Stir into the pasta and mix well. Serve hot.

MAKES 4 SERVINGS

What is curry powder?

ASK ART

Curry powder is a wonderful spice mixture rather than a specific spice. It's a blend of such spices as cumin, curry leaves, mace, turmeric, cardamom, coriander seeds, fennel seeds, mustard seeds, and fenugreek. Not surprisingly, curry powders differ from brand to brand, with some being more pungent or sweeter than others. Madras-style curry powder, available in every supermarket, is a good choice for most curry needs.

G nocchi is an Italian word for dumplings. They are commonly made with potatoes, although not always. They can be bought frozen at Italian grocers but are better when made with love by your own two hands. Gnocchi (pronounced NYOH-kee) are not hard to make, but the first time you try, you might want to do it on a Sunday afternoon so you get the hang of it without any undue pressure. If you can boil potatoes, you can make these little charmers. When you do, make a batch and freeze them for a weeknight supper. I like my gnocchi with pesto, but try them with marinara sauce another time.

POTATO GNOCCHI WITH PESTO

1 pound large baking potatoes, such as russet or Burbank, scrubbed but unpeeled

1 large egg, beaten

½ teaspoon salt

1 cup all-purpose flour

⅓ cup Kitchen Workhorse Pesto (page 226) or store-bought pesto

Freshly grated Parmesan cheese for serving

1 Place the potatoes in a large pot and add enough lightly salted water to cover by 1 inch. Bring to a boil over high heat. Reduce the heat to medium and loosely cover the pot. Cook at a brisk simmer until the potatoes are tender when pierced with the tip of a knife, but not soggy and falling apart, 30 to 40 minutes. Drain the potatoes, rinse under cold water, and cool until they can be handled.

2 Peel the potatoes and press them through a ricer into the bowl of a heavy-duty electric mixer fitted with the paddle blade. (You can also rub the potatoes through a coarse wire sieve into a large bowl and use a sturdy hand mixer or spoon instead of the standing mixer.) Mix the egg and salt in a small bowl. With the machine on low speed, gradually mix in the egg, being careful not to do it too quickly or the egg will curdle. Gradually mix in enough flour to make a soft but malleable dough with a consistency similar to Play-Doh.

3 Dust a large baking sheet with flour. Turn the dough out onto a lightly floured work surface. Working with one-fourth of the dough at a time, roll the dough under your palms on the work surface to shape it into a long ½-inch-thick rope. Using a sharp knife, cut the rope into 1-inch-long pieces. Transfer the

gnocchi to the floured baking sheet. Repeat with the remaining dough. (The gnocchi can be covered with plastic wrap and refrigerated for up to 2 hours before cooking. To freeze, cover the gnocchi with plastic wrap and freeze on the baking sheet just until frozen and firm, about 2 hours. Transfer the frozen gnocchi to self-sealing plastic freezer bags and freeze for up to 2 months. Do not thaw the gnocchi before cooking.)

4 **Bring a large** pot of lightly salted water to a boil over high heat. Fill a serving bowl with very hot water and let stand to warm the bowl. Toss the water out of the bowl and dry the bowl when the water in the pot comes to a boil.

5 **Add about a** dozen gnocchi to the boiling water and cook until 10 seconds or so after the gnocchi float to the top of the water. Using a wire skimmer or sieve, scoop the gnocchi out of the water, transfer to the warmed bowl, and cover to keep warm.

6 **Add the pesto** and about 1/3 cup of the cooking water. Stir gently to coat the gnocchi. Serve immediately and pass the Parmesan on the side.

MAKES 4 TO 6 SERVINGS

The ingredients for pesto can be purchased at almost every supermarket, and while you can buy a container of ready-made pesto and not be disappointed, homemade is always best. If you have basil growing in your garden, even better! Plus, it's worth making your own just so your house can smell like fresh basil. You'll be glad that you have it on hand to dress pasta, stir into tomato sauce or salad dressings, and spoon on top of potatoes, to name just a few uses. The addition of fresh parsley adds an extra dose of chlorophyll, all the better to keep the pesto nice and green.

PESTO

spin-off recipes

Roast Leg of Lamb with Pesto (page 167)

Chicken Breasts with Yukon Gold Potatoes, Spinach, and Fontina Gratin (page 182)

Pasta Verde with Green Beans (page 221)

Potato Gnocchi with Pesto (page 224)

Portobello Caps with White Bean–Pesto Puree (page 266)

4 garlic cloves, peeled

2 cups packed fresh basil leaves

1 cup freshly grated Parmesan cheese

½ cup packed fresh parsley leaves, preferably Italian flat-leaf parsley

½ cup walnuts, toasted (see page 251)

½ cup extra-virgin olive oil, plus more for freezing

Salt and freshly ground pepper to taste

With the food processor running, drop the garlic through the feed tube to chop it finely. Add the basil, Parmesan, parsley, and walnuts. With the machine running, gradually add the oil to make a thick, smooth paste. Season to taste with salt and pepper. Transfer to an airtight container. Cover the surface of the pesto with a thin layer of oil. (The pesto will keep, refrigerated and covered with the oil in an airtight container, for up to 2 weeks. For longer storage, transfer ½-cup portions of the pesto to small self-sealing freezer bags and freeze for up to 2 months. Thaw the pesto at room temperature before using.)

MAKES ABOUT 1½ CUPS

The briny flavor of mussels stands up to the most herbaceous tomato sauce, so I add oregano, thyme, and parsley to marinara sauce without worry. Unless you have the marinara sauce in the freezer ready to defrost in the microwave, make the sauce before starting this recipe, so it can lend its long-cooked flavor to the steamed mussel juices. And if you have the time, soak the mussels in lightly salted water (about 2 teaspoons of salt to 1 gallon of cold water) to help them expel any grit. There is a rule in Italy about not putting grated cheese with seafood, but rules are made to be broken.

MUSSELS IN HERBED TOMATO SAUCE WITH PENNE

2 tablespoons olive oil

2 garlic cloves, chopped

1 cup dry white wine, such as Sauvignon Blanc or Pinot Grigio, or reduced-sodium chicken broth

2 tablespoons fresh lemon juice

1 teaspoon dried oregano

½ teaspoon dried thyme

2 pounds mussels, tough beards removed

1 quart Kitchen Workhorse Marinara Sauce (page 234) or store-bought marinara sauce

¼ teaspoon hot red pepper flakes

1 pound regular or whole wheat penne

¼ cup chopped fresh parsley for garnish

Freshly grated Parmesan cheese for serving

1 Bring a large pot of lightly salted water to a boil over high heat.

2 Meanwhile, combine the oil and garlic in another large pot and cook over medium heat until the garlic softens, about 3 minutes. Add the wine, lemon juice, oregano, and thyme, and bring to a boil over high heat. Add the mussels and cover tightly. Cook, occasionally shaking the pot, until the mussels open, about 5 minutes. Using tongs, transfer the mussels to a platter and cover with aluminum foil to keep warm. Discard any mussels that do not open. Add the marinara sauce and red pepper to the pot and bring to a boil. Boil until the sauce is slightly thickened, about 5 minutes.

3 While the mussels are cooking, add the penne to the first pot and cook until

barely tender, about 9 minutes. Drain well. Return the penne to its cooking pot, add the tomato sauce, and mix well.

4 **Immediately serve the** pasta in deep bowls. Top each serving with a few mussels and a generous sprinkling of parsley. Pass the grated Parmesan on the side.

MAKES 4 TO 6 SERVINGS

Miso may be an unfamiliar ingredient to a lot of American cooks, but it deserves more popularity. It's a great thing to have in the refrigerator, ready to stir into a cup of hot water to turn into a nourishing, protein-rich soup. Here I use some of my favorite Asian vegetables and roast pork, but there's no reason that you can't use your own favorites or some chopped cooked chicken breast. Also, if you can't find buckwheat soba noodles, the wheat udon are a more than acceptable substitute.

SOBA NOODLES IN MISO BROTH WITH ROAST PORK AND VEGETABLES

7 ounces soba noodles

Dark Asian sesame oil for the noodles and for serving

½ pound shiitake mushrooms, stems discarded and caps cut into ½-inch-wide strips

2 cups trimmed and coarsely chopped bok choy, preferably baby bok choy (see Note)

6 scallions, white and green parts, chopped

3 tablespoons red miso, or more to taste

12 thin slices Kitchen Workhorse Roast Pork Tenderloin with Asian Glaze (page 154)

Crushed hot red pepper flakes for serving

1 **Bring a large** pot of lightly salted water to a boil over high heat. Add the soba noodles and cook until barely tender, about 5 minutes. Drain well and rinse under cold water. Toss with a drizzle of sesame oil to keep the noodles from sticking.

2 **Bring another pot** with 6 cups cold water to a boil over high heat. Add the mushrooms, bok choy, and scallions. Cook just until the mushrooms are

tender, about 3 minutes. Add the drained noodles and cook just until the liquid returns to a simmer. Remove the pot from the heat. Transfer about 1 cup of the cooking liquid to a small bowl, add the miso, and mix to dissolve the miso. Stir the dissolved miso back into the pot. If you like a stronger flavor, dissolve more miso in some cooking liquid and add it to the pot.

3   Ladle the soup and noodles into deep bowls and top each with 2 slices of pork. Serve hot and pass the red pepper and sesame oil on the side so that each person can season the soup to taste.

MAKES 6 SERVINGS

NOTE: There are two main varieties of bok choy available. Traditional bok choy has long stalks with wide white bases and leafy dark green tops, and each head weighs about 1 pound. Baby bok choy is light green and much smaller, and a single head weighs about 7 ounces, which will chop into the 2 cups required for this soup. Unless you don't mind having leftover bok choy (great in stir-fries), look for the baby ones; they can be found at Asian grocers, many natural food supermarkets, and more traditional supermarkets, too. If you can't find either bok choy, substitute napa cabbage or baby spinach leaves.

Where can I buy miso?

ASK ART

You can find miso in nearly any supermarket these days. It's in a refrigerated bin and generally is sold in small plastic tubs. If your market doesn't carry it, seek it out in an Asian market. It's well worth it.

A Japanese seasoning, miso is fermented soybean paste. It's added to hot water in Japan as a quick and soothing soup, and it's equally successful as a flavoring for any number of dishes. Depending on the grain with which the beans are fermented, miso will range in color from yellow to dark brown. I like red miso, which is sort of brick colored and made from soybeans and fermented rice. It's considered a good all-purpose miso. Try different types and choose those you like best. There is no right or wrong. Store miso in the refrigerator. It keeps for months.

Madame Luisa Tetrazzini was a famous opera singer of the early twentieth century. She would probably not be thrilled to be remembered mainly for the creamy poultry and mushroom dish named in her honor instead of her voice. (To prove my point, a recent Internet search for Tetrazzini yielded hundreds of sites with recipes and only three that referred to opera.) Turkey Tetrazzini is often baked as a casserole, but I prefer to simply toss the sauce with hot pasta and serve, which keeps the lean turkey breast nice and juicy. If you wish, substitute 2 cups of cooked broccoli florets for the peas. Garnish this with sliced black olives, toasted slivered almonds, and chopped parsley if you want to dress it up even more.

FETTUCCINE WITH TURKEY TETRAZZINI SAUCE

2 tablespoons olive oil

1 pound boneless and skinless turkey breast cutlets, cut crosswise into ¾-inch-thick strips

Salt and freshly ground pepper to taste

2 tablespoons unsalted butter

½ pound brown or white mushrooms, sliced

4 scallions, white and green parts, chopped

2 tablespoons all-purpose flour

1 cup reduced-sodium chicken broth

1 cup regular or nonfat half-and-half

¼ cup dry sherry, optional

1 cup thawed frozen peas

½ cup (2 ounces) freshly grated Parmesan cheese, plus more for serving

¾ pound dried egg fettuccine

1 **Heat the oil** in a large skillet over medium-high heat. Season the turkey breast strips with salt and pepper. Add the turkey strips in batches without crowding and cook, stirring often, just until the strips are cooked through, about 6 minutes. Do not overcook. Transfer the turkey to a platter and set aside.

2 **Heat the butter** in the same skillet over medium-high heat. Add the mushrooms and cook, stirring often, until they give off their juices, about 4 minutes. Add the scallions and cook until the mushroom juices have evaporated, about 3 minutes. Sprinkle with the flour and stir well. Stir in the

broth, half-and-half, and sherry, if using, and bring to a boil, stirring often. Reduce the heat to low and simmer until slightly thickened, about 3 minutes. Stir in the peas and Parmesan. Return the turkey to the skillet and keep the sauce warm.

3 Meanwhile, bring a large pot of lightly salted water to a boil over high heat. Add the fettuccine and cook until barely tender, about 9 minutes. Drain well and return to the pot. Add the sauce and mix well.

4 Serve immediately in deep bowls and pass additional Parmesan on the side.

MAKES 4 TO 6 SERVINGS

scarole, which is a healthy and flavorful and unfairly overlooked vegetable, adds an interesting dimension to the time-honored combination of pasta and meatballs. Regular ground turkey, which is a mixture of white and dark meat, will make juicier meatballs than the all-white-meat variety, which is too lean.

TURKEY MEATBALLS AND LINGUINE WITH ESCAROLE TOMATO SAUCE

TURKEY MEATBALLS

1¼ pounds ground turkey

¼ cup plain or Italian-flavored dried bread crumbs

2 scallions, white and green parts, finely chopped

1 garlic clove, crushed through a press

1 large egg, beaten

1 teaspoon salt

½ teaspoon freshly ground pepper

2 heads escarole (about 14 ounces each)

1 pound whole wheat or regular linguine

1 quart Kitchen Workhorse Marinara Sauce (page 234) or store-bought marinara sauce

2 tablespoons chopped fresh rosemary

Freshly grated Parmesan cheese for serving

1 **Position a rack** in the center of the oven and preheat the oven to 400°F. Lightly oil a large baking sheet.

2 **To make the** meatballs, thoroughly but lightly combine the turkey, bread crumbs, scallions, garlic, egg, salt, and pepper in a medium bowl (your clean hands work best). Shape the mixture into 12 meatballs and place them on the baking sheet. Bake, turning halfway through baking, until the meatballs are lightly browned, about 25 minutes. Set the meatballs aside.

3 **Add enough cold,** lightly salted water to a large saucepan to come 2 inches up the sides and bring to a boil over high heat. Meanwhile, trim the tough ends from the escarole heads, then coarsely chop the heads crosswise into pieces about 2 inches square. Wash well in a sink filled with cold water. Lift the escarole out of the water and transfer to a large bowl. (Do not drain the escarole.) Add the escarole to the pot, a handful at a time, and cook until it

wilts, about 2 minutes. When all the escarole is in the pot, cover and cook for 5 minutes. Drain and rinse under cold running water. When cool enough to handle, squeeze the excess water out of the escarole and set it aside.

4 **Bring a large** pot of lightly salted water to a boil over high heat. Add the linguine and cook until the pasta is barely tender, about 8 minutes. Drain well and return the pasta to the pot.

5 **While the pasta** is cooking, combine the marinara sauce, meatballs, escarole, and rosemary in a large saucepan and bring to a simmer over medium heat. Add to the pasta and stir well. Serve immediately and pass the Parmesan on the side.

MAKES 6 SERVINGS

Can I freeze a casserole that contains rice or pasta?

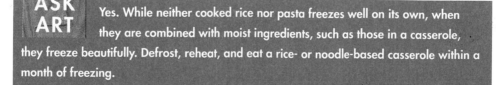

ASK ART Yes. While neither cooked rice nor pasta freezes well on its own, when they are combined with moist ingredients, such as those in a casserole, they freeze beautifully. Defrost, reheat, and eat a rice- or noodle-based casserole within a month of freezing.

There should be a culinary law that every freezer have at least one quart of this basic tomato sauce ready to defrost and turn into dinner. This recipe makes two quarts, but if you have a big enough pot and freezer, go ahead and double or even triple the recipe. You won't regret it.

MARINARA SAUCE

spin-off recipes

Turkey Meatballs and Linguine with Escarole Tomato Sauce (page 232)

Mussels in Herbed Tomato Sauce with Penne (page 227)

Chicken Breasts Primavera (page 183)

Chicken Breasts with Yukon Gold Potatoes, Spinach, and Fontina Gratin (page 182)

3 tablespoons olive oil

1 large onion, chopped

1 medium carrot, cut into ½-inch dice

1 medium celery rib, cut into ½-inch dice

4 garlic cloves, chopped

One 28-ounce can diced tomatoes in juice

One 28-ounce can crushed tomatoes

One 15-ounce can tomato sauce

1 tablespoon dried Italian herbs, or 1 teaspoon each dried basil, oregano, and rosemary

1 bay leaf

½ teaspoon crushed hot red pepper flakes

1 Heat the oil in a large saucepan over medium heat. Add the onion, carrot, and celery, and cook, stirring often, until the onion is golden, about 6 minutes. Stir in the garlic and cook until it gives off its fragrance, about 1 minute.

2 Stir in the diced tomatoes with their juice, the crushed tomatoes, tomato sauce, herbs, bay leaf, and red pepper flakes. Bring to a boil over high heat. Reduce the heat to medium-low and simmer, uncovered and stirring often, until the sauce has reduced slightly, about 1 hour.

3 Let cool completely. Transfer to two 1-quart airtight containers. (The sauce can be made, covered, and refrigerated up to 3 days ahead, or frozen for up to 3 months. Before using frozen marinara sauce, thaw in a microwave oven at 50 percent power.)

MAKES ABOUT 2 QUARTS

have a recipe for Chicken and Biscuits in my first book, *Back to the Table,* that starts with boiling a chicken until tender. This is a streamlined, creamier version, and one that can be whipped up for a weeknight supper.

CHICKEN POT PIE WITH BISCUIT CRUST

2 tablespoons vegetable oil

Three 6- to 7-ounce boneless and skinless chicken breasts, cut into 1-inch pieces

Salt and freshly ground pepper to taste

3 tablespoons unsalted butter

1 small onion, chopped

1 celery rib, finely chopped

1/3 cup plus 2 tablespoons all-purpose flour

One 10-ounce box frozen mixed vegetables (with corn, carrots, and green beans), thawed

3 cups reduced-sodium chicken broth

1 cup regular or nonfat half-and-half

1 tablespoon chopped fresh parsley

2 cups instant baking mix, such as Bisquick

2/3 cup buttermilk

1 **Position a rack** in the center of the oven and preheat the oven to 350°F.

2 **Heat the oil** in a large skillet over medium-high heat. Season the chicken with salt and pepper. Add the chicken to the skillet and cook, stirring often, just until it turns opaque and loses its raw look, about 8 minutes. Transfer the chicken to a plate.

3 **Add the butter** to the skillet and reduce the heat to medium. Add the onion and celery and cook, stirring often, until the vegetables soften, about 3 minutes. Sprinkle the flour over the mixed vegetables and mix well. Add the broth and half-and-half, and bring to a boil, stirring up the browned bits in the pan with a wooden spatula. Cook until the sauce is slightly thickened, about 2 minutes. Stir in the reserved chicken, thawed mixed vegetables, and parsley. Season with salt and pepper. Pour into an ungreased 2½- to 3-quart round casserole.

4 **Mix the baking** mix and buttermilk to make a soft, sticky dough. Drop six large spoonfuls of the dough over the chicken mixture. Bake until the biscuits are golden brown, about 25 minutes. Serve hot.

MAKES 6 SERVINGS

Frozen artichoke hearts add a fancy touch to this homey classic with a tangy, rich sauce. I really love sunchokes, also known as Jerusalem artichokes, in this dish. They aren't common in the produce market, however, so I use artichoke hearts instead, which are easy to come by. If you want to try sunchokes in place of artichoke hearts, peel and slice about five of them and steam over boiling water until tender, about eight minutes.

CHICKEN, BROCCOLI, AND ARTICHOKE DIVAN

4 broccoli crowns, cut into florets (2 cups florets)

2 tablespoons vegetable oil

3 boneless and skinless chicken breasts (about 7 ounces each), cut into bite-sized pieces

Salt and freshly ground pepper to taste

2 tablespoons unsalted butter

1 medium onion, chopped

1 small celery rib, chopped

2 tablespoons all-purpose flour

1½ cups reduced-sodium chicken broth

½ cup whole or 2% milk

1 cup (4 ounces) coarsely grated sharp cheddar cheese, divided

1 tablespoon Dijon mustard

One 9-ounce box frozen artichoke hearts, thawed and patted dry

Hot red pepper sauce to taste

¼ cup grated Parmesan cheese

1 **Position the oven** rack in the top third of the oven and preheat the oven to 375°F.

2 **Bring a medium** saucepan of lightly salted water to a boil over high heat. Add the broccoli and cook until barely tender, about 5 minutes. Drain, rinse under cold running water, and drain again. Pat completely dry with paper towels.

3 **Heat the oil** in a large skillet over medium-high heat. Season the chicken with salt and pepper. Add the chicken to the skillet and cook, turning occasionally, until the chicken is lightly browned, about 6 minutes. Transfer the chicken to a plate and set aside.

4 **Add the butter** to the skillet and melt it. Add the onion and celery, and cook, stirring often, until they soften, about 3 minutes. Sprinkle with the flour and

stir well. Stir in the broth and milk, and bring to a boil, stirring often. Reduce the heat to medium and simmer until the sauce is slightly thickened, about 5 minutes. Stir in ½ cup cheddar and the mustard. Stir in the chicken, broccoli, and artichokes. Season the sauce with salt and hot red pepper sauce. Pour into a 2-quart heatproof baking dish (preferably an oval gratin dish).

5   **Sprinkle the top** of the divan with the remaining ½ cup cheddar and the Parmesan. Bake until the cheese is melted and serve immediately.

MAKES 4 SERVINGS

This dish has been famous with Texan cooks for generations, but no one really knows how it got its name. The enormous King Ranch is known for cattle, not chickens. Perhaps it is because the casserole has a flavor as big as all outdoors. While most people know the bowdlerized canned soup version, my recipe takes a from-scratch approach—with excellent results. Because it takes a little extra effort, save this entrée for weekend suppers or company, or make it ahead and freeze it for up to 2 months.

FROM-SCRATCH KING RANCH CASSEROLE

Nonstick vegetable oil spray

9 corn tortillas

10 boneless and skinless chicken thighs (about 2¼ pounds), cut into bite-sized pieces

One 14½-ounce can reduced-sodium chicken broth

One 14-ounce can chopped tomatoes in juice, drained

One 7-ounce jar roasted red peppers, drained and chopped

One 4.25-ounce can chopped green chilies, drained

3 tablespoons unsalted butter

1 medium onion, chopped

10 ounces white mushrooms, sliced

1 teaspoon chili powder

2¼ cups milk, as needed

½ cup all-purpose flour

Salt and freshly ground pepper to taste

1 cup (4 ounces) shredded sharp cheddar cheese

1 **Position a rack** in the center of the oven and preheat the oven to 350°F. Lightly coat a 9 × 13-inch baking dish with the oil spray.

2 **Arrange the tortillas** directly on the oven racks. (You can spread the tortillas on 2 baking sheets, but baking the tortillas on the oven racks is fine.) Bake until the tortillas feel dry and leathery (they do not have to toast), about 6 minutes. Remove the tortillas from the oven and set aside.

3 **Combine the chicken** thighs and broth in a large saucepan. Bring to a boil over high heat. Reduce the heat to medium-low, cover, and cook just until the chicken shows no sign of pink when pierced with the tip of a knife, about

10 minutes. Using a slotted spoon, transfer the chicken to a medium bowl, reserving the cooking liquid. Add the tomatoes, red peppers, and green chilies, and mix well.

4   Meanwhile, heat the butter in a large skillet over medium heat. Add the onion and cook, stirring often, until it softens, about 3 minutes. Add the mushrooms and cook, stirring often, until they are tender and their liquid has evaporated, about 10 minutes. Add the chili powder and stir for 15 seconds.

5   Pour ½ cup milk into a 1-quart glass measuring cup. Add the flour and whisk until dissolved. Add the reserved broth and enough milk to make 4 cups total liquid. Stir into the mushrooms and bring to a boil. Reduce the heat to medium-low and simmer, stirring often, until slightly thickened, about 3 minutes. Season the sauce with salt and pepper.

6   Arrange 4 tortillas in the bottom of the baking dish. Tear 1 tortilla in half to cover the empty spot in the center. Sprinkle with half of the chicken. Spread with half of the sauce and sprinkle with half of the cheddar. Repeat with the remaining tortillas, chicken, sauce, and cheddar.

7   Bake until the sauce is bubbling and the cheese has melted, about 30 minutes. Let stand for 5 minutes, then serve hot.

MAKES 6 SERVINGS

amale pie is a staple of Mom Cuisine. This modern version increases the protein with the addition of beans and corn, reduces the fat by using ground turkey instead of hamburger, and substitutes an easy precooked polenta for the cornmeal topping. This packaged polenta, sold in a round tube, is often flavored with sun-dried tomatoes, garlic, or basil, all of which are compatible with the pie.

TURKEY AND BLACK BEAN PIE WITH POLENTA CRUST

1 tablespoon olive oil

1 medium onion, chopped

1 green bell pepper, seeds and ribs discarded and cut into ½-inch dice

2 garlic cloves, minced

1¼ pounds ground turkey

1 teaspoon salt

2 teaspoons chili powder

One 15- to 19-ounce can black beans, drained and rinsed

One 14½-ounce can tomatoes with jalapeños, drained

One 8-ounce can tomato sauce

1 cup thawed frozen corn kernels

One 16-ounce tube cooked polenta, plain or flavored, cut crosswise into ½-inch-thick slices

1 cup (4 ounces) shredded sharp cheddar cheese

1 Position a rack in the center of the oven and preheat the oven to 350°F.

2 Heat the oil in a large nonstick skillet over medium heat. Add the onion and bell pepper, and cook, stirring occasionally, until the vegetables soften, about 3 minutes. Add the garlic and stir until it is fragrant, about 1 minute. Add the ground turkey and cook, stirring often and breaking up the meat with a spoon, until it loses its pink color, about 8 minutes. Stir in the salt, chili powder, beans, tomatoes with jalapeños, tomato sauce, and corn. Bring to a boil over high heat. Reduce the heat to medium-low and simmer, stirring often, until slightly thickened, about 5 minutes.

3 **Transfer the turkey** mixture to a 9 × 13-inch baking dish. Arrange the polenta, slightly overlapping, on top. Sprinkle with the cheddar.

4 **Bake until the** sauce is bubbling and the cheddar has melted, about 20 minutes. Serve hot.

MAKES 6 SERVINGS

Which came first—canned mushroom soup or tuna casserole? Once you taste this version, you won't care. This is one heck of a casserole, made even better when you put in a little extra effort and use fresh ingredients. One warning: Don't try to use fresh tuna, which will dry out if baked for the required cooking time. Stay with the canned fish.

TUNA CASSEROLE WITH BOW TIES, MUSHROOMS, AND PARMESAN

Nonstick vegetable oil spray

12 ounces (about 4½ cups) bow tie pasta (also called farfalle)

5 tablespoons unsalted butter

½ cup (½-inch dice) chopped red bell pepper

10 ounces white mushrooms, sliced

3 scallions, white and green parts, chopped

⅓ cup all-purpose flour

2 cups milk

1 cup reduced-sodium chicken broth

Two 6-ounce cans albacore tuna in water, drained and flaked with a fork

¾ cup (3 ounces) freshly grated Parmesan cheese

⅛ teaspoon ground hot red (cayenne) pepper

Salt and freshly ground pepper to taste

¼ cup dried bread crumbs

1 **Position a rack** in the center of the oven and preheat the oven to 350°F. Lightly coat the inside of a 2½- to 3-quart deep baking dish with the oil spray.

2 **Bring a large pot** of lightly salted water to a boil over high heat. Add the pasta and cook until barely tender (it will cook further in the oven), about 7 minutes. Drain well. Return the pasta to the cooking pot.

3 **Meanwhile, heat the butter** in a large skillet over medium heat. Add the red pepper and cook, stirring often, until softened, about 3 minutes. Add the mushrooms and scallions, and cook, stirring often, until the mushroom juices evaporate and the mushrooms are tender, about 6 minutes. Sprinkle with the flour and stir well. Stir in the milk and broth, and bring to a boil, stirring often. Reduce the heat to medium-low and simmer until slightly thickened, about 3 minutes. Remove from the heat and stir in the tuna, ½ cup Parmesan,

and the cayenne. Stir this into the pasta mixture and season with salt and pepper.

4 **Pour the pasta** into the baking dish and sprinkle with the bread crumbs and the remaining ¼ cup Parmesan. Bake until the sauce is bubbling, 25 to 30 minutes. Let stand 5 minutes, then serve hot.

MAKES 6 SERVINGS

Should I buy water-packed tuna instead of oil-packed?

ASK ART

If you prefer tuna packed in olive oil, go for it! I like water-packed tuna because it contains fewer calories and tastes a little lighter. White albacore tuna is slightly more expensive than dark tuna and has a lighter flavor. The choice is yours. Truthfully, I buy whatever is on sale!

Instead of a long-simmered pot of chili, this is really a quick sauté of vegetables spiked with chili powder and dolled up with sour cream. Toast the tortillas in the oven while making the chili, and dinner will be on the table in no time.

QUICK VEGETABLE CHILI TOSTADOS

Nonstick vegetable oil spray

4 corn tortillas

2 tablespoons olive oil

1 medium onion, chopped

1 large zucchini, cut in half lengthwise and then crosswise into ½-inch-thick half-moons

8 ounces mushrooms, sliced

2 garlic cloves

1 tablespoon chili powder

½ cup sour cream

½ cup shredded sharp cheddar cheese

3 cups thinly shredded iceberg lettuce

⅔ cup Make-Ahead Salsa (page 92) or store-bought salsa

1 lime, cut into wedges, for serving

1 Position a rack in the center of the oven and preheat the oven to 400°F.

2 Coat both sides of the tortillas with the oil spray. Arrange the tortillas directly on the oven racks. (You can spread the tortillas on 2 baking sheets, but baking the tortillas on the oven racks is fine.) Bake until the tortillas are golden and crisp, about 10 minutes.

3 Meanwhile, heat the olive oil in a large skillet over medium heat. Add the onion and cook, stirring occasionally, until softened, about 3 minutes. Add the zucchini, mushrooms, and garlic. Cook, stirring occasionally, until the vegetables are barely tender, about 6 minutes. Sprinkle with the chili powder and stir for 15 seconds. Mix in the sour cream and cook just until heated through without boiling.

4 Place a tortilla on each of 4 dinner plates. Top with equal amounts of chili. Sprinkle each tortilla with 2 tablespoons cheddar. Add a mound of lettuce and a dollop of salsa. Serve immediately with the lime wedges.

MAKES 4 SERVINGS

Despite its low fat content, tangy flavor, and creaminess, buttermilk is too often forgotten. What a shame! This dish should help raise its profile. Here's a chance to put to work a Kitchen Workhorse you have in the freezer.

CHILI SHEPHERD'S PIE WITH BUTTERMILK POTATO TOPPING

2 pounds Yukon Gold potatoes, peeled and cut into 1-inch chunks

2 tablespoons unsalted butter

½ cup buttermilk, preferably at room temperature

Salt and freshly ground pepper to taste

1 quart Kitchen Workhorse Chunky Beef Chili (page 150), heated

1½ cups fresh or thawed frozen corn kernels

⅓ cup (about 2½ ounces) shredded sharp cheddar cheese

1 Position a rack in the center of the oven and preheat the oven to 400°F. Lightly oil an 8-inch square baking dish.

2 Place the potatoes in a medium saucepan and add enough cold, lightly salted water to cover them by 1 inch. Bring to a boil over high heat. Reduce the heat to medium and cook until the potatoes are tender, about 20 minutes.

3 Drain the potatoes and transfer to a bowl. Add the butter. Mash the potatoes with a potato masher or a handheld electric mixer on low speed, gradually adding the buttermilk as you work. Season with salt and pepper.

4 Mix the chili and corn in the baking dish. Spread the potatoes on top of the chili and sprinkle with the cheddar. Bake until the cheddar has melted and the topping is tinged with brown, 15 to 20 minutes. Serve hot.

MAKES 4 SERVINGS

Another addition to the macaroni and cheese pantheon, this one is meaty and spicy with Kitchen Workhorse Chunky Beef Chili, one of my favorites!

CHILI AND MACARONI CASSEROLE

½ pound (about 3 cups) elbow macaroni

1 quart Kitchen Workhorse Chunky Beef Chili (page 150)

1 cup (4 ounces) sharp cheddar cheese, divided

½ cup sour cream

1   **Position a rack** in the upper third of the oven and preheat the oven to 350°F. Lightly oil a 2½- to 3-quart deep baking dish.

2   **Bring a large pot** of lightly salted water to a boil over high heat. Add the macaroni and cook until it is almost tender (it will cook further in the oven), about 7 minutes. Drain well.

3   **Mix the chili,** pasta, ½ cup cheddar, and the sour cream in a bowl. Spread in the baking dish. Sprinkle with the remaining ½ cup cheddar.

4   **Bake until the** cheddar has melted and the juices are bubbling, about 30 minutes. Serve hot.

MAKES 4 TO 6 SERVINGS

FIFTEEN

ON THE SIDE

While I call this chapter On the Side, the dishes on the following pages should never be relegated to the sidelines. They are truly delicious accompaniments to main courses, but many also double as the centerpiece of a light meal. This is what I love about cooking in the twenty-first century: Anything goes.

If you feel like eating one or two of these dishes for lunch or supper, go right ahead. For instance, Kale and Tomatoes (page 262) served with Bacon-Buttermilk Corn Bread (page 258) makes a satisfying lunch. Green Beans with Turkey Sausage (page 260) spooned over hot white or brown rice is a lovely, easy supper, and Portobello Caps with White Bean–Pesto Puree (page 266) would be superb as a light weekend lunch.

I like big, bold flavors, and this penchant doesn't stop with main courses. In these recipes you will find garlic, hot chilies, Thai chili sauce, toasted nuts, freshly grated Parmesan cheese, and other flavor boosters that make these side dishes the opposite of shy and retiring. I use buttermilk in a fair number of recipes because I just love the tangy flavor it imparts as well as how its natural consistency never thins out purees the way low-fat milk can. One word of caution: Don't let buttermilk boil, or it will curdle. It's an awesome secret ingredient that I use in mashes, purees, sauces, and baking—and it's naturally low in fat!

Mashes have to be one of my favorite foods. They are so reassuring and can be happily dressed up or down with other ingredients such as peas, cheese, bacon, and garlic. When you add liquids, be sure to warm them up a little. This can be done in the microwave or a saucepan; the point is to add heated milk or stock so that the potatoes or other mashed veggies don't cool down.

Your kitchen life will be richer and fuller if you start planning dishes to serve alongside the main course rather than depend on that package of frozen peas or corn to do the job. From time to time, convenience items such as these are the ticket, but for other times try your hand at some very easy yet interesting sides. Your family will love them!

recipes

Roasted Asparagus with Lemon Zest and Black Pepper

Roasted Beets with Walnuts

Sesame Bok Choy with Balsamic Vinegar

Baby Carrots with Orange Glaze

Corn Pudding

Bacon Corn Bread and Pecan Dressing

Bacon-Buttermilk Corn Bread

VERY EASY LUNCH
Roast Chicken Waldorf Salad with Pecans and Rosemary *(page 123)*

EATING LIGHT?
Salmon Steaks with Citrus Couscous Salad *(page 128)*

QUICK BEEF DINNER
Steak Hoisin with Stir-fried Broccoli Slaw *(page 142)*

FEWER THAN 7 INGREDIENTS

Roast Pork Tenderloin with Asian Glaze *(page 154)*

PERFECT POULTRY
Chicken Breasts with Yukon Gold Potatoes, Spinach, and Fontina Gratin *(page 182)*

FAST, FANTASTIC FISH
The Best Fish Tacos *(page 204)*

KITCHEN WORKHORSE SPIN-OFF
Soba Noodles in Miso Broth with Roast Pork and Vegetables *(page 228)*

SWEET TOOTH

Mashed Cauliflower and Parsnips

Green Beans with Turkey Sausage

Kale with Tomatoes

Two-Potato Mash

"Polka-Dot" Mashed Potatoes with Peas

Portobello Caps with White Bean–Pesto Puree

Corn and Rice Pilaf

Basmati Rice and Vermicelli

Spicy Garlic Spinach

Creamy Parmesan Spinach

Zesty Roasted Vegetables

Old habits are hard to break. For years there was only one way to cook asparagus—boiling. Now cooks regularly roast and grill these tender spears. Roasting, in particular, releases the vegetable's lovely sweetness. Large asparagus are best for roasting and grilling because it is easier to gauge their doneness (and if you grill them, they won't fall through the grill rack!). If you use slender, pencil-thin asparagus, simply reduce the roasting time accordingly. And break the boiling habit!

ROASTED ASPARAGUS WITH LEMON ZEST AND BLACK PEPPER

2 pounds plump fresh asparagus, tough ends snapped off

2 tablespoons extra-virgin olive oil

Salt and coarsely cracked black pepper to taste

1 large lemon

1 **Position a rack** in the top third of the oven and preheat the oven to 400°F. Lightly oil a large rimmed baking sheet.

2 **Spread the asparagus** in a single layer on the baking sheet. Drizzle the asparagus with oil and roll the asparagus on the baking sheet to coat. Season with salt and cracked pepper.

3 **Bake until the** asparagus spears are lightly browned and barely tender, about 15 minutes. Transfer to a serving platter and grate the lemon zest over the asparagus. Squeeze the lemon juice into a wire sieve over a small bowl to strain out the seeds. Drizzle the lemon juice over the asparagus. Serve hot.

MAKES 6 SERVINGS

Roasted beets, a fine accompaniment to many grilled or roasted meat or poultry dishes, are rich. Sometimes just a few forkfuls will suffice. Regardless, roast the entire batch suggested in this recipe because extras can be refrigerated for a few days and are dynamite in salads.

ROASTED BEETS WITH WALNUTS

6 medium beets, scrubbed but unpeeled

⅓ cup walnuts, toasted (see below) and chopped

1 tablespoon extra-virgin olive oil

1 tablespoon balsamic vinegar

Salt and freshly ground pepper to taste

1 **Position a rack** in the center of the oven and preheat the oven to 400°F.

2 **Wrap each beet** separately in aluminum foil. Place on a baking sheet and bake until the beets feel somewhat tender when squeezed, about 1¼ hours.

3 **Unwrap the beets.** To peel, working one at a time, impale a hot beet at the stem end on a fork. Using a small knife, pare off the skin and then cut the beet into ½-inch-thick rounds. Transfer the beets to a serving bowl. Add the walnuts, oil, and vinegar, and mix gently. Season with salt and pepper. Serve hot.

MAKES 6 SERVINGS

Why do I have to toast nuts? So many recipes call for them, but I am not sure it's worth the effort.

ASK ART

It does seem a little fussy, but believe me, the flavor is well worth the extra effort. As they toast, the oils in the nuts release all their good flavor, and the nuts taste full and delicious. It's really not hard: Spread the nuts in a single layer in a small baking dish and put them in a preheated 350°F oven for 5 to 8 minutes, until the nuts are noticeably fragrant and have darkened slightly in color. Stir them once during toasting. When they are done, slide them onto a plate to cool (this will stop the cooking) or use them right away. Roasted nuts are the same as toasted nuts.

While bok choy is an Asian vegetable, its mild flavor takes well to many different seasonings. Sesame, balsamic vinegar, olive oil, and garlic all play a part here, while there's not a drop of soy sauce!

SESAME BOK CHOY WITH BALSAMIC VINEGAR

1 head bok choy (about 1¾ pounds)

1 tablespoon sesame seeds

1 tablespoon extra-virgin olive oil

1 garlic clove, finely chopped

1 tablespoon balsamic vinegar

Salt and freshly ground pepper to taste

1 Cut the thick bok choy stems crosswise into ½-inch-wide strips, discarding any hard core pieces. Rinse well in cold water and drain. Cut the leaves crosswise into ½-inch strips. Rinse and drain the leaves and set aside separately from the stems.

2 Heat a large skillet over high heat. Add the sesame seeds and cook, stirring often, until the seeds are toasted, about 1 minute. Transfer to a plate and set aside.

3 Heat the oil and garlic together in the skillet over medium-high heat just until the garlic softens, about 30 seconds. Add the bok choy stems and cook, stirring often, until the stems are crisp-tender, about 5 minutes. Stir in the leaves and cook until wilted, about 2 minutes. Stir in the vinegar and sesame seeds, and season with salt and pepper. Serve hot, using a slotted spoon.

MAKES 4 SERVINGS

Packaged baby-cut carrots are one of the quickest shortcuts around for an easy side dish. Cooked with orange juice and zest and a smidgen of butter and honey, they end up crisp-tender with a sweet-tart glaze. If you like tender carrots, cook them in lightly salted boiling water for 3 minutes and drain before adding them to the skillet. And if you wish, add a teaspoon or so of chopped fresh herbs near the end of cooking—sage, rosemary, or tarragon would go nicely with the orange flavor.

BABY CARROTS WITH ORANGE GLAZE

2 juice oranges

1 pound baby-cut carrots

2 tablespoons unsalted butter

2 tablespoons honey

Salt and freshly ground pepper to taste

1 Grate the zest from 1 orange. Squeeze the juice from both oranges; you should have ¾ cup.

2 Spread the carrots in a single layer in a medium skillet. Add the orange zest and juice, butter, and honey, and bring to a boil over medium-high heat. Partially cover the skillet. Cook, stirring often, until the liquid has evaporated into a glaze and the carrots are almost tender, about 10 minutes. Season with salt and pepper. Serve hot.

MAKES 4 TO 6 SERVINGS

Corn pudding is comfort food and a side dish in one warming, creamy package. I have created a reduced-fat version by making it with 2% milk instead of the cream found in many other versions. Spice it up with a chopped jalapeño (sauté it with the onion mixture) or substitute shredded sharp cheddar cheese for the Parmesan.

CORN PUDDING

3 tablespoons unsalted butter

¼ cup finely chopped onion

¼ cup finely chopped red or green bell pepper

3 cups fresh or thawed frozen corn kernels

2¼ cups 2% fat milk

3 large eggs

½ teaspoon salt

½ cup (2 ounces) freshly grated Parmesan cheese

1 **Position a rack** in the center of the oven and preheat the oven to 325°F. Butter an 8 × 8-inch (2-quart) glass or ceramic baking dish.

2 **Melt the butter** in a medium saucepan over medium heat. Add the onion and bell pepper and cook, stirring often, until the vegetables are tender, about 5 minutes. Add the corn and cook until heated through, about 2 minutes. Add the milk and bring to a simmer.

3 **Whisk the eggs** and salt in a medium bowl. Gradually whisk the hot milk and corn mixture into the eggs and then stir in the Parmesan. Pour into the baking dish.

4 **Bake until a** knife inserted 1 inch from the center of the pudding comes out clean (the center won't be quite set), about 30 minutes. Let stand for 5 minutes. Serve hot.

MAKES 6 SERVINGS

What is the difference between 1% and 2% milk?

ASK ART

About 20 calories and 2.5 grams of fat! Think of it this way: If you are trying to cut calories and fat, drink skim milk or 1%. If you prefer a milk that is a little creamier than low-fat milk but lighter than whole milk, go for 2%. A cup of whole milk has about 150 calories and 8 grams of fat; 2% has about 120 calories and 5 grams of fat; 1% has about 100 calories and 2.5 grams of fat; nonfat (skim) milk has about 85 calories and .5 gram of fat.

Where I come from, stuffing is called dressing even though they are actually the same thing. It's the ultimate side dish for turkey and works wonders alongside chicken or pork, too. While slightly stale corn bread works best because it soaks up the broth without turning the dressing soggy, I don't recommend leaving this bread at room temperature for very long because of the bacon. Instead, take a few minutes to toast the corn bread in the oven to dry it out.

BACON CORN BREAD AND PECAN DRESSING

4 tablespoons unsalted butter

1 medium onion, chopped

2 celery ribs with leaves, chopped

1 cup pecans, toasted (see page 251) and coarsely chopped

2 teaspoons chopped fresh sage, or 1 teaspoon dried sage

2 teaspoons chopped fresh rosemary, or 1 teaspoon crumbled dried rosemary

1 batch Bacon-Buttermilk Corn Bread (page 258), crumbled and toasted (see Note)

1½ cups reduced-sodium chicken broth, as needed

Salt and freshly ground pepper to taste

1 **Position a rack** in the center of the oven and preheat the oven to 350°F. Lightly butter a 13 × 9-inch baking dish.

2 **Melt the butter** in a large skillet over medium heat. Add the onion and celery, and cook, stirring often, until the vegetables are tender, about 10 minutes. Stir in the pecans, sage, and rosemary. Transfer to a large bowl and add the corn bread. Stir in enough broth to moisten the dressing as desired. Some people like moist dressing; some prefer it firmer. Season with salt and pepper. Spread in the baking dish and cover with buttered aluminum foil, buttered side down.

3 **Bake until the** stuffing is heated through, about 40 minutes. If you like dressing with a crisp top, remove the foil during the last 20 minutes of baking. Serve hot.

MAKES 8 TO 10 SERVINGS

NOTE: To toast the corn bread, position a rack in the center of the oven and preheat the oven to 400°F. Spread the crumbled corn bread on a large rimmed baking sheet. Bake, stirring occasionally, until the edges of the corn bread feel dry, about 15 minutes. Remove from the oven and cool completely; the corn bread will become crisper.

ot, piping corn bread is one of my favorite accompaniments to almost any main course, especially stews and chilies. Don't forget, I was raised in the South where hot breads are part of everyday life, and this corn bread, packed with bacon and made with buttermilk, does the tradition proud. Shake the buttermilk well before using, and if you prefer, substitute ¾ cup of plain low-fat yogurt whisked with ¼ cup of milk (whole, skim, or in between) for the buttermilk. Use this for Bacon Corn Bread and Pecan Dressing (page 256) and serve it with the Kitchen Workhorse Smoked Turkey Breast with Cranberry Mustard (page 194).

BACON-BUTTERMILK CORN BREAD

4 slices bacon

1 tablespoon vegetable oil, as needed

⅔ cup yellow cornmeal, preferably stone-ground

⅔ cup all-purpose flour

1 tablespoon sugar

½ teaspoon baking soda

½ teaspoon salt

1 cup well-shaken buttermilk

1 large egg, beaten

1 Position a rack in the center of the oven and preheat the oven to 400°F.

2 Place the bacon in a large skillet. Cook over medium heat, turning once, until crisp and browned, about 8 minutes. Transfer the bacon to paper towels. Cool and coarsely chop the bacon. Measure the bacon fat and add enough oil to make ¼ cup.

3 Pour 2 tablespoons bacon fat into an 8 × 8-inch baking pan. Bake until the fat is very hot, about 2 minutes.

4 Whisk the cornmeal, flour, sugar, baking soda, and salt in a medium bowl. Make a well in the center and add the buttermilk, egg, and remaining 2 tablespoons bacon fat. Stir just until the batter is barely smooth—a few lumps can remain. Quickly stir in the bacon. Do not overmix. Spread in the hot baking dish.

5 Bake until the top of the corn bread springs back when pressed in the center, about 20 minutes. Cool for 5 minutes. Cut into squares and serve hot.

MAKES 9 SERVINGS

When you want a comforting side dish that is not high in carbohydrates, try this mash of cauliflower and parsnips simmered in milk. As you will see when you read through the recipe, you won't use all the milk, but don't throw it out—stir it into any leftover puree to make a quick cream of vegetable soup for lunch the next day. For tangier flavor, mash the vegetables with about 1/2 cup of plain yogurt instead of the cooking liquid. Or use finely shredded sharp cheddar cheese instead of Parmesan.

MASHED CAULIFLOWER AND PARSNIPS

2 cups regular or 2% milk

3 medium parsnips, peeled and cut into 2-inch chunks

4 garlic cloves, crushed under a knife and peeled

1 cauliflower (about 2 pounds), cut into florets

1/2 cup (2 ounces) freshly grated Parmesan cheese

Salt and freshly ground pepper to taste

2 tablespoons finely chopped chives or scallion greens

1 Combine the milk, parsnips, and garlic in a large saucepan. Cover and bring to a boil over medium heat. Add the cauliflower (it will not be submerged in the milk) and season lightly with salt. Cover and cook until the vegetables are very tender, about 25 minutes. Drain the vegetables in a colander, reserving the milk. Return the vegetables to the saucepan.

2 Using a potato masher or handheld electric mixer, mash the vegetables, adding enough of the reserved milk as needed to reach your desired consistency. Stir in the Parmesan. Season with salt and pepper. Cool and refrigerate the extra milk for another use (see my suggestion in the headnote).

3 Transfer to a serving bowl and sprinkle with the chives. Serve hot.

MAKES 4 TO 6 SERVINGS

Asian cooks have long employed a trick to flavor green vegetables: They add a small amount of meat to the dish. With this in mind, a little turkey sausage goes a long way to flavor a pound of green beans cooked with Eastern flair. If you like spicy food, add a finely chopped jalapeño when you sauté the garlic. This is good enough for a light supper, served over white or brown rice— or serve it as a side dish with plainly cooked chicken or turkey.

GREEN BEANS WITH TURKEY SAUSAGE

1 pound green beans, trimmed and cut into 1½-inch lengths

1 tablespoon vegetable oil

1 medium onion, chopped

1 garlic clove, finely chopped

1 hot or mild turkey sausage (about 2½ ounces), casing discarded

1 ripe plum (Roma) tomato, seeded and cut into ½-inch dice

1 tablespoon Thai sweet chili sauce, or more to taste

Salt to taste

1 **Bring 3 cups** lightly salted water to a boil in a large skillet over high heat. Add the green beans and cook, stirring often, until they are crisp-tender, about 3 minutes. Drain and rinse under cold water. Set aside.

2 **Heat the oil** in the skillet over medium-high heat. Add the onion and cook, stirring often, until it softens, about 3 minutes. Add the garlic and stir until it gives off its aroma, about 30 seconds. Add the turkey sausage and cook until it is cooked through, about 6 minutes; stir occasionally to break up the sausage with the side of a spoon.

3 **Add the tomato** and 2 tablespoons water. Add the green beans and cook, stirring often, until they are heated through, about 3 minutes. Stir in the chili sauce and season with salt. Serve hot.

MAKES 4 TO 6 SERVINGS

ASK ART

When a recipe calls for Thai chili sauce, what should I buy?

Look for Thai chili sauces in the Asian section of the supermarket. It is sold in glass jars, and the orange sauce is a mix of sweet and spicy. The Chinese also market chili sauces with varying degrees of heat. All contain some mixture of chili peppers, salt, and oil. They usually have garlic, too, and may contain ginger, soybeans, or black beans. Once opened, either sauce should be stored in the refrigerator.

A southern favorite, kale and pork love each other. This dish goes well with the Kitchen Workhorse Roast Pork Loin with Sweet Potatoes and Apples (page 158) and Barbecued Orange-Maple Country Ribs (page 162). Some supermarkets now carry washed, stemmed, and chopped kale in a bag, which is a real time-saver.

KALE WITH TOMATOES

1¾ pounds dark kale

Salt

2 tablespoons extra-virgin olive oil

1 small onion, chopped

2 garlic cloves, finely chopped

¼ teaspoon red pepper flakes

One 14½-ounce can diced tomatoes in juice

1 **Fill a sink** with lukewarm water. Wash the kale well in the sink. Lift the kale from the sink and transfer to a cutting board. Strip the leaves from the stems. Coarsely chop the stems. Stack the leaves and cut crosswise into ½-inch-wide strips.

2 **Heat a large** pot of lightly salted water over high heat. Add the kale stems, return to a boil, and cook for 5 minutes. Add the leaves and return to a boil. Cook until the stems are barely tender, about 3 minutes more. Drain well. Squeeze the kale slightly to remove excess water.

3 **Heat the oil** in a large saucepan over medium heat. Add the onion and cook, stirring often, until softened, about 3 minutes. Add the garlic and red pepper, and cook until the garlic is fragrant, about 1 minute. Add the tomatoes with their juice and bring to a boil. Cook until the tomato juice has reduced by half, about 3 minutes.

4 **Add the kale** and cook, stirring often, until it is heated through, about 3 minutes. Season with salt. Serve hot.

MAKES 6 SERVINGS

Mashed yams sound like a good idea, but they quickly turn cloying. Adding Yukon Gold potatoes improves their color, flavor, and texture. Orange-fleshed yams are called sweet potatoes in some parts of the country, which is incorrect nomenclature. Just make sure you don't buy the other kind of sweet potatoes, which are drier and have yellow flesh.

TWO-POTATO MASH

1½ pounds orange-fleshed yams, such as Louisiana, garnet, or Jewel, peeled and cut into 2-inch chunks

1½ pounds Yukon Gold potatoes, peeled and cut into 2-inch chunks

2 tablespoons unsalted butter

½ cup well-shaken buttermilk, microwaved on high for about 20 seconds to lose its chill, as needed

Salt and freshly ground pepper to taste

1 **Place the yams** and potatoes in a large saucepan and cover with lightly salted cold water to cover. Cover the pot and bring to a boil over high heat. Reduce the heat to medium and cook until the potatoes are tender, about 25 minutes. Drain and return to the pot.

2 **Add the butter** to the pot. Using a potato masher or handheld electric mixer, mash the vegetables, adding enough buttermilk to reach the desired consistency. Season with salt and pepper. Transfer to a serving bowl. Serve hot.

MAKES 4 TO 6 SERVINGS

There are lots of little touches here (garlic, buttermilk, and Parmesan cheese, not to mention the peas) that add flavor and interest to standard mashed potatoes. This may become a way to get kids to eat their peas! To prevent the potatoes from cooling, heat the buttermilk in the microwave so that it isn't ice cold when you add it.

"POLKA-DOT" MASHED POTATOES WITH PEAS

2 pounds Yukon Gold potatoes, peeled and cut into 2-inch chunks

2 large garlic cloves

One 10-ounce box frozen petite green peas, thawed

2 tablespoons unsalted butter

½ cup well-shaken buttermilk, microwaved on high for about 20 seconds to lose its chill, as needed

½ cup (2 ounces) freshly grated Parmesan cheese

2 tablespoons finely chopped fresh chives, mint, or scallion greens

Salt and freshly ground pepper to taste

1 **Place the potatoes** and garlic in a large saucepan and add enough lightly salted water to cover the potatoes by 1 inch. Bring to a boil over high heat. Cook, partially covered, until tender, about 25 minutes. During the last minute or so, add the peas. Drain well and return to the pot.

2 **Add the butter** to the pot. Using a potato masher or handheld electric mixer, mash the vegetables, adding enough buttermilk to reach the desired consistency. Stir in the Parmesan and chives. Season with salt and pepper. Transfer to a serving bowl. Serve hot.

MAKES 4 TO 6 SERVINGS

How do I thaw frozen vegetables quickly?

ASK ART

There are several easy ways to defrost frozen vegetables without letting them stand at room temperature for hours. You can put them in a wire sieve and rinse them under running lukewarm water for a few minutes until the ice has melted and the vegetables can be separated. Or you can put the vegetables in a bowl of hot water and let them stand for 10 minutes or so, then drain. You can also microwave the vegetables for a few minutes on high in a covered microwave-safe bowl (add a tablespoon of water).

Can I mash potatoes in a food processor?

No. Use a blender, fork, or old-fashioned potato masher. The force of the blade in a food processor turns mashed potatoes gluey and unappealing.

wo earthy-flavored ingredients, portobello mushrooms and white beans, come together in this dramatic side dish. Make these about an hour before serving and then pop them into a hot oven to warm through. The size of the mushroom caps is essential. Look for medium-to-large caps about 4 inches across. Luckily, this is what most packaged portobello caps measure, which makes shopping easy. If you buy whole mushrooms, cut off and save the stems for another use (great flavoring for soups and stews). Scrape out the brown-black gills to make room for the bean puree and also to reduce the amount of exuded dark juices. Serve these alongside grilled pork chops or steaks.

PORTOBELLO CAPS WITH WHITE BEAN–PESTO PUREE

6 portobello mushroom caps, each about 4 inches across

4 tablespoons extra-virgin olive oil, divided

Salt and freshly ground pepper to taste

½ cup finely chopped onion

1 garlic clove, minced

One 15- to 19-ounce can white kidney (cannellini) beans, drained and rinsed

1 tablespoon Kitchen Workhorse Pesto (page 226) or store-bought pesto

¼ cup freshly grated Parmesan cheese

1   **Position a rack** in the top third of the oven and preheat the oven to 400°F. Lightly oil a baking sheet.

2   **Using a dessert** spoon, scrape out and discard the dark gills from the underside of each mushroom cap, taking care not to break the cap. Place the caps on the baking sheet. Brush the caps all over with 2 tablespoons oil. Season with salt and pepper. Bake until the caps are barely tender, about 7 minutes. Remove the baking sheet with the caps from the oven. (The caps can be prepared up to 2 hours ahead and stored at room temperature.)

3   **Meanwhile, heat 1 tablespoon oil** in a medium saucepan over medium heat. Add the onion and cook, stirring often, until the onion is golden, about 6 minutes. Add the garlic and cook until fragrant, about 1 minute. Add the beans and ½ cup water. Bring to a boil over high heat. Cook, stirring often,

until the water has almost completely evaporated, about 6 minutes. Transfer the beans to a food processor and puree. Add the pesto and pulse until combined. Season with salt and pepper. Fill the mushroom caps with the bean puree. (The mushrooms can be filled 1 hour before serving and stored at room temperature.)

4 Sprinkle the tops of the mushrooms with the Parmesan. Drizzle with the remaining 1 tablespoon oil. Bake until the Parmesan has melted, about 10 minutes. Serve hot.

MAKES 6 SERVINGS

It's a simple matter to prepare a pot of rice, and with the tiniest bit of extra effort, you can turn that familiar dish into something special. Here's a chance to use that frozen corn in the freezer. I told you it would come in handy! If you have extra, reheat the pilaf in a little oil in a nonstick skillet. No one ever said that "fried rice" had to be Chinese.

CORN AND RICE PILAF

1 tablespoon olive oil

1 small onion, chopped

1 garlic clove, finely chopped

1 teaspoon cumin seed

1½ cups long-grain rice

1½ cups canned low-sodium chicken broth

½ teaspoon salt

1 cup frozen corn, rinsed under warm water to defrost and drained

1 tablespoon chopped fresh cilantro, optional

1   **Heat the oil** in a medium saucepan over medium heat. Add the onion and cook, stirring often, until softened, about 3 minutes. Add the garlic and cumin, and stir until the garlic is fragrant, about 30 seconds. Add the rice and stir well.

2   **Add the broth,** 1½ cups water, and the salt. Bring to a boil over high heat. Reduce the heat to medium-low and cover tightly. Simmer, without stirring, until the rice is tender and has absorbed the liquid, about 18 minutes. During the last minute or so of cooking, add the corn (do not stir it in). Remove from the heat and let stand for 5 minutes.

3   **Add the cilantro,** if using, and fluff the rice with a fork, stirring in the corn and cilantro at the same time. Serve hot.

MAKES 6 SERVINGS

Cooking rice by first sautéing it in oil with some chopped onions turns it into something special but takes very little effort. You could omit the broken pasta to eliminate a step, but I like it for added texture and color. And kids think it's fun to find pasta in their rice! Basmati is an aromatic long-grain rice that we associate with Indian cooking, but it is now grown in the United States and is not hard to find. You don't have to use it, but once you start, it surely will become a regular in your pantry.

BASMATI RICE AND VERMICELLI

2 tablespoons olive oil, divided

½ cup (1-inch lengths) broken vermicelli pasta

½ small onion, chopped

¾ cup basmati rice

2 cups reduced-sodium chicken broth

½ teaspoon salt

1 Heat 1 tablespoon oil in a medium saucepan over medium heat. Add the vermicelli and cook, stirring almost constantly, until the vermicelli is golden brown, about 1 minute. Don't worry if a few strands remain untoasted. Drain in a wire sieve.

2 Heat the remaining 1 tablespoon oil in the saucepan over medium heat. Add the onion and cook until the onion is softened, about 3 minutes. Add the rice and cook, stirring often, until the most of the rice has turned chalky white, about 2 minutes. Stir in the broth, reserved pasta, and salt, and bring to a boil. Cover and reduce the heat to medium-low. Cook until the liquid is absorbed and the rice is tender, about 18 minutes.

3 Remove from the heat and let stand for 5 minutes. Fluff the rice with a fork and serve hot.

MAKES 4 TO 6 SERVINGS

BASMATI RICE AND VERMICELLI WITH PEAS: When the rice is cooked, add ¾ cup thawed frozen baby peas to the saucepan but do not stir. Remove from the heat and let stand 5 minutes. Fluff the rice with a fork and serve hot.

Spinach travels to Asia in this quick sauté! And it's a delicious trip. If you don't have chili sauce with garlic, which is sold in Asian markets and the Asian section of the supermarket, use an additional garlic clove and spike the spinach with crushed hot red peppers. Heat the garlic along with the oil for even more garlic flavor and to reduce the chance that the garlic will burn when it hits the hot oil in the skillet.

SPICY GARLIC SPINACH

1 tablespoon vegetable oil

1 garlic clove, thinly sliced

Two 10-ounce bags baby spinach, rinsed but not dried

1 tablespoon Chinese chili sauce with garlic

Salt to taste

1 **Combine the oil** and garlic in a large skillet and cook over medium heat until the garlic is softened, about 3 minutes.

2 **Add the spinach** to the skillet, one handful at a time, stirring until the batch is wilted before adding the next handful. Cook until the spinach is tender, about 5 minutes. Stir in the chili sauce. Season with salt and serve hot.

MAKES 4 SERVINGS

R emember creamed spinach? When I was a child, we thought it a great treat in restaurants. This recipe brings back many fond memories and makes the reality so much better! It takes only about ten minutes to cook fresh spinach (it takes that long to thaw and cook frozen spinach), and when you stir it with a simple cream and cheese sauce, it's luscious.

CREAMY PARMESAN SPINACH

Two 10-ounce bags spinach, stems removed

1 tablespoon unsalted butter

1 tablespoon all-purpose flour

1 cup regular or nonfat half-and-half, warmed

1/8 teaspoon freshly grated nutmeg

1/2 cup (2 ounces) freshly grated Parmesan cheese

Salt and freshly ground pepper to taste

1 Wash the spinach well in a large sink of lukewarm water. Lift the spinach leaves out of the sink (do not spin dry) and transfer to a large bowl.

2 Place about half of the spinach and any water clinging to the leaves in a large saucepan. Cover and cook over medium-high heat, stirring often, until the spinach wilts, about 5 minutes. Stir in the remaining spinach and cook until all the spinach is wilted and tender, about 5 minutes more. Drain in a colander and rinse under cold water.

3 Squeeze the excess water from the spinach, one handful at a time, and set the spinach aside.

4 Melt the butter in a medium saucepan over medium-low heat. Whisk in the flour and let bubble without browning for 1 minute. Whisk in the half-and-half and bring to a simmer over medium heat. Cook just until slightly thickened and no raw flour flavor remains, about 3 minutes. Stir in the spinach and nutmeg, and cook until the spinach is heated through, about 3 minutes. Stir in the Parmesan. Season with salt and pepper. Serve hot.

MAKES 4 TO 6 SERVINGS

If you aren't in the habit of roasting vegetables, you're missing out on one of the easiest and tastiest ways to cook them. The time in the oven allows the vegetables to caramelize just a little; this means their natural sugars develop, so they are exceptionally flavorful. I boost the flavor here with a few tablespoons of salad dressing mix, which eliminates the need for seasoning them with salt and pepper. So handy!

ZESTY ROASTED VEGETABLES

1 small eggplant, cut into 1-inch chunks

1 teaspoon salt

4 large red-skinned potatoes, scrubbed but unpeeled and cut into 1-inch chunks

3 tablespoons extra-virgin olive oil, divided

One 0.7-ounce envelope salad dressing mix, such as Good Seasons

2 medium zucchini, scrubbed but unpeeled and cut into 1-inch chunks

1 medium red onion, unpeeled and cut into 6 wedges

1 **Position a rack** in the top third of the oven and preheat the oven to 425°F. Lightly oil a large rimmed baking sheet, preferably a 17 × 13-inch half-sheet pan.

2 **Toss the eggplant** and salt together in a colander and let stand for 30 minutes to drain off excess bitter juices. (This is about the time it will take to preheat the oven and begin roasting the potatoes.) Rinse the eggplant well and pat dry with paper towels.

3 **Put the potatoes,** 1 tablespoon oil, and 1 tablespoon salad dressing mix in a large bowl and toss until the potatoes are coated. Spread on the baking sheet and roast for 10 minutes.

4 **Put the eggplant,** zucchini, red onion, and the remaining 2 tablespoons oil and 1 tablespoon salad dressing mix in the bowl and toss until the vegetables are coated. Add to the potatoes, mix as well as you can, and spread them out. Roast until the vegetables are tender, about 40 minutes. Serve hot.

MAKES 6 TO 8 SERVINGS

SIXTEEN

OUTRAGEOUS DESSERTS

There's always room for dessert in my house! I was raised in the South where we treasure our baked goods, so I never feel a meal is really complete without a sweet ending. I assembled some of my favorite, good, old-fashioned desserts for this chapter, and in keeping with the rest of the recipes in the book, they are all downright easy.

You can never have too many recipes for brownies, blondies, and cookies, and the ones here will be surefire hits with your family. The cookies fall into the category of cookie jar cookies—easy to make and nothing fussy about them. But this doesn't mean you should store them in a ceramic cookie jar. They'll stay fresher if stored in a rigid plastic container with a tight-fitting lid.

Despite my southern heritage, I don't offer recipes for pies except for a remarkably easy Frozen Key Lime Pie (page 292). Instead, I include warm, fruit-filled, deep-dish puddings, ultimate comfort foods that some of you may call cobblers or crisps.

You won't find recipes for layer cakes, as you found in *Back to the Table,* my first book. Try the cupcakes instead; they are far easier to decorate and just as celebratory. Kids love them for birthdays. The four cupcakes I offer here are as different from each other as cupcakes can be, and I love them all. If I had to choose, my favorite would be the Coconut Cupcakes with Fluffy White Frosting (page 284) because they remind me of the coconut cakes that played such a starring role during my north Florida childhood.

At the end of the chapter are three recipes for very simple sauces. Use these to dress up ice cream, frozen yogurt, sliced fruit, brownies, or pound cake. I always have one or two of these in the refrigerator.

I believe dessert should be the stuff of memories. If you take the time to make these easy, straightforward desserts every now and then, your family will thank you and your kitchen life will be ever so sweet!

recipes

Apple-Cranberry Pudding

Baked "Risotto" Pudding

Baked Berry Pudding

Chocolate Custards

Carrot Cupcakes with Cream Cheese Frosting

Chocolate Pecan Tassies

Chocolate and White Chocolate Chunk Brownies

Coconut Cupcakes with Fluffy White Frosting

Devil's Food Cupcakes with Chocolate Fudge Frosting

Vanilla Tea Cookies

Lemon Bars

Frozen Key Lime Pie

Gingersnaps

Peanut Butter Cookie Sandwiches

Chocolate and Pine Nut Biscotti

Oatmeal and Dried Cherry Cookies

Butterscotch Blondies

Banana–Peanut Butter Cupcakes with Peanut Butter Frosting

Easy Granola Bars

Homemade Fruit Sauce

Coconut Caramel Sauce

Chocolate Sauce

This warm apple dessert is a fine way to use up extra cranberry sauce from holiday dinners. Try making it with sliced Comice or Anjou pears, too, instead of apples—or mix the two fruits. With the topping this will remind you of a cobbler.

APPLE-CRANBERRY PUDDING

1¼ cups all-purpose flour

1 teaspoon baking powder

⅛ teaspoon salt

6 Golden Delicious apples, peeled, cored, and sliced

1 cup whole cranberry sauce

½ teaspoon ground cinnamon

⅔ cup granulated sugar, divided

5 tablespoons (½ stick plus 1 tablespoon) unsalted butter, at room temperature

1 large egg, beaten

⅓ cup whole milk

½ teaspoon vanilla extract

Vanilla ice cream for serving

1 **Position a rack** in the center of the oven and preheat the oven to 350°F. Lightly butter an 8 × 8-inch glass or ceramic baking dish.

2 **Whisk the flour,** baking powder, and salt together. Set aside.

3 **Mix the apples,** cranberry sauce, cinnamon, and ⅓ cup sugar in a medium bowl and spread in the baking dish.

4 **Beat the butter** and remaining ⅓ cup sugar in a medium bowl with an electric mixer on high speed until light and fluffy, about 2 minutes. Beat in the egg. Gradually stir in the flour and then the milk and vanilla to make a thick batter. Using a rubber spatula, spread the batter over the apples.

5 **Place the baking dish** on a baking sheet or aluminum foil to catch any juices. Bake until the apple juices are bubbling and the topping springs back when pressed in the center, about 40 minutes. Serve warm with vanilla ice cream.

MAKES 4 TO 6 SERVINGS

Personalize this old-fashioned treat with your favorite dried fruit. Raisins may be classic, but dried cherries, cranberries, or blueberries are all wonderful, too. Medium-grain rice (such as arborio or other varieties used for risotto) makes an especially creamy pudding, so use it if you have some in the pantry. Otherwise, use long-grain rice, which isn't as starchy but still makes a very good dessert.

BAKED "RISOTTO" PUDDING

½ cup rice for risotto, such as arborio, or long-grain rice

2 cups whole milk

⅔ cup half-and-half

⅔ cup granulated sugar

¼ teaspoon freshly grated nutmeg or ground nutmeg

2 large eggs plus 2 large egg yolks, beaten together

½ cup dark or golden raisins

1 teaspoon vanilla extract

Ground cinnamon for garnish

1 **Position a rack** in the center of the oven and preheat the oven to 300°F.

2 **Place the rice** and milk in a small saucepan. Bring to a boil over medium heat, stirring often and being careful not to let the milk boil over. Reduce the heat to low and cover the pan. Cook, stirring occasionally to avoid scorching, until the rice is tender and the milk has been absorbed, about 20 minutes.

3 **Transfer to a medium bowl.** Mix in the half-and-half, sugar, and nutmeg. Gradually stir in the beaten eggs. Mix in the raisins and vanilla. Spread in an unbuttered 8 × 8-inch glass or ceramic baking dish.

4 **Bake until the blade** of a dinner knife inserted about 2 inches from the edge of the dish comes out clean, about 45 minutes. Cool until the custard is warm. If you prefer chilled custard or are not ready to serve it, cool the custard to room temperature, cover, and refrigerate until chilled or up to 2 days.

5 **Just before serving,** sprinkle the top of the custard with cinnamon. Serve warm or chilled.

MAKES 4 TO 6 SERVINGS

New Englanders will recognize this as a "buckle"—ripe berries covered with a cake batter and baked until the berries are juicy and the cake sets. You can use any berry in season or even frozen berries. If you wish, serve this with whipped cream, ice cream, or yogurt and more berries, but this is good enough to stand on its own.

BAKED BERRY PUDDING

1¼ pounds fresh or thawed frozen blackberries, blueberries, or raspberries

⅓ cup granulated sugar

1 cup all-purpose flour

½ teaspoon baking soda

⅛ teaspoon salt

⅓ cup packed light brown sugar

1 large egg, at room temperature

5 tablespoons (½ stick plus 1 tablespoon) unsalted butter, melted

½ cup whole milk

1 teaspoon vanilla extract

1 **Preheat the oven** to 350°F. Lightly butter a 2½-quart round baking dish.

2 **Mix the berries** and granulated sugar in the baking dish.

3 **Sift the flour,** baking soda, and salt together and set aside.

4 **Beat the brown sugar** and egg in a medium bowl with an electric mixer on high speed until the mixture is thick and the sugar dissolves, about 2 minutes. On low speed, mix in the melted butter, flour, milk, and vanilla. Spread the batter over the fruit with a rubber spatula.

5 **Bake until the berry juices** are bubbling and the topping springs back when pressed in the center, about 40 minutes, or until the topping is evenly golden brown. Serve warm.

MAKES 4 TO 6 SERVINGS

ASK ART

If a recipe calls for milk, can I use skim or 1%?

I prefer whole milk for baking. Although I drink low-fat milk, I always keep a quart of whole milk in the house in case I get the urge to bake. Most recipes will work with low-fat milk, but the finished product won't be quite as moist and delicious.

These rich and creamy chocolate custards are fancy enough to serve to company. You can add a dollop of sweetened whipped cream on top.

CHOCOLATE CUSTARDS

2 cups heavy cream

6 ounces semisweet chocolate, coarsely chopped

4 large eggs, at room temperature

⅓ cup granulated sugar

1 teaspoon vanilla extract

1 **Position a rack** in the center of the oven and preheat the oven to 325°F.

2 **Heat the cream** in a medium saucepan over medium heat until bubbles form around the edges. Remove from the heat and add the chocolate. Let stand 3 minutes, then whisk well to melt the chocolate and blend it with the cream.

3 **Whisk the eggs,** sugar, and vanilla in a medium bowl. Gradually whisk in the hot chocolate mixture. Ladle or pour the custard into six ¾-cup custard cups. Place the custard cups in a 9 × 13-inch baking dish. Pour hot water around the cups to come ¼ inch up the sides. Carefully transfer the dish with the custards to the oven.

4 **Bake until** a dinner knife inserted in a custard about 1 inch from the edge of the dish comes out clean, about 20 minutes. The centers will still seem jiggly but will set when cooled.

5 **Remove the cups** from the water and let cool. Cover each cup with plastic wrap and refrigerate until chilled, at least 2 hours. Serve chilled. (The custards can be made, covered, and refrigerated up to 2 days ahead.)

MAKES 6 CUSTARDS

Why do some recipes instruct me to pour water into a pan holding filled custard cups?

ASK ART

Cooking food in a water bath (another term is "bain marie") cooks it gently, which is why this is a preferred method for custards and other fragile foods. To avoid splashing water into the food or spilling it on the floor, put the pan on a partially extended oven rack and pour the water from a tea kettle or pitcher into the pan.

What is carrot cake without a topping of cream cheese frosting? Well, in this case it's dressed-up carrot muffins! So with this recipe you are getting two for the price of one: cupcakes and muffins.

CARROT CUPCAKES WITH CREAM CHEESE FROSTING

CUPCAKES

1½ cups all-purpose flour

1½ teaspoons ground cinnamon

1½ teaspoons baking soda

¾ teaspoon salt

¾ cup granulated sugar

¾ cup packed light or dark brown sugar

3 large eggs

¾ cup vegetable or sunflower oil

⅓ cup applesauce

1½ cups coarsely grated carrot (use the large holes on a box grater)

½ cup raisins

½ cup coarsely chopped walnuts

CREAM CHEESE FROSTING

One 3-ounce package cream cheese, at room temperature

2 tablespoons unsalted butter, at room temperature

1 teaspoon fresh lemon juice

¼ teaspoon vanilla extract

1½ cups confectioners' sugar, sifted

½ cup coarsely chopped walnuts

1 **To make the cupcakes,** position a rack in the center of the oven and preheat the oven to 350°F. Coat twelve 2¾ × 1½-inch muffin cups (preferably nonstick) with vegetable oil spray. Place paper cupcake liners in the cups.

2 **Stir the flour,** cinnamon, baking soda, and salt together in a medium bowl. Mix the granulated and brown sugars, eggs, oil, and applesauce in a medium bowl with an electric mixer on medium speed until combined, about 1 minute. Reduce the mixer speed to low. Mix in the flour and then the carrot, raisins, and walnuts. Divide the batter evenly among the muffin cups (an ice cream scoop works well).

3 **Bake until** a toothpick inserted in the center of a cupcake comes out clean, about 25 minutes. Cool the cupcakes for 5 minutes. Remove from the muffin cups, transfer to a wire cooling rack, and cool completely.

4 **To make the icing,** beat the cream cheese, butter, lemon juice, and vanilla with an electric mixer on high speed until well combined. Reduce the mixer speed to low. Gradually add the confectioners' sugar to make a smooth icing.

5 **Spread the icing** over the cupcakes. Sprinkle the cupcakes with the chopped walnuts, pressing the walnuts gently into the icing so they adhere. (The cupcakes can be prepared 1 day ahead, covered, and stored at room temperature.)

MAKES 12 CUPCAKES

How long can I store baking powder and baking soda?

ASK ART

Both can be stored for up to six months, although it's best to replace them within four months. While these leaveners are not identical, we tend to group them together. This is understandable because they are often paired in a recipe. Both react with liquids to release gasses that in turn lift a baked good. The difference is that baking powder is both an alkaline and an acid; baking soda is alkaline alone and needs an acid to react with, such as sour cream, buttermilk, yogurt, or lemon juice.

How should I store flour?

Most of us who like to bake buy flour in 5-pound sacks, but if you don't bake often, buy flour in amounts you will use within six months. Flour does best kept in a cool, dark, dry place. Once you open the flour sack, store the flour in a tightly covered, opaque canister. Whole wheat flour should be refrigerated to keep it from turning rancid, and all flour can be frozen for up to a year. Wrap the flour sack well in plastic wrap and then put it in a large, freezer-safe plastic bag.

Tassies are miniature pecan pies. Cream cheese in the pie pastry makes the dough especially easy to handle. You will need two mini-muffin pans for this recipe. Nonstick pans work best.

CHOCOLATE PECAN TASSIES

CREAM CHEESE PASTRY

One 3-ounce package cream cheese, at room temperature

8 tablespoons (1 stick) unsalted butter, at room temperature

1 cup all-purpose flour

¼ teaspoon salt

FILLING

¾ cup packed light brown sugar

1 egg, beaten

1 tablespoon unsalted butter, melted

⅛ teaspoon salt

1 teaspoon vanilla extract

½ cup finely chopped pecans

⅓ cup semisweet chocolate chips

1 **Position a rack** in the center of the oven and preheat the oven to 350°F. Coat twenty-four 2-tablespoon-capacity mini-muffin cups with vegetable oil spray.

2 **To make the pastry,** mix the cream cheese and butter in a medium bowl with an electric mixer on high speed until they are well combined. On low speed, gradually mix in the flour and salt until the dough clumps together. Gather up the dough and press it into a thick disk. Wrap in plastic wrap and refrigerate until chilled, about 1 hour.

3 **Roll the dough** into twenty-four 1-inch balls. Press 1 ball firmly into each muffin cup to line the cup with pastry dough. Freeze the pans while making the filling.

4 **To make the filling,** whisk the brown sugar, egg, melted butter, salt, and vanilla in a medium bowl or a 1-quart measuring cup until smooth. Combine the pecans and chocolate chips, and sprinkle the mixture into the pastry-lined cups. Ladle or pour the filling into the muffin cups in equal amounts.

5 **Bake until the crusts** are golden brown and the filling is evenly puffed, about 20 minutes. Cool in the pans for 5 minutes. Remove the tassies from the pans and cool completely on wire cooling racks.

MAKES 24 TASSIES

Brownies can be cakey, fudgey, or somewhere in between. These fall firmly in the cakey camp. For a quick icing, sprinkle one cup of semisweet chocolate chips over the brownie just as it comes out of the oven and let stand for five minutes to soften the chips. Spread the soft melting chips in a thin layer on the brownie and let cool completely. If you don't have white chocolate chips and have a yen for brownies, make these with semisweet chocolate chips.

CHOCOLATE AND WHITE CHOCOLATE CHUNK BROWNIES

½ pound (2 sticks) unsalted butter, cut into pieces

1 cup (6 ounces) semisweet chocolate chips

¾ cup sugar

4 large eggs, beaten

1 teaspoon vanilla extract

2 cups all-purpose flour

1½ teaspoons baking powder

¼ teaspoon salt

1 cup (4 ounces) coarsely chopped walnuts

1 cup (6 ounces) white chocolate chips

1 **Position a rack** in the center of the oven and preheat the oven to 350°F. Lightly butter a 13 × 9-inch metal baking pan.

2 **Melt the butter** in a large saucepan over very low heat, stirring often. Stir in the chocolate chips and let stand for 3 minutes. Whisk to melt the chocolate. Cool the chocolate mixture to lukewarm (place the pan in a large bowl of cold water to speed up this process if you wish). Whisk in the sugar. Whisk in the eggs, one at a time, and then the vanilla. In another bowl, whisk the flour, baking powder, and salt. Using a wooden spoon, stir the flour into the chocolate. Stir in the walnuts and white chocolate chips, and spread the mixture evenly in the baking pan.

3 **Bake just until** a toothpick inserted in the center comes out clean, about 20 minutes. Let cool completely in the pan on a wire cooling rack. Cut the brownies into 12 rectangles. (The brownies can be made, covered tightly, and stored at room temperature for up to 3 days.)

MAKES 12 BROWNIES

oconut cake is a classic of southern cooking. I don't know how many I ate as a boy, but as an adult, it is still a favorite. Coconut cupcakes are a little easier to deal with than a towering triple-layer cake, and a lot easier to fit into lunchboxes or to offer as an after-school snack. The frosting recipe makes enough to create a tall billow of icing on each cupcake, but use as much as you like. It's not worth making this frosting with only one egg white, so the recipe yields a lot.

COCONUT CUPCAKES WITH FLUFFY WHITE FROSTING

1¾ cups all-purpose flour

2 teaspoons baking powder

¼ teaspoon salt

½ cup whole milk

1 teaspoon vanilla extract

1 cup sugar

8 tablespoons (1 stick) unsalted butter, at room temperature

3 large eggs, separated, at room temperature

1⅓ cups sweetened flaked coconut, divided

FLUFFY WHITE FROSTING

2 large egg whites

¾ cup sugar

¼ cup water

1 tablespoon light corn syrup

1 teaspoon vanilla extract

1 Position a rack in the center of the oven and preheat the oven to 350°F. Coat twelve 2¾ × 1½-inch muffin cups (preferably nonstick) with vegetable oil spray. Place paper cupcake liners in the cups.

2 Sift the flour, baking powder, and salt together. Set aside. Mix the milk and vanilla in a glass measuring cup.

3 Beat the sugar and butter in a medium bowl with an electric mixer set on high speed until the mixture is light in color and texture, about 3 minutes. Beat in the egg yolks one at a time. Reduce the mixer speed to low. In three additions, alternating with two additions of the milk, add the flour.

4 Using clean, dry beaters, whip the egg whites in a small, clean, dry bowl with the electric mixer on high speed just until stiff peaks form. Fold the whites

into the batter. Mix in 1 cup coconut. Divide the batter evenly among the muffin cups (an ice cream scoop works well).

5   **Bake until the tops** of the cupcakes are golden and a toothpick inserted in the center comes out clean, about 20 minutes. Cool in the pan for 5 minutes. Remove the cupcakes from the pan and cool completely on a wire cooling rack.

6   **Meanwhile, heat a small** nonstick skillet over medium heat. Add the remaining ⅓ cup coconut. Cook, stirring occasionally, until the coconut is lightly toasted, 2 to 3 minutes. Transfer to a plate and let cool.

7   **To make the icing,** mix the egg whites, sugar, water, and corn syrup in the top of a double boiler. Place the insert over lightly boiling water (the water should not touch the bottom of the pan). Whip the mixture with a handheld electric mixer on high speed just until it forms stiff peaks, about 7 minutes. Do not overbeat. Remove from the heat and stir in the vanilla.

8   **Use the icing** immediately to frost the cupcakes. Top with a sprinkling of the toasted coconut. (The cupcakes can be made 1 day ahead, loosely covered, and stored at room temperature.)

MAKES 12 CUPCAKES

How should I separate eggs?

ASK ART

Experts say the safest way to separate eggs is with an egg separator, a small, bowl-shaped tool sold in kitchenware shops. I separate eggs with my hands. Wash your hands well and crack the egg so that it falls into your cupped hand. Let the whites slide between your fingers into a bowl and then put the yolk in another receptacle. Whatever you do, don't separate eggs by passing the yolk back and forth from shell to broken shell. This is a good way to contaminate the egg if there is any bacteria on the shell. A cold egg is easier to separate than a room-temperature egg.

Here is a chocolate cupcake classic in all its glory. Use this fudgy chocolate frosting or, for a change of pace, the Fluffy White Frosting on page 284.

DEVIL'S FOOD CUPCAKES WITH CHOCOLATE FUDGE FROSTING

CUPCAKES

4 ounces unsweetened chocolate, coarsely chopped

1½ cups cake flour

¼ teaspoon baking powder

¼ teaspoon baking soda

¼ teaspoon salt

½ cup buttermilk

1 teaspoon vanilla extract

8 tablespoons (1 stick) unsalted butter, at room temperature

1½ cups packed light brown sugar

½ cup granulated sugar

4 large eggs, separated, at room temperature

CHOCOLATE FUDGE FROSTING

2 cups confectioners' sugar

¼ cup unsweetened cocoa powder

8 tablespoons (1 stick) unsalted butter, at room temperature

½ teaspoon vanilla extract

3 tablespoons milk, as needed

Multicolored sugar sprinkles or nonpareils for decorating

1 To make the cupcakes, position a rack in the center of the oven and preheat the oven to 350°F. Coat twelve 2¾ × 1½-inch muffin cups (preferably nonstick) with vegetable oil spray. Place paper cupcake liners in the cups.

2 Melt the chocolate in the top part of a double boiler over hot, not simmering water or in a microwave oven at 50 percent (medium) power. Cool the chocolate until tepid.

3 Whisk the flour, baking powder, baking soda, and salt together. Mix the buttermilk and vanilla in a glass measuring cup.

4 Beat the butter in a medium bowl with an electric mixer on high speed until creamy, about 1 minute. Gradually beat in the brown sugar and granulated sugar, and continue beating until the mixture is light in color and texture, about 3 minutes. Beat in the egg yolks one at a time. Mix in the cooled

chocolate. Reduce the mixer speed to low. In 3 additions, add the flour, alternating with 2 additions of the buttermilk.

5   **Using clean, dry beaters,** whip the egg whites in a small, clean, dry bowl with the electric mixer on high speed just until the whites form stiff peaks. Fold the whites into the batter. Divide the batter evenly among the muffin cups (an ice cream scoop works well).

6   **Bake until** a toothpick inserted in the center of a cupcake comes out clean, 20 to 25 minutes. Cool in the pans for 5 minutes. Remove the cupcakes from the pan and let cool completely on a wire cooling rack.

7   **To make the frosting,** sift the confectioners' sugar and cocoa together. Beat the butter in a medium bowl with an electric mixer on low speed. Gradually beat in the cocoa-sugar; the mixture will be crumbly. Add the vanilla and then beat in enough milk to make a thick, spreadable icing.

8   **Spread the frosting** over the tops of the cupcakes and decorate with the colored sprinkles. (The cupcakes can be made up to 2 days ahead, covered tightly, and stored at room temperature.)

MAKES 12 CUPCAKES

What is the most effective way to melt chocolate?

ASK ART

Melting chocolate in the microwave is the most foolproof way. Chop the chocolate into large chunks and put it in a microwave-safe dish. With the microwave on 50 percent (medium) power, heat the chocolate for thirty to sixty seconds, or until the chocolate looks shiny. This could take longer than a minute; it depends on the wattage of the microwave, the amount of chocolate, and the size of the container. Do not expect the chocolate to melt to a liquid pool in the microwave. When it is soft and shiny, take it out and stir until it's smooth. You may have to stir for half a minute or longer. If you're melting chocolate chips, follow the same procedure. You can also melt chocolate in a double boiler over barely simmering water or, if you are extremely careful, in a heavy pan set over very low heat. With these two methods the chocolate is more likely to stiffen or scorch if you are not vigilant.

Don't wait until teatime to enjoy these buttery sugar-glazed treats. If you like lemon-scented cookies, add the grated zest of two large lemons to the dough after beating in the eggs.

VANILLA TEA COOKIES

4¼ cups all-purpose flour

1 teaspoon baking soda

1 teaspoon cream of tartar

1½ cups granulated sugar, divided

1 cup confectioners' sugar

½ pound (2 sticks) unsalted butter, at room temperature

1 cup vegetable or safflower oil

2 large eggs, at room temperature

1 teaspoon vanilla extract

1 teaspoon salt

1 **Position oven racks** in the top third and in the center of the oven. Preheat the oven to 350°F.

2 **Sift the flour,** baking soda, and cream of tartar together; set aside. Beat 1 cup granulated sugar, the confectioners' sugar, butter, and oil in a large bowl with an electric mixer on high speed (a heavy-duty mixer with a paddle blade works best) until the mixture is light and fluffy, about 3 minutes. Beat in the eggs one at a time, beating until they have been completely absorbed. Add the vanilla and salt. Beat in the flour at low speed. (If not using a heavy-duty mixer, stir the flour in by hand with a sturdy wooden spoon.) Cover the dough with plastic wrap and refrigerate until it is firm and easy to handle, about 1 hour or up to 4 hours.

3 **Place the remaining** ½ **cup** granulated sugar in a small bowl. Form the dough into balls, using a level tablespoon for each. Place the balls on ungreased baking sheets, spacing them 2 inches apart. Dip the bottom of a flat drinking glass in a small bowl of water, then dip it into the bowl of sugar. Use the glass to flatten and coat the cookies with sugar, continuing to add more water or sugar as needed.

4 **Bake until the cookies** are lightly browned around the edges, about 10 to 12 minutes. Transfer the cookies to wire cooling racks and cool completely. (The cookies can be made, covered tightly, and stored at room temperature for up to 5 days.)

MAKES ABOUT 5 DOZEN COOKIES

What is the best way to store eggs?

ASK ART Store eggs in their carton. The carton retains the cold air of the refrigerator and protects the eggs from odors. Always refrigerate eggs where temperatures stay about 40°F. For an egg, a day at room temperature is as aging as a week in the refrigerator.

Who doesn't love cookies that have tender shortbread bottoms topped with tangy lemon topping? Some recipes for the lemon layer are complicated, but not this one. The topping is stirred up and baked right on the cookie crust.

LEMON BARS

CRUST

1 cup all-purpose flour

¼ cup sugar

Pinch of salt

8 tablespoons (1 stick) unsalted butter, cut into tablespoons, at room temperature

FILLING

2 large eggs

1 cup granulated sugar

2 tablespoons all-purpose flour

2 tablespoons fresh lemon juice

Grated zest of 1 lemon

½ teaspoon baking powder

Confectioners' sugar for sprinkling

1 **Position a rack** in the center of the oven and preheat the oven to 350°F. Lightly butter an 8 × 8-inch metal baking pan. Line the bottom and short sides of the pan with a 14-inch-long piece of aluminum foil (nonstick foil works best), pleating the foil lengthwise down the middle to fit the foil into the pan. Fold down the overhanging foil to create "handles." (If you use regular foil, lightly butter the foil.)

2 **To prepare the crust,** mix the flour, sugar, and salt in a medium bowl. Add the butter and, using an electric mixer on low speed, beat the mixture until it clumps together. Gather up the dough and press evenly into the bottom of the baking pan. Bake until the crust is set and very lightly browned, about 15 minutes. Refrigerate until cooled, about 10 minutes. Leave the oven on.

3 **To prepare the filling,** whisk the eggs in a medium bowl until combined. Add the sugar, flour, lemon juice, zest, and baking powder, and whisk well. Pour over the cooled crust.

4 **Bake until the filling** is set, 20 to 25 minutes. Cool completely in the pan on a wire cake rack.

5 **Lift up on** the foil to remove the entire lemon bar from the pan. Peel off and discard the foil. Using a sharp knife dipped in hot water, cut into 8 bars. Sift confectioners' sugar over the bars. (The bars can be made up to 3 days ahead, covered tightly, and refrigerated. Sift additional confectioners' sugar over the bars before serving.)

MAKES 8 BARS

Is one kind of baking pan better than another?

ASK ART The best bakeware is the kind you like using. Everyone has favorite cake pans and baking sheets that are almost old friends. When you buy bakeware, invest in heavy, well-made pans. You won't regret the expense, especially if you like to bake, as I do. Bargain brands warp and dent and don't bake evenly. I like to use metal bakeware for cupcakes, bars, and cookies, but I also rely on glass for some desserts. The 11 × 8½-inch size baking dish is far easier to find in glass. The food in glass browns nicely and bakes differently from that baked in metal, so watch it carefully. It is a good idea to reduce the oven temperature by 25 degrees when using glass bakeware.

Here is one of the easiest desserts I know of—and one everyone loves. No baking required. It's perfect as a refreshing dessert on a hot summer day or anytime you feel the urge for its tangy-sweet kick. Ordinary supermarket limes are usually the Persian variety. If you have Key limes, use four or five (they're quite small) for the zest, but they aren't essential. And if your supermarket doesn't carry limeade, substitute lemonade and lemon zest.

FROZEN KEY LIME PIE

One 14-ounce can condensed milk

¾ cup thawed frozen limeade (half of a 12-ounce container)

Grated zest of 2 limes

One 8-ounce container thawed whipped nondairy topping, such as Cool Whip

One 6-ounce prepared graham cracker crust

1 **Whisk the condensed milk,** limeade, and lime zest until well combined. Fold in the nondairy topping with a large spatula. Heap the filling into the graham cracker crust.

2 **Freeze, uncovered,** just until the filling sets, about 1 hour. Cover loosely with plastic wrap and freeze until the filling is firm, at least 4 hours. For a softer filling, refrigerate until the filling is set and chilled, at least 2 hours or up to overnight. (The pie can be made up to 1 day ahead and then frozen or refrigerated.) To serve a frozen pie, dip a sharp knife in hot water before slicing.

MAKES 8 SERVINGS

What is the difference between a buckle, a cobbler, and a pie?

ASK ART

All these are warm, comforting, lovely baked goods usually made with fruit. A buckle is a dessert in which fruit is mixed with sweet batter and then spooned into a fairly deep baking dish. It's topped with a crumbly streusel, which, together with the fruit, causes the cake to buckle so that pockets form and the final result is sort of haphazard and totally delicious. A cobbler is a fruit mixture with a top crust only. (Well, sometimes there's a bottom crust, proving that these terms are subject to interpretation!) The top crust may be made from cake batter, pastry dough, or, more commonly today, sweetened biscuit dough. Some people think the name comes from the fact that the dessert is "cobbled together." Others say the rustic topping resembles cobblestones. A pie has either a bottom crust or two crusts. It is baked in a pie plate with sloping sides, and the crust is usually made from flaky pastry dough. A pie may have a crumb crust, too. I make it easy by calling these kinds of desserts "puddings."

Not only do these snap at your taste buds with sharp, gingery flavor, but they are nice and crisp, too. The lack of eggs in the dough contributes to the crunchy texture.

GINGERSNAPS

3½ cups all-purpose flour

1 tablespoon ground ginger

1 teaspoon ground cinnamon

½ teaspoon ground cloves, optional

1 teaspoon baking soda

½ teaspoon salt

½ pound (2 sticks) unsalted butter, at room temperature

1½ cups sugar, divided

1 cup unsulfured molasses

3 tablespoons finely chopped crystallized ginger

1 **Sift the flour,** ginger, cinnamon, cloves (if using), baking soda, and salt together. Mix the butter and 1 cup sugar in a large bowl with an electric mixer on high speed (a heavy-duty mixer fitted with the paddle blade works best) until the mixture is light and fluffy, about 3 minutes. Gradually beat in the molasses. Reduce the speed to low and gradually mix in the flour and then the crystallized ginger. Cover the dough with plastic wrap and refrigerate until slightly chilled and easier to handle, at least 30 minutes and up to 2 hours.

2 **Position oven racks** in the top third and in the center of the oven. Preheat the oven to 350°F.

3 **Place the remaining** ½ cup sugar in a small bowl. Using a level tablespoon for each one, roll the dough into balls. Roll each ball into the sugar to coat. Place the balls about 1½ inches apart on ungreased baking sheets.

4 **Bake until the edges** of the cookies are crisp (the centers will be soft), about 12 minutes. Switch the positions of the baking sheets from top to bottom halfway through baking. Cool the cookies on the baking sheets for 3 minutes, then transfer to wire cooling racks to cool completely. (The cookies will keep, stored in an airtight container, for up to 5 days.)

MAKES ABOUT 4 DOZEN COOKIES

ASK ART

Do I really need to sift the flour and other dry ingredients together for baking?

It's a good idea, particularly if the recipe includes baking soda. Sifting integrates the flour with the leavening, salt, and spices (such as ground cinnamon or ginger) and gets rid of any lumps. If it's a mixture of flour and baking powder, you can get away with giving the mixture a good whisking with a wire whisk, but baking soda can clump, and sifting alleviates this problem. It guarantees that you won't bite into a nugget of baking soda. If baking soda is part of the mix, sift the dry ingredients at the beginning or after you've whisked. You don't need a sifter; any mesh strainer will work, although a sifter makes it a little easier. I grew up in the South where we baked with self-rising flour, which includes leavening and does not always need sifting. (I still use it for biscuits and some other baked goods.)

Talk about gilding the lily! By themselves these are first-class members of the peanut butter cookie school. Take two of these babies and sandwich them together with peanut butter icing, and wow! An indulgence your kids will love and you will admit is worth every minute of exercise you'll need to burn off the calories.

PEANUT BUTTER COOKIE SANDWICHES

COOKIES

1¼ cups all-purpose flour

½ teaspoon baking powder

⅛ teaspoon salt

8 tablespoons (1 stick) unsalted butter, at room temperature

½ cup chunky peanut butter

1 cup sugar

1 large egg, at room temperature

1 teaspoon vanilla extract

FILLING

½ cup chunky peanut butter

2 tablespoons unsalted butter, at room temperature

1 cup confectioners' sugar

1 teaspoon vanilla extract

3 tablespoons milk, as needed

1 **To make the cookies,** position oven racks in the top third and center of the oven and preheat the oven to 350°F.

2 **Whisk the flour,** baking powder, and salt together. Beat the butter, peanut butter, and sugar in a medium bowl with an electric mixer on high speed until the mixture is light and fluffy, about 3 minutes. Beat in the egg and then the vanilla. Reduce the speed to low and gradually beat in the flour.

3 **Using a level** tablespoon for each, form the dough into balls. Place the balls 2 inches apart on ungreased baking sheets. Press each ball of dough with a dinner fork to make a crosshatch pattern and flatten the ball.

4 **Bake until the** edges of the cookies feel crisp, about 15 minutes. Switch the positions of the baking sheets from top to bottom halfway through baking. Cool the cookies on the baking sheets for 3 minutes, then transfer to wire cooling racks to cool completely.

5 **To make the** filling, beat the peanut butter and butter in a small bowl with an electric mixer on low speed. Add the confectioners' sugar and mix until crumbly. Mix in the vanilla and enough of the milk to make a thick, spreadable filling.

6 **Sandwich 2 cookies,** flat sides facing each other, with the filling. (The cookies will keep, stored in an airtight container, for up to 2 days.)

MAKES 10 LARGE COOKIES

What is a half-sheet pan?

ASK ART

These are shallow, rimmed rectangular metal pans. Most cooks have a jelly roll pan; a half-sheet pan looks similar but is slightly larger. They measure 12 × 17 inches, half the size of a commercial sheet pan. Half-sheet pans are extremely handy to have in your bakeware collection. I like to use them as baking sheets.

If you like your biscotti so crunchy that you must dip them in coffee, tea, wine, or milk so they will soften enough to eat, these cookies are for you. Sometimes I substitute toasted, coarsely chopped pecans for half of the pine nuts.

CHOCOLATE AND PINE NUT BISCOTTI

½ cup (about 3 ounces) pine nuts

2 cups all-purpose flour

1 teaspoon baking powder

1 teaspoon ground cinnamon

Pinch of salt

2 large eggs, at room temperature

⅔ cup sugar

2 teaspoons vanilla extract

One 3½-ounce bar bittersweet chocolate, chopped into chunks about ½ to ¾ inch square

1 **Heat a medium skillet** over medium heat. Add the pine nuts and cook, stirring often, until the nuts are lightly toasted, 1 to 2 minutes. Immediately transfer the nuts to a plate and cool completely.

2 **Position a rack** in the center of the oven and preheat the oven to 350°F.

3 **Whisk the flour,** baking powder, cinnamon, and salt together. Beat the eggs and sugar in a medium bowl with an electric mixer on high speed until the eggs have doubled in volume and are pale yellow, about 3 minutes. Beat in the vanilla. On low speed, gradually add the flour to the eggs. Add the cooled pine nuts and chocolate, and work them into the dough with your hands.

4 **Divide the dough** in half. Form each portion into a thick 8-inch log. Place the logs 2 inches apart on an ungreased baking sheet. Bake until the logs feel set when lightly pressed, about 25 minutes. Cool the logs on the baking sheet for 30 minutes. The logs will be slightly warm but easier to cut.

5 **Using a serrated knife** held at a slight diagonal, saw each log into ½-inch-thick slices. Arrange the slices close together but without touching on the baking sheet. Bake for 10 minutes. Turn the slices and bake until the biscotti are crisp, about 10 minutes more. Transfer the biscotti to wire cooling racks and cool completely. (The biscotti will keep, stored in an airtight container at room temperature, for up to 1 week.)

MAKES ABOUT 30

Is there a difference between semisweet and bittersweet chocolate?

ASK ART

There is not much difference, and these two products can be used interchangeably in baking, frostings, and sauces. Both are referred to as dark chocolate. Bittersweet must have at least 35 percent of chocolate liquor (unsweetened chocolate), while semisweet can have up to 35 percent chocolate liquor. This means that they often are almost identical. What's more important is to use chocolate you like. Neither should be used when a recipe calls for unsweetened or baking chocolate. And you should not substitute milk chocolate for dark chocolate, either.

What is the best way to measure flour?

I dip and sweep the flour, but some bakers prefer to spoon and sweep it. Please use the dip and sweep method for my recipes. Any other method will result in a different measurement, which is courting disaster. It is important to use the right kind of measuring cup so that you can level the flour with the sweep of a table knife. A dry measuring cup is made of metal or rigid plastic and holds the exact amount needed. These usually are sold in nests with measures for ¼ cup, ⅓ cup, ½ cup, and 1 cup. Liquid measures, on the other hand, are made of clear glass or plastic with the measurements marked on the side (like those Pyrex measuring pitchers most of us have).

These oatmeal cookies do not spread but stay nice and plump. Of course, other dried fruits, from cranberries to good old raisins, can be substituted for the dried cherries, but the oatmeal and cherries are a wonderful duo. Use rolled oats, also called old-fashioned oatmeal, not quick-cooking, instant, or steel-cut oats.

OATMEAL AND DRIED CHERRY COOKIES

½ cup all-purpose flour

½ teaspoon baking powder

½ teaspoon salt

10 tablespoons (1 ¼ sticks) unsalted butter, at room temperature

½ cup sugar

1 large egg, at room temperature

1 teaspoon vanilla extract

2 cups rolled (old-fashioned) oatmeal

1 cup dried sweet or tart cherries

½ cup (2 ounces) coarsely chopped walnuts

1 **Position racks in** the top third and center of the oven and preheat the oven to 350°F.

2 **Whisk the flour,** baking powder, and salt together. Mix the butter and sugar in a medium bowl with an electric mixer on high speed until the mixture is light and fluffy, about 3 minutes. Beat in the egg and then the vanilla. Reduce the speed to low. Gradually mix in the flour. Stir in the oatmeal, dried cherries, and walnuts.

3 **Drop tablespoons** of the dough onto ungreased baking sheets, spacing them about 1½ inches apart. Bake until the cookies are lightly browned, about 15 minutes. Switch the positions of the baking sheets from top to bottom halfway through baking. Transfer to wire cooling racks and cool completely. (The cookies will keep, stored in an airtight container, for up to 5 days.)

MAKES ABOUT 2 DOZEN

Chocolate lovers have brownies, and brown sugar lovers have chewy butterscotch blondies. For a double (or is it triple?) dose of butterscotch, stir ½ cup of butterscotch chips into the batter.

BUTTERSCOTCH BLONDIES

3 cups all-purpose flour

1 teaspoon baking powder

½ teaspoon salt

1¾ cups packed light brown sugar

½ pound (2 sticks) unsalted butter, at room temperature

2 large eggs, at room temperature

2 teaspoons vanilla extract

1 cup coarsely chopped pecans or walnuts

¾ cup butterscotch chips for icing

1 **Position a rack** in the center of the oven and preheat the oven to 350°F. Lightly butter an 11½ × 8-inch baking pan. Line the bottom and short sides of the pan with a 15-inch length of nonstick aluminum foil, pleating the foil in the center to fit the pan. Fold down the foil at the short ends to make handles. (If you use regular aluminum foil, butter and flour the foil, shaking out the excess flour.)

2 **Whisk the flour,** baking powder, and salt together. Beat the brown sugar and butter in a large bowl with an electric mixer on high speed until the mixture is light in color and texture, about 3 minutes. Beat in the eggs one at a time and then the vanilla. Reduce the mixer speed to low. Gradually mix in the flour and the pecans. Spread the batter evenly in the pan.

3 **Bake until** the blondie is an even golden brown and a toothpick inserted in the center comes out clean, about 40 minutes. Sprinkle the butterscotch chips over the warm blondie and let stand for 5 minutes to soften. Spread the chips with a metal icing spatula into a thin layer. Let cool completely in the pan on a wire cake rack.

4 **Lift up** on the handles to remove the cooled blondie from the pan. Peel off the aluminum foil and cut into 12 bars. (The blondies can be made up to 3 days ahead, wrapped individually in plastic wrap, and stored at room temperature.)

MAKES 12 BLONDIES

The all-American duo of banana and peanut butter makes these moist, flavorful cupcakes. The peanut butter theme is carried out in the frosting as well. The banana should be well ripened and soft, and have lots of tiny brown spots. Blackened, overripe bananas will not give the best results. If you are a chocolate lover, frost the cupcakes with the Chocolate Fudge Frosting on page 286.

BANANA–PEANUT BUTTER CUPCAKES WITH PEANUT BUTTER FROSTING

CUPCAKES

2 cups all-purpose flour

2 teaspoons baking powder

¼ teaspoon salt

⅓ cup vegetable shortening

⅓ cup chunky peanut butter

1½ cups packed light brown sugar

2 large eggs, at room temperature

1 teaspoon vanilla extract

½ cup mashed ripe banana

½ cup milk

PEANUT BUTTER FROSTING

⅓ cup chunky peanut butter

2 cups confectioners' sugar, sifted

½ teaspoon vanilla extract

⅓ cup milk, as needed

1 **To make the cupcakes,** position a rack in the center of the oven and preheat the oven to 350°F. Coat twelve 2¾ × 1½-inch muffin cups with vegetable oil spray. Place paper cupcake liners in the cups.

2 **Whisk the flour,** baking powder, and salt together. Mix the vegetable shortening and peanut butter in a medium bowl with an electric mixer on high speed to combine. Add the brown sugar and beat until the mixture is pale and crumbly, about 2 minutes. Add the eggs one at a time, beating well after each addition, then add the vanilla. Beat in the mashed banana. Reduce the speed to low. In 3 additions, alternating with 2 additions of milk, mix in the flour. Divide the batter evenly among the muffin cups (an ice cream scoop works well).

3   **Bake until a** toothpick inserted in the center of a cupcake comes out clean, about 20 minutes. Let the cupcakes cool in the cups for 5 minutes. Remove from the muffin cups, transfer to a wire cooling rack, and let cool completely.

4   **To make the frosting,** beat the peanut butter with an electric mixer on low speed for 15 seconds. Gradually add the confectioners' sugar to make a smooth icing; it will look crumbly. Beat in the vanilla. Gradually mix in enough milk to make a thick frosting.

5   **Spread the frosting** over the cupcakes. (The cupcakes can be prepared 1 day ahead, covered, and stored at room temperature.)

MAKES 12 CUPCAKES

How are eggs graded and sized? Why do most recipes call for large eggs?

ASK ART The AA and A grades refer to the freshness of the eggs at the time of packing. Without question, AA are freshest. Eggs are sized from jumbo to peewee. Smaller sizes don't usually make it to the supermarket, so most eggs in retail stores are jumbo, extra-large, or large. Almost universally, recipes are developed using large eggs. I am not sure why, but I imagine it's because large eggs are a pretty common size, and it just happened this way. You can use other sizes, but you may have to adjust the number of eggs. For instance, three large eggs can be replaced by two jumbo or three extra-large eggs, while six large eggs can be replaced by five jumbo or five extra-large eggs. This math makes my head swim. I suggest using the size called for.

Chewy, filled with fruit and nuts, and pretty irresistible, these bars will provide tasty energy any time of the day, from a mid-morning snack to a midnight raid on the cookie jar. They are great as lunchbox and after-school treats, too. Best yet, they couldn't be easier to make.

EASY GRANOLA BARS

One 14-ounce can sweetened condensed milk

2 cups graham cracker crumbs

½ cup old-fashioned (rolled) oatmeal, not quick or instant oatmeal

1 cup sweetened flaked coconut

1 cup (6 ounces) dark raisins

1 cup (4 ounces) coarsely chopped pecans or walnuts

1 **Position a rack** in the center of the oven and preheat the oven to 350°F. Lightly butter an 11½ × 8-inch baking pan. Line the bottom and short sides of the pan with a 15-inch length of nonstick aluminum foil, pleating the foil in the center to fit the pan. Fold down the foil at the short ends to make handles. (If you use regular aluminum foil, butter the foil.)

2 **Stir the condensed milk,** graham cracker crumbs, oatmeal, coconut, raisins, and pecans in a medium bowl until all the ingredients are moistened. Press the mixture into the baking pan.

3 **Bake until** the edges look crisp, about 30 minutes. Cool completely in the pan on a wire cake rack. Lift up on the handles and peel off the foil. Cut into bars. (The bars can be made up to 3 days ahead and stored in an airtight container at room temperature.)

MAKES 9 BARS

What are evaporated milk and condensed milk?

ASK ART

To make evaporated milk, more than half of the water is removed from milk, and it is then canned. It can be reconstituted with water and used in place of other milk. Evaporated milk keeps for six months on the shelf, but once opened it should be transferred to a glass or rigid plastic container and refrigerated for no longer than a week. It is usually made from whole milk but is available in low-fat and nonfat versions, too.

Condensed milk (sometimes called sweetened condensed milk) is evaporated whole milk with added sugar. It is lovely and thick and pretty high in calories.

Both are used in cooking and baking because they don't curdle easily and provide body and thickness. I keep cans of both in the pantry for times when I don't have milk in the refrigerator and for those recipes that I like better when made with condensed milk. My mother used it a lot in baking, and I have a great fondness for the flavor.

How do I make graham cracker or cookie crumbs?

The easiest way to make graham cracker or cookie crumbs is in a food processor or blender (the processor holds more). Pulse the cookies until crumbs form, and take care not to overdo it. The crumbs can lose their texture in an instant. Another technique is to put the cookies or crackers in a plastic bag and use a rolling pin to roll over them. I find this is better than buying packaged crumbs, which tend to be tasteless.

Frozen fruit is more than convenient; it's often just as tasty as fresh fruit and can be counted on for all sorts of culinary uses. I sometimes defrost a bag of fruit and turn it into a big batch of fruit sauce to pour over cake, ice cream, and even pancakes and waffles. It is also handy to whirl with frozen yogurt for a quick smoothie. You can match up the fruit with the same flavor preserves, or mix and match for variety. There's no reason that you couldn't use strawberry preserves to sweeten frozen raspberries, for example.

HOMEMADE FRUIT SAUCE

One 16- to 20-ounce bag of frozen fruit, such as strawberries, peaches, or raspberries, thawed as directed on the bag

½ cup fruit preserves

¼ cup apple or orange juice or canned fruit nectar, as needed

Puree the thawed fruit, preserves, and juice in a food processor or blender, adding more juice as needed to get the desired thickness. Transfer to a covered container and refrigerate until chilled, at least 2 hours. Serve chilled. (The sauce can be made up to 5 days ahead, covered, and refrigerated.)

MAKES ABOUT 2½ CUPS

rizzle some of this decadent sauce over plain pound cake or vanilla ice cream to turn them into anything but plain treats.

COCONUT CARAMEL SAUCE

One 14½-ounce can unsweetened coconut milk (not cream of coconut)

½ cup packed light or dark brown sugar

2 tablespoons unsalted butter

1 teaspoon vanilla extract

Bring the coconut milk, sugar, and butter to a simmer in a medium heavy-bottomed saucepan over medium heat. Cook, whisking often to be sure that the sauce doesn't scorch and to blend it, until it is reduced to about 1 cup, 15 to 20 minutes. Transfer to a bowl and stir in the vanilla. Cool until warm or cool further to room temperature. (The sauce can be made up to 5 days ahead, covered tightly, and refrigerated. Reheat gently in a small saucepan, whisking almost constantly until the sauce is warm.)

MAKES ABOUT 1 CUP

When I need something to dress up dessert, it's easy to whip up this chocolate sauce with ingredients from the pantry. For a richer version, substitute heavy cream for the evaporated milk.

CHOCOLATE SAUCE

One 12-ounce can evaporated milk

1½ cups (9 ounces) chocolate chips

2 tablespoons unsalted butter

½ teaspoon vanilla extract

Bring the evaporated milk to a simmer in a medium saucepan over medium heat. Remove from the heat. Add the chocolate chips and butter, and let stand for 3 minutes. Add the vanilla and whisk until smooth. Transfer to a bowl and cool until warm or cool further to room temperature. (The sauce can be prepared up to 3 days ahead, covered, and refrigerated. Reheat gently in a small saucepan, stirring often, just until the sauce is warm.)

MAKES ABOUT 1½ CUPS

PART
THREE

SEVENTEEN

REAL PEOPLE, REAL MEALS

Because I know everyone has different needs in the kitchen and their families have varieties of tastes, I have sorted my recipes into handy categories. Pick and choose from these lists and make the most of your kitchen life!

dinner in under thirty minutes

Pork Tenderloin with Mushroom Marsala Sauce, page 160

Parmesan and Sesame Chicken Breasts on Spicy Garlic Spinach, page 180

Asian Chicken Wrap with Hoisin Sauce, page 192

Flounder Fillets with Cornmeal-Mustard Crust, page 205

main courses with fewer than seven ingredients*

Fragrant Lamb Chops with Tomatoes and Cinnamon, page 170

Kitchen Workhorse Roast Pork Tenderloin with Asian Glaze, page 154

Bacon, Spinach, and Cheddar Frittata, page 164

Capellini with Summer Tomato-Basil Sauce, page 216

snacks with fewer than seven ingredients*

Asian Snack Mix, page 87

Habanero and Garlic Popcorn, page 89

Make-Ahead Salsa, page 92

High-Protein Shake, page 102

sides with fewer than seven ingredients

Two-Potato Mash, page 263

Baby Carrots with Orange Glaze, page 253

Roasted Asparagus with Lemon Zest and Black Pepper, page 250

Spicy Garlic Spinach, page 270

make ahead and freeze

Cabbage and Bacon Soup, page 108

Kitchen Workhorse Chunky Beef Chili, page 150

Sicilian Chicken Thighs, page 186

Cauliflower and Penne Gratin, page 218

eating light

Roasted Chicken Soup, page 114

Salmon Steaks with Citrus Couscous Salad, page 128

Beef and Tomatoes in Black Bean Sauce, page 136

Chicken Breasts in Orange Sauce, page 178

Does not include ordinary seasonings and garnishes

ACKNOWLEDGMENTS

First, I would like to thank:

My beloved Jesus Salgueiro, friend and lifetime partner. There were only words, and you painted the picture. Through your love and guidance we have created a wonderful way to teach the families of America the importance of being family. You have helped me realize that family is whomever you choose to love. Together, we have one mission: to love. Thank you for teaching me that valuable lesson and enabling me to reach my potential.

Dear Oprah Winfrey. You brought America back to the table with the greatest television show on earth and gave me this once-in-a-lifetime opportunity to teach people the importance of being family. I am grateful to you, Stedman Graham, and Wendy Graham and appreciate all your love and support.

I also would like to thank my extended families, those who help me create my books, and those who support me through it all.

Thanks to:

Everyone at Hyperion. For one great book to follow another takes a publisher that cares. Will Schwalbe—you have your finger on the pulse of America's food life. You and your wonderful company, under the guidance of Bob Miller and Ellen Archer, have framed my work beautifully and taken me to so many places. And love to you, Kiera Hepford, Emily Gould, Claire McKean, and the rest of the team that helped bring my book to life.

If there were saints in food-dom, Mary Goodbody and Rick Rodgers would be hailed as most sacred of all. America would have never gotten *Back to the Table* without your professional and candid guidance and your hard work. Mary, you are the best cookbook writer in America, and I thank you for making my books sound so good! Rick, America learns to cook from you. When *Bon Appétit* named you Best Cooking Teacher in America, they were right on. You both took my ideas and helped me create a book for American families.

Linda Ekhardt. You are my love and my muse. I so appreciate the magic that you created by helping me assemble recipes that America can cook with ease. A big thanks to George Burns, the photographer at Harpo, and to Lori Allen and Chad Soderholm for their photographic mastery. Thanks, too, to their son Chaz!

My agents, Jan Miller and Michael Broussard. From day one, you said to me, "Art, families need cookbooks that help them get food on the table." I have never forgotten your advice.

The wonderful people at Harpo who make *The Oprah Winfrey Show* all that it is, including Tim Bennett, Dianne Hudson, Ellen Rakieten, Katy Davis, Dana Newton, Jill Van Lokeren, Lisa Morin, Sheri Salata, Lisa Erspamer, and their amazing production teams and crew. And a special thanks to Jack Mori, Jill Barancik, Andrea Wishom, Doug Pattison, and Caren Yanis. To Lisa Halliday, Harriet Seitler, and their teams. And to Libby Moore, Angelique McFarland, Kelly Donnelly, Novona Cruz, and the executive offices of Oprah Winfrey. You continually inspire me with your passion and dedication.

To my many friends at *O, The Oprah Magazine,* Oprah.com, and the newest addition to the Oprah family, *O at Home* magazine. You allow me to share my vision and passion for food, families, and helping others. Amy Gross, who believes in teaching people how to cook; Gayle King, for giving advice on what families need and can afford; Adam Glassman, for his friendship and making it all look beautiful; Susan Slesin and Dan Shaw, for their encouragement and ideas; Jill Seelig and Stefanie Manning, for supporting my work. And to the talented and dedicated team that puts it all together.

William Farley and Tom Pollock. You have enabled me to extend my love for families by creating amazing opportunities. I appreciate your friendship and partnership.

My beloved Evan Orensten. From the early days of cooking together in your Chicago kitchen, you have given me the confidence to follow my dreams. I so appreciate all your hard work, your great taste, and your candid advice. You organized *Kitchen Life* from the beginning and became its ambassador. Although you now live in New York and we don't cook together as often as we once did, your encouragement and support have kept me going. Thank you, my friend!

Connie Pikulas. My dear Connie—it just couldn't happen without your talent and hard work. We met in the test kitchen at *Martha Stewart Living* all those years ago. It's hard to believe that I now have the pleasure and privilege of having you by my side. Having you with me for cooking shows and special events across the country is reassuring. You are the lady who gets it going and keeps it going! And you never forget the love in your cooking. I love you!

PJ Gray, friend and writing coach. Thank you for helping me organize my thoughts to bring *Kitchen Life* to a reality. Ron Bilaro, Domenica Catelli, and Karen Armijo, my chefs. Your kind, warm, nurturing instincts have helped me live a better life and allowed me the time to help others. My beloved Margie Geddes. You took the time to teach me a lot about how America shops, and for that I am grateful. Jan Walters, "Empress of Chocolate." Thank you for being my advisor, psychologist, and friend. Jeffrey Pawlak, friend and mentor. You have been with me all these years, and I appreciate all your love and support.

Linda Novick, Nic O'Keefe, and all the Board of Directors of Common Threads. Thank you for bringing my vision for a comprehensive, not-for-profit, after-school program for kids to a reality. I now have a greater purpose and will do my best to give back and help children have a brighter future. With your help, we will teach them the common threads that bring us all together.

Charles Falarara, Charles Berghammer, Chuck Turow, and Dale Hilleman. Thank you for creating a warm and welcoming home so that I was able to focus and make *Kitchen Life* a reality.

Our beautiful families in North Florida, Tennessee, Texas, and Venezuela.

Mother, Grandmother Mabel, Daddy, Gene, Anise, Addie, Marsha, Diane, Jessica, Auntie Evelyn, Uncle Franklin, Aunt Diane, Uncle Raymond, Aunt Annette, Aunt Lois and Uncle Jerry, Uncle Buddy, Uncle John, Aunt Wanda, Aunt Brenda, Uncle Sammy, and all the many children and many, many grandchildren. To the Salgueiros: Mama Hilda, Evelyn, Thais, Moraima, Yoli, Kelly, Orlando, and Ramon. To the Edwards: Andrea, David, Christian, Lauren, Peggy, Scott, Allison, and Chad. Here's to celebrating family!

ABOUT COMMON THREADS

Art Smith and Jesus Salgueiro founded Common Threads to provide a sanctuary where children can find the common threads that allow them to celebrate their diversity and differences. With food and other arts as the vehicle for change, children can share, learn, teach, and embrace their own and each other's common threads. These threads promote understanding of shared interests and enhance appreciation for cultural diversity.

Art Smith has enlisted the help of top chefs like Gale Gand, Paul Kahan, Jamie Oliver, and Charlie Trotter to guest-teach cooking classes that emphasize ethnic cooking. In addition, he has also enlisted chef friends Susan Goss and Karen Armijo to spearhead the Common Threads World Garden. The Common Threads World Garden provides an educational environment, using horticulture to teach children how we, as a world family, share in the common threads of growing food. Our mission is to promote a nurturing relationship with the earth, encourage healthy eating, and learn to embrace our cultural differences. We believe that our interactive approach can make a difference in understanding the ways in which food connects our communities.

It is our belief that all children—regardless of race, belief, religion, and socioeconomic status—deserve equal educational opportunities. Common Threads works with neighborhood schools to bring together children from different cultural and socioeconomic backgrounds to participate in both cooking and gardening programs. Scholarships are awarded to students who demonstrate financial need.

A portion of the author's proceeds will go to Common Threads. You can find out more about Common Threads by going to *www.ourcommonthreads.org*, or by calling Linda Novick, executive director, at 312-876-1289.

INDEX